TRANSITION TO SURVIVAL

To my mother, who could light up a room with her smile.
A szeretet soha el nem fogy.

Transition to Survival

Enterprise restructuring in twenty East German and Hungarian companies, 1990-1997

ENESE LIEB-DÓCZY
University of Warwick

Routledge
Taylor & Francis Group
LONDON AND NEW YORK

First published 2001 by Ashgate Publishing

Reissued 2018 by Routledge
2 Park Square, Milton Park, Abingdon, Oxon OX14 4RN
711 Third Avenue, New York, NY 10017, USA

Routledge is an imprint of the Taylor & Francis Group, an informa business

A Library of Congress record exists under LC control number: 00110696

ISBN 13: 978-1-138-73367-1 (hbk)
ISBN 13: 978-1-315-18758-7 (ebk)

Contents

List of Diagrams

List of Tables

Summary

Using case studies from twenty East German and Hungarian companies this book examines the process of enterprise restructuring in transition economies. The focus is on the crucial 'initial' restructuring phase of 1990–97. The broad theme is one of disintegration and integration. The aim is to provide a comprehensive picture of the restructuring process as it affects the crucial aspects of a company's operations. I examine how in response to increasing market pressures companies change their vertical integration, including the in-house provision of social services, how they functionally integrate with their investors and restructure their forward and backward linkages.

A noticeable pattern in my data is that the academic literature and investors frequently endorsed restructuring measures which turned out to be 'right' for the East German companies and 'wrong' for the Hungarian ones. The second startling feature of my case studies is the evidence of total industrial devastation in East Germany. I argue that these observations are related to three recurring themes: local idiosyncrasies matter, the past matters and the future should not be rushed.

Acknowledgments

This book is the result of a research project which would not have been possible without the cooperation of the over 100 managers interviewed. It is them I have to thank most profoundly for giving up their time for something that yielded little immediate tangible benefits to them. I hope that their openness and intellectual curiosity will contribute to their and their companies' future success.

This book was written during my time at the University of Warwick. I thank all the members of the Department of Economics, University of Warwick, for providing me with an excellent working environment and especially Mike Waterson and Morten Hviid for their support and comments on endless versions of this book. Without the financial assistance of the Research Innovation Fund of the University of Warwick, it would have been difficult to complete this research project.

I very much benefited from discussions with colleagues at Warwick and other universities, especially Saul Estrin, Paul Hare, Klaus Meyer, Keith Cowling, Dennis Leach, Aydin Hayri, Bruce Lyons, Gernot Grabher and Csaba Makó. Peter Lankes and Nick Stern at the European Bank of Reconstruction were of great help in negotiating access to Hungarian companies. At a crucial juncture their help was central in making this project happen.

My friends, grown-up and small, provided me with lots of laughter, encouragement and regular reminders of the important things in life. Finally and most importantly, I am indebted to my family, especially my parents and Duncan, for their unshakeable faith and support.

Errors and omissions remain my own.

Enese Lieb-Dóczy
NERA, previously University of Warwick

1 Introduction

This book examines the initial restructuring challenges posed by the transition, using comparative case study evidence on the fate of 20 East German and Hungarian enterprises between 1990 and 1997. The broad theme is one of disintegration and integration. I examine how in response to increasing market pressures companies change their vertical integration, including the in-house provision of social services, how they functionally integrate with their investors and restructure their forward and backward linkages. Enterprise restructuring in transition economies is an extraordinary economic and historical occurrence. This process is not only interesting in its own right, but also poses a multitude of academic, policy and practical challenges.

The aim is to provide a comprehensive picture of the restructuring process as it affects the crucial aspects of a company's operations. Transition economics still suffers from data scarcity, particularly when questions at the company-level are concerned. Especially in the early transition phase this scarcity has arguably contributed to the dogmatism based on preconceptions, which is occasionally evident in the academic literature. This book aims to make a contribution by providing detailed empirical evidence which will help in distinguishing the relevant theories and interpretations from the less relevant ones. In doing so this study benefits from a relatively large number of in-depth comparative case studies enjoying an unusual amount of consistency. Only one researcher was involved who spoke each interviewee's native language and used the same extensive questionnaire throughout.

Chapter 2 provides a selection of restructuring accounts. The aim is to provide the reader with a feel for the issues and problems encountered. I do not claim that these accounts reflect objective reality, that they are statements of truth which could be defended in court. Rather they serve to show not just facts but also people's perceptions, the rumours that accompany restructuring and the memories which remain. However, as well as making use of newspaper articles and archival material, each write-up is based on interviews with several managers and a trade union representative and hence a certain degree of inter-subjectivity should have been hopefully obtained. Chapter 2 provides some of the flesh, the soft tissue, for which subsequent chapters try to provide the organising structure, the bones.

Chapter 3 examines the way in which previously highly integrated enterprises have restructured their vertical boundaries. In particular I ask whether, as suggested by the literature on enterprise restructuring, vertical disintegration leads to transaction cost savings and efficiency gains.

Chapter 4 maintains a focus on the firms' boundaries by examining the way in which enterprises have restructured the extensive social services they used to provide. Empirical hypotheses are examined which suggest that the extent to which a company stops the internal provision of social services is a good indicator of its overall restructuring effort.

Chapter 5 deals with the role of foreign direct investors in the strategic restructuring of their subsidiaries. The notion that companies with FDI will outperform their rivals because of knowledge transfer from their investor and his role in introducing new products and production methods is examined both qualitatively and statistically.

Using the literature on economic geography as an interpretative framework Chapter 6 deals with the changes which have occurred in the companies' forward and backward linkages.

Chapter 7 concludes by arguing that in enterprise restructuring local idiosyncrasies matter, the past matters and the future should not be rushed.

Despite the fact that surveys rather than case studies are typically used in economics, case studies play a significant role in other areas of social science. Case studies allow us to focus on naturally occurring units, such as an individual company. By relinquishing typicality, they make possible the 'thick' description of a phenomenon. Case studies allow for an in-depth understanding of context and situation, which is especially important when examining the complex and multifaceted process of adaptation and change companies in transition economies are subject to. Case studies complement surveys because they are able to indicate the qualitative reasons behind statistical regularities, which on their own can be consistent with several explanations or interpretations. In addition the big transition induced changes in the boundaries of firms make the traditional use of large firm databases (even if these were readily available with reliable data) largely irrelevant in the key initial restructuring phase.[1]

A comparison between East Germany and Hungary can yield insights which are relevant to other transition economies as well. Both Hungary and East Germany benefit from a relatively stable political and social environment. For this reason these countries allow us to focus on the 'economic' side of transition, rather than on questions as to how economic agents behave under political, legal and social uncertainty. Consequently both Hungary and East Germany provide an example of what one might expect to happen at the enterprise level in other countries once there is some stability and legality in the overall framework they operate in. At the same time Hungary and East Germany represent important differences within this relatively advanced and 'smooth' transition group, in particular along the shock therapy and gradualism dimension; their comparison can provide a more general indication of the relative merits of these two approaches to transition.

The reader will find that in many instances the changes examined have also occurred over time in companies in more advanced market economies. For example, I find that in restructuring their boundaries firms closed some product lines and replaced them with new ones. They stopped in-house input production and started using some subcontractors for physical and non-physical inputs. The reader might well be left with a feeling of 'so what?'. The answer to that question lies not so much in the individual changes themselves, but rather in the magnitude and diversity of the pressures which the companies examined simultaneously faced and the resulting speed and complexity of change.

To gain an impression of the pressures which companies in transition economies face, one has to consider that they are not just – as is common for companies operating in more stable and advanced market economies – faced with rapidly changing market conditions but that also the entire legal, political and economic framework within which they operate is simultaneously changing as well. To put it differently, companies in a transition environment are not just faced with a situation where the parameters of the game are changing but one where also the rules of the game have suffered a structural break.

It is the all-encompassing nature of the changes which all companies are simultaneously exposed to which makes a sit-and-wait response almost infeasible. Companies have to try and adapt by introducing targeted changes to all aspects of their operations if they do not want to be entirely left behind by their fast-moving environment.[2] It is not activism which is called for, but genuine change. The company has to find new markets, new products, new supply networks, new ways of organising production and learn the new rules of the game (that is, for example, learn about marketing, consumer wants, quality control, legal requirements, new political lobbies etc.). Furthermore, a company has to find and learn all these things more or less at the same time and as soon as possible.

Information about the Companies Visited and the Empirical Evidence Collected

Although one cannot speak of strictly matched, randomly selected or representative samples, the companies in my data set were selected to allow for meaningful comparisons between Hungary and East Germany.

- The first selection criterion was that in both the Hungarian and East German data I have focused on manufacturing companies. A few construction companies were included in order to be able to examine, for example, issues arising from the extent to which a company's operations are localised due to factors such as high transportation costs for its final products and inputs.[3]
- Secondly, in both countries I have focused on companies which used to be very large, that is have at least 2,000 employees, before 1990. These are companies which by their very size, prominence and high degree of vertical integration were likely to face big restructuring challenges. In both countries I included some medium-sized companies in order to be able to examine under what circumstances a company's initial size effects its restructuring outcomes. Overall the Hungarian and East German companies included had a very similar mean size in 1990.
- Thirdly, although companies with FDI dominate my data set, in both data sets I included companies without a direct investor for comparative purposes.

It has to be noted, however, that the ultimate composition of my data set was not determined by my selection criteria but by the companies' willingness to participate. This is likely to lead to a bias in favour of companies which are generally cooperative, open, have nothing to hide and are hence more likely to be dynamic and successful. However open a company is, the promise of anonymity generally was a precondition for their participation.

I collected data pertaining to a company's situation in 1990 and data on subsequent changes. With the aim of allowing for all aspects of a company's restructuring challenge I focused on changes in each company's

- vertical integration;
- its integration with and relationship to its investor;
- changes in its human resource policies and the general handling of labour shedding,
- changes in its product range, production methods, product markets, competitive situation; as well as

Table 1.1 The companies

	Sector	Main products	FDI	Sales[4]	Employees 1996/7 (1990)[5]
D1	Construction	Housing	YES	150	600 (2000)
D2	Construction	Housing	YES	33	248 (330)
D3	Manufacturing	Steel products	YES	69,3	270 (2021)
D4	Manufacturing	Tyres	YES	135	722 (9500)
D5	Manufacturing	Pharmaceuticals	YES	256	1033 (2700)
D6	Construction	Power stations	NO	58	320 (6500)
D7	Construction	Civil engineering	NO	220	800 (6800)
D8	Manufacturing	Gas turbines	YES	120	500 (4500)
D9	Manufacturing	Gears	YES	213	700 (3000)
H1	Manufacturing	Food: refined oils	YES	292	640 (2100)
H2	Manufacturing	Food: instant drinks, sweets	YES	133	1396 (2400)
H3	Manufacturing	Food: cookies, chocolate	YES	101	800 (2500)
H4	Manufacturing	Pharmaceuticals	YES	265	2550 + 200 (4500)
H5	Manufacturing	Chemicals: polyolefin feedstocks and products	NO	569	3500 + 1600 (5000)
H6	Manufacturing	Buses, vehicle parts	NO	354	3200 + 4300 (10500)
H7	Manufacturing	Lamps, lamp equipment	YES	442	9.952 + 2000 (14297)
H8	Manufacturing	Packaging materials	NO	9.7	580 + 400 (1000)
H9	Manufacturing	Packaging materials	YES	10	100 (450)
H10	Construction	Civil engineering	YES	23	250 (650)
H11	Manufacturing	Petroleum and gas products	NO	4159	14500 + 17000 (40.000)

- the regional effects of FDI and on changes in the company's procurement policies.

The companies have been numbered though from 1 to 9 in Germany, with the prefix D indicating that this is a German company and from H1 to H11 in Hungary. In each company I used the same 38 page questionnaire (see Appendix A) and every interview was conducted in the interviewee's native language. Although I made sure that the basic questionnaire was answered in all companies, I regularly encouraged interview partners to elaborate and digress, since this is usually the context in which the most interesting information was revealed. I revisited a company until I felt that all my questions had been answered satisfactorily and truthfully, frequently asking several different people to give their version of events. As a matter of principle the trade union representative and the personnel manager were asked the same set of questions. Overall I conducted in-depth interviews with (at least) the managing director, personnel manager, trade union representative, procurement manager and production manager in each company. Each individual interview was semi-structured and lasted at least one hour. The information obtained in the interviews was supplemented with company reports, archival material and newspaper articles.

Company D1 belongs to the building sector and currently has 600 employees. In 1995 the value of its sales was about 150 million DM. In 1990 it had 2,000 employees and was one of the most important employers in the small town just outside Berlin in which it is located. In March 1991 the company was acquired by a Swedish investor operating in the same industrial sector. I visited company D1 on 13 August 1996 and conducted interviews with the procurement manager, the Vice-trade union representative, the personnel manger and the manager in charge of logistics and organisation. Each interview lasted for about two hours and all of these managers had been with the company for many years. I obtained back issues of the magazine for employees of company D1, company reports, brochures of building projects in which the company has been involved in over the years, a brochure on quality management and copies of algorithms used by the manager in charge of procurement when evaluating suppliers and subcontractors and quality control documents. I also obtained a case study report published in the book *Privatisierte und was aus ihnen geworden ist* (Verlag Die Wirtschaft, 1994).

Company D2 belongs to the building sector as well and has currently 248 employees. In 1995 the value of its sales was about 33 million DM. In 1990 the company had 330 employees and was only active in the quarter of East Berlin in which it is located. In July 1992 it was acquired by a local investor with a lot of experience in the West Berlin building sector. To complement my interviews with the managing director, trade union representative and procurement manager I obtained a company report and a list of references for the company. Furthermore there exists a case study report published in the book *Privatisierte und was aus ihnen geworden ist* (ibid.).

Company D3 is a steel processing plant with 270 employees and sales of 69.3 million DM in 1995. The company is a very interesting case study since in 1993 it was acquired by the East Slovak Steel Works, a company with 15,000 employees. Not only is it most unusual to find FDI into Eastern Germany coming from another transition economy but also the vertical integration is the other way around as is usually expected, with the investor supplying its acquisition with inputs. Company D3 had 2,021 employees in 1990 and is located in town which used to be one of the industrial centres of the Brandenburg region but has experienced a significant decline in its industrial base since reunification. I visited the company on 11 and 20 September 1996. I conducted interviews with the manager in charge of procurements, the manager in charge of logistics, who had been until recently in charge of sales for the last 20 years, the personnel manager and the worker's representative. I was also given an extended tour of the factory with an explanation of the machines and production processes. Further supporting material was obtained in the form of the company brochure and report as well as in numerous newspapers from the local as well as national and international press, including an article in Business Central Europe, October 1996, on the East Slovak Steel Works.

Company D4 is a tyre manufacturer located in the same town as Company D1. The company has 722 employees currently and used to have 9,500 employees, which made it the single most important employer in its home town. Current sales amount to 135 million DM (1995), with 170 million DM being planned for 1996. In January 1995 company D4 is acquired by a West German tyre maker, who in turn belongs to a Japanese conglomerate. I visited company D4 20 August 1996 and conducted two-hour interviews with the manager in charge of production, the personnel manager, the worker's representative and the manager in charge of procurements. Further supporting material was obtained in the form of a copy of the contract between the employees and the managers of the company concerning working hours, wages and employee numbers which is in force while the company transfers from one trade union (Chemie-Papier-Keramik) to another (Bergbau-Chemie-Energie), cuttings from local newspapers, back issues of all press releases made by the company as well as a copy of the quality management booklet compiled for the managers of the company which includes, among others, documents dealing with the internal organisation of quality control, internal and external audits, project management and customer relations.

Company D5 is a pharmaceuticals company in (East) Berlin with 1,033 employees, down from 2,700 employees in 1990. In 1992 company D5 was acquired by an Italian pharmaceuticals company. In 1995 its sales amounted to 256 million DM. I visited company D5 on 5 and 6 September 1996 and conducted interviews with the manager in charge of *Gesundheitspolitik und Unternehmensführung* (health policies), the manager in charge of sales and the manager in charge of procurements, the personnel manager and the worker's representative. Supporting material was obtained in the form of a complete set (starting in 1991) of back issues of the magazine published for the employees of company D5, company reports of 1995 and 1991 product price lists and brochures as well as several confidential audit reports of suppliers. Furthermore there is a case study report of this company in *Privatisierte und was aus ihnen geworden ist* (ibid.).

Company D6 is of interest because it is an example of a failed privatisation. This company used to belong to the VEB Kombinat Kraftwerksanlagenbau in which 40,000 employees were organised in 20 companies. The company out of which D6 developed had 6,500 employees. Before 1990 company D6 designed and built components for both nuclear and fossil fuel power stations, but had an exclusive responsibility within the conglomerate for designing and building nuclear power stations. In 1995 the company had 320 employees and sales amounting to 58 million DM. Since 1990 company D6 has been specialising in designing and coordinating the building of small and medium sized fossil fuel power stations. In 1992 the company had been sold to a consortium consisting of an American pipeline operator and a West German power station builder, with the latter however pulling out of the deal at the last moment. The privatisation to the pipeline operator did not prove a success and to save company D6, the Treuhand intervened by instituting a *treuhandlerischer Verwalter*, that is an administrator who is the formal owner of 100 per cent of the company's shares and is supposed to restructure the company with the aim of reprivatisation. Thus the Treuhand in effect bought back company D6. When I visited the company in 1996, it was conducting negotiations with several potential investors and was hoping to be privatised before the end of the year. It was facing serious economic problems as was reflected both by the lack of hope its employees had for the future of the company and in comments made by managers in company D8 which used to belong to the same Conglomerate as company D6.

In a follow-up call in May 1998 I was told that the company D6 went bankrupt on 30 November 1997. It was then taken over with a third of its employees by a consortium consisting to 51 per cent of a German and to 49 per cent of an English power station builder.

I visited the company on 21 August and 24 September 1996 and interviewed the manager in charge of public relations, the worker's representative, the manager in charge of procurements and the personnel manager. Supporting material was obtained in the form of the 1994 and 1995 company reports as well as a list of references for the company.

Company D7, a civil engineering company, is an unusual case because its investor, an internationally operative Austrian holding company with 10000 employees worldwide, went bankrupt in the beginning of 1995. Interestingly the investor had also bought what managers in company D7 refer to as their 'sister company', an industrial site builder who was of a similar size as D7 before reunification and belonged to the same Conglomerate. The sister company, together with the investor's numerous acquisition in all of Eastern Europe followed the investor into bankruptcy. Company D7 is the only member of the conglomerate who survived and is currently up for sale by the Treuhand again. Company D7 had 6,800 employees in 1990 of which 800 are left by the end of 1996. Its sales amounted to 220 million DM in 1996 with 210 being expected for 1997. I visited the company on 17 December 1996 and conducted interviews with the personnel manager, the trade union representative, the *Technischer Leiter* (the manger in charge of technical questions) and the procurement manager. I further obtained a case study published in *Privatisierte und was aus ihnen geworden ist* (ibid.) as well as company reports for 1995 and 1994, an internal exposé concerning developments since 1990, copies from the internally developed training programme, evaluation sheets for suppliers, the investor's company report for 1992 and excerpts from training documents provided by the investor.

Company D8 is a power station components supplier specialising in gas turbines. In 1991 D8 was bought by a large Swedish-Swiss conglomerate. In 1990 the company had 4,500 employees, down to 500 by the end of 1996. Its sales volume in 1996 amounted to 120 million DM. Company D8 used to belong to the same conglomerate as company D6 and still occasionally supplies turbines or services for projects coordinated by company D6. I visited company D8 on 19 December 1996 and conducted interviews with the manager in charge of PR and the management of change. He seemed to be the only manager left who had a good historical experience of the company and overview of the parameters of change. He also answered questions concerning industrial relations, because the position of the personnel manger was just being filled with a new candidate. I also talked to the trade union representative and obtained a case study published in *Privatisierte und was aus ihnen geworden ist* (ibid.), as well as a company report for 1995 and an expose of the history of the company.

Company D9 is a gear factory acquired by a West German company operating in the same industrial sector. Company D9's investor has shares in 34 companies in 15 countries, including South and North America and Eastern Europe, a sales volume of 7.2 billion DM and 33,892 employees. Company D9 itself has 750 employees, down from 3,000 in 1990 and a sales volume of 213 million DM (1996). I visited the company on 18 December 1996, conducted interviews with the manager in charge of controlling, the trade union representative and was allowed to join an end of year inspection of the entire factory. I also obtained a company report of the investor for 1996, a brochure on quality management, an exposé of the products, a case study published in *Privatisierte und was aus ihnen geworden ist* (ibid.), as well as back issues of the magazine for employees.

Company H1 belongs to the food industry. The company is active in crushing and refining oilseeds and has a virtual monopoly in the Hungarian market for sunflower oil. In 1996 the net value of sales generated by company H1 was 292 million DM. At the time of its privatisation in 1992 to a French investor from the same sector the company had 2,100 employees in six factories. By 1997 the overall number of employees in the three remaining factories had been reduced to 640. I visited the head offices of the company on 15 April and 29 July 1997. I conducted a two and a half hour interview with the general manager and a one hour interview with a trade union representative. The general manager thought it unnecessary for me to talk to the personnel and procurements managers separately since in his opinion I would receive the very same answers from them as from him, after all 'we have all been here for very long.' From the head of marketing I obtained leaflets which the company publishes as part of a heart awareness campaign along the lines of 'eat less animal fat and more vegetable fats', the investor's annual reports of 1995 and 1996 and a collection of newspaper articles published in the national media about the company.

Company H2 is also active in the food industry. Its main product groups are instant drinks, convenience foods and sweets, generating net sales of 133 million DM in 1996. Overall, the company has currently 1,396 employees, down from 2,400 in 1992, the year of its privatisation to a Swiss multinational from the same industrial sector. The factory I visited produces chocolate drinks and wafers. Since 1992 the number of its employees has fallen from 600 to just 50 people. I visited the head office of the company as well as its factory on 20, 21 and 22 May 1997. I conducted interviews with the general manager of the factory, the manager in charge of product development who also acts as a trade union representative, the personnel manager and the head of procurement. Each interview lasted for about one and a half hours. In addition I also obtained the investor's company report for 1995.

Company H3 belongs to the food industry as well. Originally it was part of the same industrial structure as most of what was become company H2. H3 specialises in chocolates and cookies. Its net sales amounted to 101 million DM in 1996. In 1992 H3 was privatised with 3400 employees to the German subsidiary of an American multinational company. In the same year two of the four factories acquired by the investor were sold on to the investor of company H2, thus transferring 900 employees between the two companies. Today H3 employs 800 employees in two factories. I visited company H3 on 17 April 1997 and conducted interviews with the general manager, the personnel manager, a trade union representative and the head of procurement. I also obtained press releases by the company, back issues of the employee's magazine and newspaper articles from the national press.

Company H4 is a pharmaceuticals company with 2,550 employees (1997) and net sales totalling 265 million DM in 1996. When the French investor acquired a 40 per cent stake in H4 in 1991, company H4 had 4,500 employees. The stake of the investor, who is also a pharmaceuticals company, was gradually increased to 51 per cent in 1993, 76 per cent in 1995 and 100 per cent in June 1996. I visited the company on 15 May 1997 and conducted interviews with the operation director of industrial resources, the trade union representative, the personnel manager and the head of purchasing. I also obtained relevant newspaper articles and a company profile.

Company H5 is a large chemicals company specialising in polyolefin feedstock and products. The company is based on a vertical structure and produces ethylene, propylene and polymers from naphtha. H5 has 20 per cent of Central Europe's petrochemical capacity.[6] It is one of the two remaining Hungarian chemicals companies of this size and importance and generated net sales worth 569 million DM in 1996. Company H11 is a major input supplier of H5, who purchases refined petroleum products, in particular naphtha and gasoil, from H11. There were several potential foreign investors who wanted to acquire a controlling stake in the company, but H5 resisted being privatised to any of them on the grounds that the prospective investors did not have long-run plans with H5 which were in the interest of H5 as perceived by its management and workforce. The company made a conscious decision to resort to institutional investors instead and floated in 1996, becoming one of the most liquid stocks on the Budapest stock exchange. The company is also listed on the London stock exchange. In 1997, 51 per cent of shares were held by foreign institutions, 23.4 per cent by domestic institutional investors and 8.2 per cent of shares were held by the company's employees.[7] In 1990 the company had 5,000 employees. Today H5 itself has 3,500 employees. About 1,600 employees were transferred to 32 affiliated companies which have been separated out from H5 as part of its restructuring plan or which are joint venture greenfield developments with a foreign investor.

I also visited companies H5b and c. Since in these companies it was not possible to obtain complete data sets, they have been omitted from the statistical parts of this study. H5b is a joint venture on-site greenfield development between H5 and an American investor (the shareholdings are 40 per cent and 60 per cent respectively). Using inputs from H5, H5b produces carbon, which is needed, for example, for the production of tyres. Since its foundation in 1992, H5b has been profitable throughout and has increased its employee numbers from 60 in 1992 to 88 in 1997. In 1996 its net sales totalled 53 million DM. H5c used to be fully integrated with company H5. Using plastic fibres produced by H5, H5c specialises in the production of polypropylene and polyethylene sacks. In 1991 H5c was separated out from H5 and a 50 per cent stake was sold to an Austrian investor. H5c's employee numbers have risen from 150 in 1994 to about 500 in 1997.[8] Net sales in 1996 amounted to 16 million DM.

I visited H5, b and c on 5 and 6 June 1997. All three companies are located on one site in northern Hungary. I interviewed the managing directors of companies H5b and H5c respectively, the deputy CEO of H5, the personnel manager of company H5, a representative of the trade union to which employees in all three companies belong and the personnel manager of company H5. Furthermore I obtained back issues of the employee's magazine of H5, a company brochure for H5c, relevant newspaper articles from the national press, stock exchange reports of H5 for 1996 and 1997, the annual report of H5 for 1996 and the script for a PR presentation introducing H5 to prospective business partners. I was also given a guided tour of the main production facilities and of the extensive on-site recreational facilities for employees.

Company H6 used to be one of the best-known manufacturing companies in Hungary. The company is still state owned although there are ongoing negotiations with potential investors. The only investor so far is a Russian consortium which has a 30 per cent stake in the company. It has been claimed towards me by the TUR that this is however a sleeping investor, who is represented through the Hungarian state property agency, ÁPV Rt. Articles in the Hungarian equivalent of *The Economist*, *HVG*, document, however, in great detail the rather stormy past this 'sleeping' investor has had with the state property agency.[9] H6's main products are buses of all categories, vehicle parts and vehicle manufacturing equipment. At the height of its output throughout the 1980s, the company produced in excess of 12,000 buses a year. In 1989 an accelerated decline set in and production in H6 fell to about 500 buses in 1996. The net value of sales in 1997 was about 203 million DM, generated by the sale of about 1,750 buses. Employee numbers reflect this overall decline: they fell from 10,500 to 3,200 overall and in the factory visited from 3,500 to 850. Considering that in its main markets demand for the product of this company has not collapsed as much as would be the case for some other manufacturing products, this rapid decline is as much intriguing to the researcher as it seems to be baffling and de-motivating to highly trained workforce. In 1996 the company got a new managing director and there are hopes to stabilise the output of the company in the medium term at 3,500 buses and increase output in 1998 to 2,500 buses, hopefully generating targeted net sales worth 354 million DM that year.

I visited company H6 on 13, 14 and 20 May 1997 and conducted interviews with the head of logistics, a trade union representative, the head of corporate strategy and the personnel manager. I also had a discussion with some junior engineers and met an intern from America, Todd Calamita, who gave me a working paper written by him on the situation and strategic options of the company. I also obtained a company profile and the script for a PR presentation introducing H6 to prospective business partners.

Company H7 is another well-known Hungarian manufacturing company. Its products are lamps, lamp equipment and components. In 1989/90 H7 was acquired by an American investor. At the time H7 had 14,297 employees. The number of employees has been reduced to 9,952 by 1997. Production increased between 1989 and 1995 by over 50 per cent with net sales totalling 442 million DM in 1995 and 600 million US $ in 1996. The privatisation of H7 is now widely viewed as very successful, also because the investor has not only maintained the R&D activities of H7 but even transferred large R&D capacities to H7 from Europe and the USA. I visited H7 on 3 June 1997 and 7 August 1997. I conducted interviews with the Director of Manufacturing of the European division of H7's investor, the manager in charge of compensation and benefits, the trade union representative, the manager heading services sourcing, the head of R&D and the communication manager. I also obtained a company profile, a publication on the history of the company, back issues of the employees' magazine, ongoing leaflets to the employees outlining and arguing for the company's most recent advancements in quality management, the 1996 annual report of the investor and articles from the national press.

Company H8 is active in the printed matter and packaging industry. Its main products are folding cartons, flexible-wall packaging materials, labels as well as books and newspapers. H8 is an input supplier to H7. In 1996 the company had net sales worth 97 million DM. It was acquired in 1990 with 1,000 employees by a French institutional investor. By 1997 employee numbers had been reduced to 580. I visited H8 on 6 August 1997 and conducted an interview with the technical director of the company, the personnel manager and a trade union representative. I was also given several promotional publications on both H8 and its investor and was shown some of the products made by H8.

Company H9 is also in the packaging industry, specialising in the production of paper boards and folding cartons. In 1996, the company had net sales worth 10 million DM. The company was acquired in 1993 by an American investor. Between 1990 and 1997 employee numbers fell from 450 to 100. I visited thė company on 13. and 29 August 1997. The managing director of the company preferred to take the questionnaires home hand fill them in his own time. Consequently I could only have an unstructured discussion with him at our first meeting and I have to rely on the answers he gave me on the questionnaire. I was unable to see the trade union representative, who could not make any proposed meeting times. I also obtained a fact sheet about the company.

Company H10 belongs to the construction industry. Its activities include road and railway building, the production of asphalt and the building of water and gas pipelines. In 1996 it generated net sales of 23 million DM employing 250 people. In 1991 H10 was privatised to an Austrian investor with 650 employees. I visited H10 on 14 and 15 August 1997. I interviewed the managing director of the company and the chief accountant. Since the employees showed no interest in their trade union, the local trade union structure has withered away and there was no trade union representative to be interviewed. I obtained two different PR booklets introducing the company to potential business partners and the investor's annual report for 1995/6.

Company H11 is one of the largest Hungarian companies. Its field of activity is the exploration and production as well as the refining and marketing of gas and oil. H11 also has a telecommunications division, whose main asset is a switched network of over 6,000 km laid alongside the company's pipelines. H11 produces petrol, runs a network of petrol stations, produces heating oils, lubricants, kerosene, propane, butane and is involved in gas and oil production and transportation but not in distribution. Company H5 is one of the three most important wholesale customers of H11. In some areas of its activities the company still has an effective state monopoly. The company was floated in 1991 on the Budapest stock exchange, where, due to the profitability of H11, it has proven to be one of the most popular shares. In 1996 the net value of sales reached 4,159 million DM and had 14,500 employees. In 1990 the company had 40,000 employees. As part of a pre-flotation restructuring 33 companies with overall 17.000 employees were separated out of H11. H11 was floated with 22,000 employees in 1991, so that the overall direct reduction of employee numbers between 1990 and 1997 is no more than 8500.

I visited H11 on 25 May 1997. I conducted interviews with the deputy finance manager, the deputy marketing manager, a trade union representative and the personnel manager. I also obtained the report for the shareholders' meeting of 28 May 1997, back issues from the employees' magazine from several years, the company report for 1996/7, an investors' news leaflet from February 1997 and a document outlining the company's business development since 1993 and its business plans up to 1999.

In addition to the research done in companies D1–9 and H1–11 I also conducted interviews with the following people, whom I thank for their participation and help:

1 on 22 September 1996 I conducted a two-hour interview with Mr Harald Braun, Bezirkssekretär at the IG Bauen-Agrar-Umwelt, Landesverband Berlin-Brandenburg. Mr Braun has been active in the trade union movement in Brandenburg for many years before reunification even though he was not a member of the SED. From 1981 to 1987 he was *Betriebsgewerkschaftsleiter* (the head of the trade union in that company) in a medium sized company. He is one of the very few remaining trade union officials who have stayed in their positions after 1990. Mr Braun has been known to be very critical of the political regime of the GDR, a stance which caused personal problems for him in the past, such as being denied a university education;
2 on 11 April 1996 I conducted a three-hour interview with Professor Hilmar Schmidt from the *Bundesanstalt für Vereinigungsbedingte Sonderaufgaben* (BVS). Professor Schmidt has been previously working for the *Treuhandanstalt* in a high-ranking position;
3 in Hungary I interviewed the President and Managing Director of Douwe Egberts Hungary, a subsidiary of the American company Sara Lee. He declined an interview based on my questionnaire, but kindly gave me a two hour unstructured interview on 3 June 1997. Sara Lee took over the former state monopolist in food packaging, Compac, and also developed some greenfield sites. The company belongs to the food industry and specialises in coffee (40 per cent market share), tea (65 per cent), spices (50 per cent), groceries, sweeteners and salt. The turnover of Douwe Egberts Hungary was about 22 billion HUF in 1996. The interview provided an insight into a Western manager's point of view concerning the attitudes

and qualification of the Hungarian workforce, the professionalism of Hungarian trade unions, the conditions with the ÁPV Rt., the role of local government, the reliability and attitude of Hungarian business partners and the image of Western investors with the general public. Since my interview partner gets interviewed by the Hungarian media, including television quite frequently, his opinions seem to be regarded by the Hungarian media as fairly representative;

4 I also conducted a two hour interview with a senior Hungarian diplomat who was involved, among other things, in post-1990 trade negotiations with Russia;

5 I am grateful for the discussions conducted with Hungarian academics working in related fields, especially Prof. Csaba Makó from the Hungarian Academy of Science, Dr Annamária Inzelt from the Budapest University of Economics and Dr Gábor Papanek from the GKI Economic Research Unit.

Notes

1 These advantages of case studies have to be weighed against the fact that they are only able to provide us with snapshots of what is happening and that they do not allow us to generalise to entire populations, only to empirical and theoretical hypotheses. An ideal procedure is, of course, to combine case study evidence with survey evidence. In this study this is partly done by explicitly taking account of the findings made in and puzzles raised by surveys conducted by other researchers.

2 This assumes that the force for change in the country and industrial sector at hand has already developed so much momentum that it is not a feasible policy for managers of the company to try and obliterate it or at least try and control it through forming alliances with political and bureaucratic forces.

3 I consider construction companies to be serving final product markets, so that in both the East German and Hungarian data set companies which produce intermediate products are the exception.

4 1995 figures for the German companies and 1996 figures for the Hungarian ones, all in million DM.

5 2550 + 200 means, for example, that in 1997 the company in question employs 2550 people, while 200 of its former workers are now employed by fully operative separated out units (that is, newly founded companies under independent management, but not necessarily without ownership ties to the parent company).

6 Source: H5's company report for 1996.

7 Source: H5's stock market report for 1996. The remainder is held by H5's local government.

8 Source: script of a presentation held in May 1997 by the manager in charge of investor relations.

9 See, for example, *HVG*, 1995, June 10; *HVG*, 1995, November 25; *HVG*, 1996, October 12.

2 Subjective Realities: Restructuring Accounts[1]

Born from a desire to 'tell it as it is', case studies easily become rather verbose transcriptions of interviews. Personal accounts are, however, important. They show the subjective reality of restructuring. All stories contain grains of truth which taken together can yield insightful patterns. I look for patterns in later chapters by using correlation analysis, but to gain a feel for the topic and the context, let us start with the flesh, before searching for the bones. The accounts in this chapter are by no means exhaustive, they are merely meant to set the scene.

Company D1: Smooth Sailing with Confidence Boosters from Sweden

Company D1 started breaking even in 1994 and by 1998 has experienced three years of healthy profits in a highly competitive industry. Before 1990, company D1 specialised in commercial buildings and engaged in some road-building, but was not at all active in the housing sector. Today the company concentrates on large housing projects, that is estates, hospitals, hotels and still engages in some industrial projects, for example extending a local cement factory. The company has totally stopped its activities in the road-building area as well all earthworks. Furthermore the company operates on a smaller section of the value-added chain now, completing projects up to the building shell and using subcontractors for all successive production stages, while maintaining overall responsibility.

Between 1990 and 1996 accumulative investment in the company has amounted to about 30 million DM. This investment has been mainly into replacing the company's machinery and the introduction of new production methods, mainly the establishment of a comprehensive computer network covering the administrative area and in the coordination of production. As a result of these investments, the company now has machinery with an average age of about five years, while its technical lifetime is about 10 years.

The company had 2,000 employees in 1990. By 1996 D1 had 512 full-time employees and 68 trainees. It is expected that these numbers are going to stay constant in the medium-run.

Transition resulted in 1,420 jobs being lost in this company. The personnel manager gave the following description of this process: restructuring on the labour front started in 1989 when the Bau und Montagekombinat Ost to which company D1 belonged was dissolved and company D1 became a GmbH. This however was more a legal process than anything else because the change in the legal status of the company was not followed by any organisational changes. Reunification proved to be the decisive signal that radical changes had to be implemented in order for the company to survive.

The management decided to try to restructure in such a way so that company D1 would become attractive for an investor, they wanted to become 'sellable' rather than have MBO. Quite a few workers and managers left the company at this point, frequently in order to work for companies whose future seemed more assured at the time. In order to achieve the restructuring needed to attract an investor, the old management looked at companies in West Germany who are active in the same sector and what kind of activities they engage in.

This type of thought process lead them to define a core activity which should be carried out *within their company.* It was decided that the other activities, such as transportation and supplies but also all social community activities like kindergartens, which had been previously integrated into the company should be separated out of company D1 and organised into new, independent companies.

Company D1 was reorganised into several new companies, with the largest, the successor to the original company D1 focusing on core activities (that is the planning of projects and their execution up to the completion of the building shell) and using a network of subcontractors for the later production stages. In this way about 500 former employees found employment in these new companies, many of which have however gone bust. Then several hundred (that is all employees between 50 and 70 years old) benefited form an early retirement programme supported by the state. Others were induced to leave voluntarily by being given a 2,000 DM incentive, however the company tried to make sure that this incentive was not taken by its most valuable employees. It is hard to judge whether any employees were 'strongly advised' to make use of this opportunity.

As a result of these actions, by the time of the sale to the investor in March 1990, the company had only 1,000 employees. Altogether there were about 200 employees over the years who did not fall into any of the above measures and had to be plainly fired. Directly after the sale to the investor 30–40 people were fired. However this, as were all the other measures, was always done together with extensive social plans amounting to three million marks so that, in the words of the personnel manager, the dismissals did not create any problems for the company in the local community. One important reason was that no-one was fired or pensioned off anonymously, but the management tried to have personal talks with everyone concerned in order to create an understanding for the situation in which the company was and the reasons for the measures they were taking. The personnel manager claimed that the company had showed a strong sense of social responsibility because it needed a maintain a cooperative environment for its future success. The personnel manager expects no further changes in the number of employees in the medium run and states that in 1996 80–90 per cent of the company's employees is made up of people who have been with the company in 1990 as well.

The workers' representative tells the same story and agrees with the statement (made by the management) that the management tried everything possible to make the very difficult personnel restructuring in a socially as responsible way as possible. He thinks that this emphasis on the social aspect of restructuring on the labour side originated also from a 'Swedish way of thinking about these things' which emphasises cooperation and informational exchange between labour and management. The workers' representative was able to experience at first hand this Swedish thinking on a few trips to Sweden where he talked to Swedish trade union representatives.

According the company employees, the biggest problem for the remaining personnel was a total lack of self-esteem and a confidence in their capabilities. People generally were very confused by the huge changes in their environment and one of the first things the new Swedish owner did was to have some courses for all personnel with leadership positions (that means down to the Polierer level) to build their self-confidence. These courses seem to have had a very positive impact as almost all managers employed mentioned how important it had been to them to be explicitly told that their input into the company was very important and valuable and that the investor had confidence in their abilities. The managers interviewed claimed that these courses had been instrumental in making it possible that the past was used in constructively shaping a new future for the company.

Further courses, partly held in Sweden, were aimed at creating an open and cooperative company culture and get people acquainted to the idea of taking responsibility. With this aim the company also used the magazine for employees and in addition organised internal project weeks in which the aim was to try to explain the new company philosophy and strategy to the employees. Again, the East German managers found it particularly important that they were given the feeling of bringing something into these courses, which felt more like an exchange of experiences and a search for a realistic judgement of the situation than being lectured to or being indoctrinated. It was probably important that the Swedish company had had experience with doing business in the former GDR and thus had an appreciation for the needs of managers in East Germany. It was probably these experiences in the past as well as its own company culture which made the investor refrain from an 'organisational and ideological annihilation campaign'.

According to the workers' representative the biggest achievement of the workforce is not so much coping with the new technical job requirements, but rather in mentally adjusting to the new system. Apparently the work intensity has increased and there were some unexpected problems with work attitudes. Some employees on the Polierer level did not adjust well to having more responsibility (and thus implicitly more direct power over subordinates) which lead to some unacceptable behaviour. However apparently the management took an extremely strong stance against bullying and tried to improve attitudes through training courses for Polierer. In the judgement of the workers' representative work satisfaction has increased since reunification. More is being achieved and the workers feel that they receive recognition for the achievements mainly in the form of higher real wages and the fact that the company, unusually for the East German building industry, pays full Tarif wages. At the same time the workers' representative showed a great deal of nostalgia for a sense of community and belonging which in his opinion got lost in this new 'elbow-society'.

In the process of restructuring the company as also introduced new forms of work organisation, in particular quality management groups, flexible working hours and project groups. Job rotation was judged to be desirable but due to time and monetary considerations had not been implemented. These changes in work organisation were introduced with the aim of making the workings of the company more creative and rationalised. The workers' representative thinks that they mainly resulted in quality improvements. As a result of the improved motivation at all levels, the changes in work organisation and the access to new technology, productivity has dramatically improved, lying above the average for Bradenburg but, before 1997, slightly below the West German average for the industry.

According to the personnel manager there are no significant demands made by the employees. In his words 'there is currently no *Verteilundsmentalität* [that is a mentality according to which there is a distributional fight between management and employees]' because good communication between the management and workforce shows, what is possible and what is not in these unusual circumstances. Both the personnel manager and the workers' representative agree that this good communication increases trust between management and the workforce and enables them to find and implement solutions to unexpected problems.

Company D7: How to Survive your Investor

Company D7 shed 6,000 jobs between 1990 and the end of 1996. This company has introduced the usual restructuring measures by separating our smaller units, concentrating on core activities and trying to maintain high training standards.

Before 1990 company D7 specialised in all types of civil engineering projects, that is: 1) the building of tunnels and subway systems; 2) of streets and railway tracks; of 3) bridges and water treatment plants; as well as 4) demolishing existing buildings. The company was further involved in the planning of large projects as well as in the production of asphalt and concrete.

Already before the investor moved in 1993 the company abandoned the production of inputs and stopped having an overall planning role for entire projects as well as its R&D activities. D7 frequently uses subcontractors for ancillary services such as transportation which previously belonged to the company. These companies typically still depend to 80–90 per cent on the contracts given by company D7 and, usually for the East German data set, D7 has tended to keep shareholdings of about 33 per cent in these companies.

What makes D7 unusual is that it had been taken over in 1993 by an investor together with what the personnel manager calls 'our sister company' a construction company specialising in industrial sites and formerly belonging to the same Kombinat as company D7. In the end of 1995 the investor and all other companies belonging to it went bankrupt, except for company D7.

We have got two companies (D7 and its sister) of equal size and having belonged to the same Kombinat before restructuring and operating in the same sector and one investor. Only one of them survives. The personnel, procurement and technical manager gave the following picture in a round table discussion (sections with quotation marks are direct quotations from this discussion round).[2] The investor

> got all these young, dynamic people from Austria in who did not understand the situation here and wanted to introduce revolutionary changes. However if a company has been run differently for 40 years, then one cannot expect that even after two years of schooling everybody will support the new measures, that even if we understand the theory, in practice everything will work as people in the head offices have thought it out. The new people who were supposed to run the company from the top did not know the market and had no contact with the people here. This lead to arguments and disagreements with the 'old' management and workforce.

It is significant that in the sister company the investor rid himself of all old managers, whereas this did not happen in company D7. The reason seems to have been that in company D7:

> We [the old managers] had the trust of the workforce and nobody volunteered to take our place. The trust and backing of the workforce carried us through our disputes with the investor. They trusted us because we were achieving the right results in terms of profits and survival and because the workforce had the conviction that our plans for the company were the right ones. After all we [the old management] worked out our alternative business plan by continuously involving the workers (in the form of their representatives) in the process.

The manager in charge of change management in company D8 explains why it was so important to the workforce in his company that the investor eventually implemented the policy of relying on the local management:

> Some 'old' managers were simply untenable, everybody knew who they were. But with every competent and respected old manager the investor sacked, the investor signalled to the workforce that they were regarded as useless as well, the workforce identifies with these managers and thus is de-motivated with every further manager being sacked.

Ironically by showing all this initiative the old management in company D7 was doing to a large extent what the investor was busily trying to train them to do. Training documents provided by the investor as late as 1995 emphasise the ideals of being 'victors together', of participation, empowerment, subsidiarity and partnership. Success was to be built on 'better information, orientation, training and motivation' for the workforce. Strategies were to arise out of a continuous analysis of the environment and reassessment of goals. Individuals were supposed to aim for continuous learning and to sharpen their ability to recognise trends faster than the competition.

In practice these modern buzzwords and principles resulted in rather more conservative attitudes and policies. Information was perceived as strictly one way only, that is from the investor to the subsidiaries and strategies and analysis were also supposed to come from above. In the judgement of the 'old' management:

> These are very fine principles, but those young whizz kids lacked the insight into the realities here to be able to translate them into sound company policies. They also lacked respect for us [the old management and workforce], it was a sort of generational conflict, I suppose, in the beginning we even had to learn their language first.

Although the old management agreed with the company philosophy in principle, there was also strong disagreement with the investor as to how to spread it. The investor tried to follow a bottom-up approach within company D7: at one time all the Poliere, that is several hundred people, were sent into a training programme to be told about the new company philosophy. The investor had overlooked the fact, however, that 50–70 per cent of the people in this training scheme had already been notified that they would have to leave the company by the end of the year. This mistake could have been avoided had there been less centralism in trying to implement the new philosophy of empowerment. The old management favoured a more top to bottom approach to cultural change. 'We came to believe that the company philosophy has to be learned and internalised by the leadership first and should then be disseminated through the ranks through further qualifications and practical example.'

It is probably a sign of a latent lack of respect for the old management which lead the investor in company D7 to make the mistake of not listening to information coming from below. Another good example was the arguments surrounding training schemes for the workforce.

> One day we got this letter from Austria notifying us that we should train people in the following software package. When we have a closer look at it, we [the old management] realise that the package is concerned with Austrian accountancy procedures, that the training programme includes lessons on Austrian law. So we refused to do any of the training, after all we need to know about German accountancy procedures and law, not about software packages used by the investor in his head offices in Austria. We simply refused and worked out an alternative training scheme, identified the training needs we have and where to get the training from. Our training scheme has even been adopted by other East Berlin companies in the industry. After many arguments and the demise of a

> particularly intolerant Austrian manager the investor finally stopped meddling with us and just let us get on with our own plans. Our independently developed business plans as much as our good results served the Berlin banks as a security so that in the end they backed us against the investor. The banks refused to use us as a security when the investor wanted to use us to obtain further loans for himself before going bankrupt. We had the backing and protection of the Berlin banks and the investor did not, that is why we survived and the rest did not.

Both the personnel manager and the trade union representative stress that the general level of expertise has been always high in the company, but that further training became necessary, especially in brick laying, quality control and new technologies. Both interview partners state, however, that acquiring this additional training was not problem for the existing workforce. The training programmes had as a result that all of the company's products and activities conform with DIN norms. In the winter months when demand is low the company has comprehensive and training programmes which are obligatory for different employee groups. It is hence not surprising that both the personnel manager and the trade union representative agree that training is taken very seriously in the company and is given a high priority. The acquired skills are transferable within the building sector.

Quality control groups existed before 1990 but the company is now making more extensive use of them. To maintain its competitiveness and lower its costs, D7 has also introduced flexible working hours. Productivity has doubled and the personnel manager estimates that D7's labour productivity is at about 90–100 per cent of that of Western companies in the sector. The aim is to overtake Western competitors, who have been creating a lot of price pressure but employing (frequently illegally) cheap and less qualified foreign labour.

The company used to provide a multitude of social services to its employees. These included apartments, comprehensive childcare and sporting facilities, holiday camps and cultural activities. Very unusually the company has still kept the holiday camp for children, presents for anniversaries and activities centred at former employees who are now retired, such as company fetes with special emphasis on the elderly and young. The personnel manager points out that H7 is the only company in the entire building sector to have kept such services. He attributes this fact to H7 still having a different management culture in this respect than other companies where investors are in the driving seat.

Company D8: Restructuring Successfully, but Falling Victim to the Investor's Global Strategy

Company D8 was, together with a company in Görlitz, the monopoly producer in the former GDR for turbines and generators. T he company was acquired by its investor in March 1991, but there was a cooperation agreement between the two companies already since February 1990. Company D8 continues building power station components, especially turbines, which however have a different specification (supplied by the investor) from the old ones.

A major change is that the company has discontinued the production of generators and has added and is expanding its activities in repairing, servicing and modernising of Eastern European built turbines. This is the market niche in which the companies competitive advantage and the value of its historical knowledge lies. Furthermore this activity gives the company the opportunity shift its focus away from the rather saturated German market to the global one. This shift in focus also means however that the company is becoming increasingly service rather than production orientated. However representatives of the company are keen to stress that this does not mean that the company is purely an assembling plant.

Accumulative investment in D8 has amounted to about 80 million DM.[3] By 2001 this figure is expected to rise to 110 million DM at most. The main investments since the acquisition were into machinery aimed at metal processing, computing facilities and into work safety and buildings. As a consequence of this investment drive, the average age of the relevant machines and tools is between three to four years old, with none being older than six years. The technical life-span of the company's machines is at least 10 years.

Company D8 lost 4,000 jobs between 1990 and the end of 1996. It was a precondition of being acquired by the investor in 1991 that the number of employees should be reduced to 1850 from 4,500 in 1989. The company had few problems with law suits surrounding restructuring. According to the manager in charge of PR and change management 'the only people we had problems with were West German managers who had played a guest role and wanted to get as much money out of us upon leaving as possible'. By 1998 D8 intends to reduce its workforce to 400 people only. In 1996 it was hoped that employee numbers will stay stable at this level or even expand slightly again over time.

In a follow-up call in May 1998 I obtained the information that although the company generated a 3.5 million DM profit on a sales volume of 100 million DM in 1997, D8 is having to fight for its survival within the conglomerate it belongs to. In the judgement of the manager in charge of change management D8 has in part achieved more modern and efficient production methods and is of a higher productivity than many other parts of its parent company. The investor has nevertheless transferred the entire production of gas turbines (D8's main product) to a site in Mannheim. At one stage there were plans to entirely close D8 down, but now it is going to continue as a component manufacturer and a service provider to its parent. Negotiations are still on their way to determine the exact extent of further labour shedding. The manager in charge of change management estimated, however, that in May 1998 that about 50 per cent of the current workforce would be sent away, that is that in the end of this latest restructuring D8 would employ no more than 200 people. The investor justifies these moves with the increasing competition, consolidation and price falls in the gas turbine manufacturing sector.

Company D6: A Slow, Lingering Death

Company D6 used to specialise in nuclear power stations and has now shifted its focus onto being a turn-key contractor for small and medium sized fossil fuel power stations. There have been no investments in the company since 1990, nor has the company introduced any changes in its production methods. However, since the company is mainly involved in the planning and execution of projects, questions relating to changes in production processes are not applicable. The average age of the machinery used in D6 is about 13 years, while its technical lifetime is estimated to be about 15 years.

When I visited company D6 in 1996, it had not been able to generate profits since reunification. Its future was generally uncertain and crucially depended in whether it would be able to attract an investor who was genuinely interested in the company's long-term survival. In a follow-up call in May 1998 I was told that the company D6 went bankrupt 30 November 1997. It was then taken over with a third of its employees by a consortium consisting to 51 per cent of a German and to 49 per cent of an English power station builder. Hence, by 1998 only 105 people are left of the originally 6,500 employees which means that only 1.6 per cent of the original workforce has survived. The investor has taken over the financial and general management of the company and it is hoped that the successor to D6 will become profitable within the next few years. Apparently the investor is not planning to change the company's product range from what it was in 1996.

My data refers to the situation as it was in 1996. D6 has shed 6,180 employees between 1990 and 1996. Since the company did not separate out rather than liquidate units outside its newly defined core activities, almost all of these employees have become unemployed or gone into short-term state employment programmes.

Because of the importance of training and qualifications in this sector[4] the youngest and least experienced employees were made redundant first, which has resulted in a current problem of the company, mentioned by the TUR, namely a very high average age for its employees. Again, the Betriebsrat was involved in designing the social plans, and the company made extensive use of part-time work. Nevertheless there was a *large number of law suits surrounding redundancies*, for which the personnel manager gives the same explanation as the personnel manager in company D5. The TUR points out the that the financial help for cushioning redundancies and the possibility of employees entering into a state scheme are becoming less and less due to the efforts of the federal government to keep the fiscal debt under control.

The new product range (that is fossil fuel power stations rather than nuclear ones) requires according to the personnel manager the same level of qualifications and further training became only necessary in English, computing, quality management and contract law. This training took place on weekends and was financed by the company. However lack of time does not allow as much training to take place as the personnel manager would like to see. Flexible working hours have been continued to be used and were in place already before reunification. Productivity has increased and the work motivation is high, employees work overtime when needed even when they do not receive payment for it. However it is a big problem for many employees that since 1991 there has been constant uncertainty surrounding the privatisation of the company and many do not believe any longer that the company has got a future or that they can influence the course of the company.

D6 used to provide the same types of social benefits before 1990 as all other big companies. Although the company is doing very badly, it has kept the internal provision of a few benefits. The employees can still send their children to a company-owned holiday camp at subsidised rates and there also continues to be a sports' club. Employees furthermore receive presents on every five-year anniversary of their time at the company. When asked why these benefits were kept, the TUR claims that they are a small compensation and sign of appreciation for the employees in a situation where the company cannot give them many of the financial fringe benefits which employees of West German companies receive. Apparently these social services are very popular and increase the loyalty of employees.

The personnel manager is aware that the workload within the company is very unevenly distributed with some working an unacceptable amount of overtime because their specific skills are scarce and in high demand. The trade union representative would like to see a stop to redundancies and some long-term personnel plans to give the employees an aim and hope. She is amazed that the employees are not making any pay demands but in her words 'everybody has been with the company for very long and knows what is obtainable and what is not in the current situation'. The employees are satisfied with receiving the Tarif 'with no frills'. She also would like to see improvements in the flow of information in the company, between the management and Betriebsrat as well as between project managers and the company as a whole. But the main thing that the employees need is hope and an investor who is interested in the continued existence of the company, something some employees are cynical about.

Company D9: Doing Well as Part of a Worldwide Conglomerate

Company D9 used to specialise in manual gears for trucks before 1990. After the acquisition in 1991, the investor totally changed the company's product line. In the context of a large regrouping and specialisation of production sites within the conglomerate, the investor transferred entire production lines, including all of the physical capital, from other, West German, production sites to company D9. Consequently since 1992 company D9's main product are manual gears for cars (constituting 60 per cent of total sales). A further 30 per cent of sales is generated with the production of parts for automatic gears. The remaining 10 per cent are generated by manual gear parts.

Company D9 shed 2,300 jobs between 1990 and 1996, reducing its workforce from 3,000 people in 1990 to 700 in 1996. It is expected that employee numbers will stabilise at this level or possibly even increase slightly over time. The company was taken over by its investor July 1991.

A condition for the sale to take place was that the company reduces its workforce to 600 prior to privatisation. Great effort was invested into avoiding direct unemployment as a result of labour restructuring. Apparently this was a consequence not only of the personal convictions of the representative from the Treuhand supervising restructuring and of the managing director, but is was also the 'fear of mutiny by the workforce'. The TUR continues that 'all activities which did not belong to our core business were separated out'. About

250 jobs had been taken up by inmates from a nearby prison, who together with several hundred 'guest workers' on short-term contracts from Vietnam and Cuba were the first to go. All social institutions such as the kindergarten and the doctor's surgery were given to the local government and are still operating. Many former younger employees were taken over by subsidiaries of West German companies who were locating themselves in the neighbourhood. Almost everybody older than 55 was sent into early retirement. It is not without pride that the trade union representative estimates that in the end only about 400 employees were fired rather than directed into new employment elsewhere, many of which went however directly into state-run training or employment programmes.

The company increased its employee numbers after privatisation, only to reduce them again by 200 people when there was a slump in sales in 1993. This proved to be a very expensive policy for the company because demand for its product recovered unexpectedly. As a consequence only six weeks after employees had been made redundant and compensations had been paid, the very same people had to be re-employed because their company specific qualifications were needed. The company has concluded that in times of a slump it is more cost effective to hold on to its core workforce.

D9 has been profitable for tax purposes since 1995, but it is only in 1997 that it also became profitable according to internal accounting procedures.

In the judgement of the trade union representative and personnel manager the new production techniques introduced by the investor require differently rather than higher qualified workforce. They claim that in GDR times more improvisation was required in the day-to-day running of the factory, something 'that people are slowly unlearning'. Further qualifications were obtained by a few people from every administrative area, including procurement and logistics who then showed their colleagues how to deal with problems. The TUR claims that '*most of our learning has been learning by doing*'. People employed in technical jobs were generally sent to certified training programmes as needed. These training measures were financed by the investor. Overall both the trade union representative and personnel manager think that the qualifications obtained are highly specific to the company and that at times due to time pressure the employees receive less further training than would be desirable.

New forms of work organisation, such as quality control teams and flexible working times were introduced in order to obtain the requisite ISO quality standards reduce costs. Apparently there are severe problems surrounding work organisation in the company. Due to the high average age of employees, absences due to illness are not uncommon. At the same time employee numbers have been drastically reduced over time, so that there is very little slack on the labour side: According to the TUR foremen are overspecialised, frequently lack knowledge of production processes in their entirety and it is very difficult to find replacements for them should anyone fall ill. It seems that the root cause of the problem is understaffing and a too rigid separation of labour.

Solutions, such as job rotation, however are frequently resisted by the workers themselves. The trade union representative states that:

> Many changes are greeted with the suspicion that just like in the past we are dealing with propaganda and nothing else. Furthermore many foremen resist empowering other employees because they fear for their power base and job security.

The manager in charge of controlling reflects the sentiments of the manager in charge of change management in company D8 when stating that is was very difficult to introduce groups work, for example, without people saying: 'I know this, this is just like brigade work, you have only changed the label, this is just propaganda, just like in the old system.'

The main impulse for this restructuring of the product range came from the investor, who 'decided what should be produced for which customers'. In this sense, important customers were important influences as well, especially since the sales of company D9 are strongly focused on a single West German car manufacturer. The local management was an important secondary force behind the changes, especially by initiating them. The manager for controlling relates the following incidence:

> In 1990, before there was even the currency union, the management of company D9 packed a huge canister of petrol – they did not have enough foreign currency to stop for petrol in the West – and a few gears into a minibus and drove all the way to our head offices in West Germany. There they were with their truck, as if they had come from another planet, and they gave us a presentation trying to convince us to buy them, even though this was the first time we had really heard about company D9. We asked them, were their market was. They answered: We have not got one.

Productivity is now above western levels. Indeed, it was a condition for the investor to transfer some of its production lines from West German factories to D9 that productivity in D9 would lie 30 per cent above the West German factory's.

The manger in charge of controlling states that the investor was lucky by choosing a gradual approach to organisational change. The new West German and 'very fatherly' managing director was integrated into the existing old management but left within a year, leaving the company without any West German leadership at all between 1992 and 1994. Instead the existing management was extensively trained through courses and internships in West German subsidiaries and managerial hierarchies were flattened.

> Like this we maintained the internal networks intact, which are of great value. People know who can get things done, who can solve particular problems. Networks external to the company, Seilschaften, are downright dangerous however. People give, for example, supply or research contracts on the basis of non-economic considerations, which harms performance of course.

In 1994 a new West German managing director and a West German manager for controlling (the interviewee) joined the company. Apparently 'this experiment was a fiasco'. The new West German managing director was not respected by the workforce and they did not support him. After one year the managing director had to leave. As a consequence the entire current management consists of 'old' mangers with the exception of two West German experts who have joined the team. One of these, the manager for controlling, states that 'it is very important that West German managers behave in a way which is not guided by and which does not confirm stereotypes.'

Company H2: Drinking Chocolate with a Bitter Aftertaste

Company H2 was privatised in 1992 when 100 per cent of its shares were acquired by a Swiss investor from the same industrial sector. The company's results have fluctuated around the break-even point since privatisation. H2 had 2,400 employees in 199–92. This number has been reduced to 1,396 by 1997. No further redundancies are expected in the next five years. Of the 1,396 employees at least 90 per cent are directly employed on the production side. The middle management consists entirely of Hungarians, while about 18 of the top managers are from abroad. According to the TUR the longer term aim is to reduce this latter number by training local managers.

According to the personnel manager the largest challenge which the company is currently facing is the aim of making the company consistently profitable and a market leader in its product groups in a highly competitive market. Both he and the TUR state that the investor had expected much more demand growth than had actually taken place. These depressed demand conditions are something all the companies in the food industry which have been interviewed complain about. A further challenge facing the company is having to adapt to rapidly changing sales networks, with the multitude of traditional corner shops going bankrupt due competition from aggressively entering hyper- and supermarkets. Concerning challenges relating to the area of human resource management the personnel manager emphasises that as a company with a 75 year tradition in Hungary H2 needs to keep the social peace in the company while introducing changes and new approaches to the organisation of work.

The factory of company H2 which I visited used to produce cookies, coffee, drinking chocolate (for which it acquired a licence from its later investor in 1986). This factory had been originally bought by H3's investor and was immediately sold on to H2's. H2's major production centres are located in northern Hungary and the sections on production cannot be viewed as entirely representative of these factories as well. After 1992, the factory I visited specialised in producing instant drinking chocolate, while the product group of H2's other main factory in northern Hungary proliferated from sweets production only to include convenience foods.

The northern Hungarian production sites received the lion's share of the overall 5–6 billion HUF (@ 48 million DM) invested into H2. The last big investment into the Budapest factory took place in 1988, when the licence for producing instant chocolate drinks was acquired. The biggest investment by the investor into this factory was the introduction of wafer production in 1993. 350 million HUF (@ 3.09 million DM) were invested into this project, which however failed and was facing closure when I visited in 1997. The factory's general manager blamed insufficient market research before the product's introduction[5] and inadequate marketing subsequently.

Only two new production methods have been introduced since 1992: computers in stock management and CAD systems. As a result production of instant chocolate powder has increased from 400 kg per hour (1988) to 700 kg (1997). The average age of the machinery used in production is about 10 years, while its technical lifetime is about 15–20 years. According to its general manager the packaging of the instant drinking chocolate powder has improved, but 'product quality has continuously declined following investment. We are forced to use more and more substitute ingredients.' Furthermore the investor does not provide its Hungarian subsidiaries with state of the art machinery. 'Usually we get machines which have been replaced in Western factories. We are expected to be happy with outdated machines and generally there is very little investment by foreigners which is of a high quality.' The uncertain future of the Budapest factory is reflected in the fact that although it has a capacity of 26,000 tonnes per year, it is currently only producing 3,000 tonnes. According to the factory's general manager the main problem is that H2's Budapest factory is located on too big a property and it is very expensive to pay all the taxes and maintain the buildings on the property. At the moment the investor would like to sell the factory.

In the judgement of the factory's general manager, the production of the core product requires the same amount of technological know-how as before and the same basic production technology. He requires, however, better-trained employees. On the question whether the same or more organisational know-how is required, he has a rather differentiated opinion. According to him there has been an increasing trend to centralise all decision-making functions and activities in the head office, reversing the trend towards functional decentralisation to the individual factories and away from the central authorities which had marked economic policy in Hungary between 1968 and 1992. He claims that the advantages of such internal centralisation are that orders are placed centrally which increases the company's monopsony power vis a vis suppliers and also enables the head office to impose more uniform processes on the factories.

The factory manager claims, however, that a major problem resulting from centralisation is information loss, which is augmented through the fact that decision-makers in the factories are spatially separated from decision-makers in the head offices. In his perception mental and cultural differences are also developing between the factories and the head offices, especially since 'there is a very high proportion of ex-pat managers in the head office'. The factory's general manager's conclusion on internal centralisation is that:

> the investor tries to have coherent organisational methods on a worldwide scale. This leads to excessive hierarchies and to a situation where these uniform methods do not adjust well every time to local conditions. Hungary is too small and idiosyncratic. H2 suffers from informational problems and ends up reacting in retrospect. The management consists mainly of ex-pat managers[6] who have learnt some Hungarian, but nevertheless it still has great problems in picking up information from the surroundings in which H2 operates. This is a particular problem for the marketing department.

His overall conclusion on the issue of organisational know-how is that:

> the masses are required to be disciplined and reliable, but the attitude is that the average employee does not have to understand the bigger picture. In this respect

the average employee or even the factory manager is required to have the same or even less organisational know-how than before. A few top employees, however, face greatly increased demands since everything has to be centrally planned and designed etc.

The main determining force in the restructuring of H2's products and production processes was the investor. The Budapest factory's general manager claims that 'in theory market forces play an important role', but in practice H2 is not innovative or very aggressive. The market is saturated and all the players have a large excess capacity.'The 'old' management had a secondary influence on the restructuring process of production, but this was not for lack of trying. Apparently there were large clashes between the old management and ex-pat managers in the factory in northern Hungary. My interview partner described them as follows:

Two internally closed groups were facing each other. My colleagues had to deal with ex-pats who had little understanding of our products. The ex-pats wanted to get rid of all local brands. Many local managers got sacked over this issue and the ex-pats got their way. But the introduction of the Western brands was a flop: There was a big price difference between the new brands and the local brands which had been scrapped and this price difference was, in the eyes of the Hungarian consumer, not justified by quality differences. Introducing new brands also entails large advertising costs etc. The ex-pats learned it the hard way that it is worth keeping local Hungarian brands and have re-introduced the very brands they had been so keen to scrap and re-place by their own Western ones.

When asked about the development of labour productivity, the trade union representative claims that it has greatly increased and that 'in our attitudes, aptitude and degree of willingness we are totally on a Western level. However our productivity is also influenced by factors such as our suppliers and customs and excise regulations.' The personnel manager added:

In the West one factory produces one product. Before privatisation, different factories in the food industry specialised as well. Now these factories have been privatised to different investors and all the new companies want to produce everything, reversing the previously existing division of labour within the food industry. This leads to a very high degree of complexity in each factory and when you compare such a factory to a specialised Western factory, you are not comparing like with like. Our one factory which is specialising in one product almost fulfils Western standards.

Concerning the persistence of social service provision in the company the personnel manager states that 'In Hungary there are two types of companies: Firstly there are greenfield sites, where employers pay a fair wage but all social questions are left to the state. Secondly there are old companies like us, who inherit a multitude of social obligations.' The social institutions which have been inherited and kept by H2 include doctors' surgeries on all sites, a holiday camp, interest free loans for house building or purchasing, free babyfood for the children of employees, children's days, sport events and a shop where employees can purchase the products of the company at reduced rates. The kindergarten has been given to the local council and the company is currently trying to sell the apartments it owns. The trade union representative stresses that not only have almost all the social institutions been kept but also a new canteen has been built and air conditioning has been introduced where only possible. When asked why these social institutions have been kept, not only the generally 'humane' company philosophy of the investor is mentioned but the personnel manager also mentions that:

> Hungarians now understand that a higher productivity is needed. At the same time foreigners are starting to understand that we not only have a work culture and traditions of our own[7] but also that we are highly qualified and have experiences which are of value. Cooperation is starting to work by learning on both sides.

Company H5: Satellite Structures in a Company Town

Company H5 has essentially the same product range today as it did previously (polyolefin feedstocks and products). Since the company's privatisation in 1995 production methods have been continuously upgraded, but no radical changes have been introduced, since the company employed Western-type production methods already before 1995.[8] The Deputy CEO was, however, keen to stress that H5 always invests into the best technology it can conceivably afford when making new capital investments.[9]

Company H5 had 5,000 employees in 1990. Of these, about 1600 employees were transferred to 32 affiliated companies which from 1991 onwards have been separated out from H5 as part of its restructuring plan or which are joint venture greenfield developments with a foreign investor. These 32 affiliated companies can be grouped into:

- petrochemical and trading companies (eight companies, with H5 having a 75 per cent, 40 per cent, 33 per cent, 40 per cent, 100 per cent, 100 per cent, 51 per cent and 65 per cent stake respectively);
- technical and environmental companies (nine companies, with H5's share being typically, with the exception of one minority holding, about 98 per cent);
- service companies (nine companies, except in the case of two minority holdings, H5 averages again about a 98 per cent stake);
- plastic processing companies (three companies, with H5 having a 50 per cent, 25.1 per cent and 83.1 per cent stake respectively); and
- financial companies (3 companies with majority stakes).[10]

All the affiliated companies operate as independent divisions and profit centres. In 1997 H5 itself employs 3,500 people.

H5 has floated on the Hungarian stock exchange in 1996 in preference to finding an investor and has not experienced mass redundancies, a factor which both the management and the workforce see as a big achievement. There seems to be a belief among the management and workforce that had the company been privatised to a foreign direct investor, then mass redundancies would have occurred. The reason given is that an investor would have simplified the product profile of the company (that is focus on the lower end of the vertically integrated ladder) to fit his own need for input supply. According to the trade union representative, H5 would be employing only about 1,200 people today had it been privatised to a foreign direct investor. In his judgement this would have had detrimental regional consequences in an area of Hungary where unemployment rates are well above the national average and were in his opinion 50,000–60,000 jobs depend indirectly on the activities of H5. He states that the Western companies who showed an interest in acquiring H5:

> wanted to use us for input production only. They had the idea that the biggest profits can be gained from pure input production and they thought that they could buy all ancillary activities and services later. Even disregarding the human and regional consequences of this stance, what they did not realise, is that in Hungary the necessary background industries do not exist.

The trade union representative is convinced that it is due to the very active stance of the local trade union that such a course of events was averted:

> Between 1990–94 we had yearly changing MDs[11] due to the interference of political interests with the company. Consequently the management could not represent the interests of the company, the union had to do this and we tended to get our way because we were the only stable group. In 1995 we got a new and very dynamic management who finally took a pro-active stance.

The company's profits are highly influenced by fluctuations in world prices for its in- and outputs. Consequently the company's profits have been fluctuating but consistently positive since 1995. I do not have information on the preceding five years when the company did not publish official accounts.

When asked what in his opinion were the greatest challenges the company was currently facing, the personnel manager of H5 stated that this was certainly the management of the restructuring process. He sees it as his task to find solutions which are 'as humane as possible: we are human and hence can empathise with employees and have to consider the human consequences of our decisions. We try and talk to each affected employee on an individual basis. ' The trade union representative emphasises the need to secure the long-run future of the company. He is concerned that the institutional investors which the company has been privatised to might be unwilling to tie their money down for long enough to enable H5 to invest into sufficient R&D activities.

Productivity has greatly increased with sales (in HUF millions) per head increasing from 5.7 in 1993 to 7.8 in 1994, 12.5 in 1995 and 15.0 in 1996.[12] The trade union representative estimates that today the company's productivity level is about 90 per cent of a Western chemicals company of similar size, while the personnel manager puts this figure at 80 per cent. They both claim that the company operates with the newest Western technologies and is just as productive on the production side as a Western counterpart, but the discrepancy in productivity is due to the fact that H5 engages in many (social) activities that Western companies do not engage in.

In this context it is relevant that the company has kept all its social activities and benefits. These include a very large recreational facilities on the premises, the provision of medical services, lunches, holiday camps, transportation and financial aid for house building. The trade union representative claims that these services were kept because of a well-organised union which was willing to fight for them every year. He concedes that making sure that employees are looked after socially is also in the management's interest in a country where wages are extremely low when compared to Western levels. The personnel manager agrees that many of these activities detract from the company's profitability but are essential in maintaining morale.

Company H6: How did it Come to This?

In an international comparison, the buses of company H6 are in the middle to upper middle quality range. H6 constitutes an interesting case which is very difficult to categorise even along the lines of whether we are dealing here with a failed privatisation or with a privatisation delayed by valid concerns. It is also unclear whether we are examining an example of how a company with prospects can be ruined by political meddling or examining an example of how political interference keeps alive what is really a dinosaur with no real prospects for commercial success. What emerges from the interviews however, is that the employees and middle managers of the company do not seem to have themselves a very clear picture or coherent story of what has lead to the decline of what was once a showpiece of the Hungarian manufacturing industry. Nor do they have a consistent vision of the future. The only unifying factor seems to be that many of them are pinning all their hopes on the new MD who took over in October 1996.

H6's main products are buses of all categories, vehicle parts and vehicle manufacturing equipment. H6 used to specialise on all types of buses, including models aimed at mass transportation and long-range luxury coaches. After 1990 the major change in H6's product range has been to produce less luxury models and focus more on mass transport models. The aim has been to make quality improvements and develop new models in the latter product group. Nobody could (or was willing to) give me a precise number concerning total investment into the company since 1990. The manager of logistics volunteered that since the company has been loss making throughout the 1990–97 period, there has been only very little investment, mainly in the area of CAD and CAM systems. Overall only the investments 'which were absolutely unavoidable' (manager for logistics) were undertaken.

In 1990 company H6 had 10,500 employees. There were two main factories producing finished buses and another five factories producing components and parts. In 1997 the company employed 3,200 people. This number includes the 700 people who were hired at the beginning of 1997. If one includes the employees who have been transferred to newly founded companies, then of the original workforce about 7,500 people are still employed either by H6 itself or one of the companies separated out from it. The overall number of people who have been made redundant is about 4,000.

According to the personnel manager in 1991–92 quite a few people wanted to actually leave voluntarily: at this time unemployment benefits were fairly generous and people figured that they could have quite a comfortable life living off these benefits and their earnings in the black market economy. This however lead to a very undesirable outcome for H6: it was the most able and highly trained workers who had the best outside options and for this reason the 'worst' administrators etc. were the ones staying, leading to the increase in the proportion of white collar workers.

The trade union representative is particularly disappointed at the attitude which employees showed during the restructuring process.

> The union and management organised an information day where we brought in people from many large companies and employment agencies to give talks and advice. They also brought many jobs with them, because they were hunting for people with certain qualifications they hoped to find among the pool of people becoming unemployed in our factory. Of the 40 people invited to attend, only 12 turned up. Employees were behaving as if they were 'hurt' and like sulking children. They thought they could manage on their own, they did not respond to the questionnaires sent out to them, were incredibly passive and still believed in the old slogan: 'The factory belongs to us!' People believed that nobody would take the hammer out of their hands and nobody in their right mind would want their job. Society and individuals were very surprised by the changes.

The problems H6 was having in terms of labour shedding were also reflected on the production side. At the height of its output throughout the 1980s, the company produced in excess of 12,000 buses a year. In 1989 an accelerated decline set in and production in H6 fell to about 8,000 buses in 1990, 4,500 in 1991, 3,800 in 1992 and via a particularly marked fall from about 3,500 buses in 1993 to 1,574 buses in 1994 and about 500 buses in 1996. Production recovered to 1,500–2,000 buses in 1997.[13] This fall in sales was mainly due to a strong decline in exports since during this period the domestic demand was fairly stable at about 300 buses per annum.[14]

The question as to what exactly cause H6's startling decline is rather intriguing. In 1995 a *HVG* article (June 10) the author György Heimer claimed that the problems company H6 faces are due to three main factors: firstly, by this time the company was facing a disastrous financial situation, with its debts amounting to about 16.1 billion HUF by 1995.[15] By 1997 the debt burden of the company was larger than its official book value.[16] This severe debt burden also went together with life-threatening liquidity problems, which at times questioned the continuation of day-to-day production and the payment of wages. The second problem referred to by György Heimer is the large overcapacity which the company was facing and its outdated top-heavy organisational structure. Thirdly the article mentions the ongoing disagreements between the company's two main owners at the time, the ÁPV Rt and a Russian consortium.

Between 1990 and 1995 the company had its 'old' management. The strategy of this management team had two main discernible tenants: one was to aim for a financial consolidation with the assistance of the Hungarian state and the other to hope for the company's major export market, Russia, to pick up again. This management approach is categorised by Iván Major and Éva Voszka[17] as 'conservative-traditional', where the management lobbies the government to obtain debt consolidation, but does not re-focus itself on market-orientated behaviour. The ÁPV Rt and Ministry of Trade and Industry were open to efforts to obtain financial injections for the company because the existence of a domestic bus producer continued to be viewed to be of strategic importance. It was also estimated that about 50,000 jobs were directly or indirectly connected with the company's operations in 1990. Even in 1997, with the activities of H6 being greatly reduced this number is still put at about 16,000 (interview with the trade union representative). The achieved debt consolidation was insufficient to solve the company's spiralling debt problem.

The second element of this old management's strategy had as its main result that for 50 million US $ a Russian consortium acquired a 30 per cent stake in the company in 1991 together with the right to veto major business decisions.[18] The idea behind this sale was that the Russian consortium, which included the government of Belarus, as well as local governments and municipalities, could guarantee H6 a demand of about 6,000 buses per annum. The export into the former SU averaged about 7,500 buses per annum in the 1980s. Unfortunately, this promise was never formulated in a written, contract-ually binding form.[19] Comments obtained in interviews on what happened instead vary from 'this is just a number which was mentioned verbally' to 'I suppose that, as usual, everybody got pretty drunk by the time the contract was signed.'[20]

The relationship which evolved between the two owners of the company, that is the Russian consortium and the Hungarian state property agency, ended up being very acrimonious. Due to the inability of the Russian side to pay, the export into the former SU almost entirely collapsed to 800 buses in 1994. This lead the ÁPV Rt to hold the Russians responsible for the company's lack of orders, while the Russians were pointing the finger at the Hungarian state's insufficient financial infusions and threatening with law suits. The personnel manager of H6 has, for example, claimed that strong anti-Soviet feelings did not help the company because they kept the Hungarian state from granting the company the financial assurances it needed in order to be able the export illiquid Russian customers.

During all this the management of the company continued in its passive stance and was unable to achieve a resolution of the conflicts between the two owners or to force decisions.[21] According to the trade union representative the MD of the company was very ill with heart problems and nobody wanted to step in because it was unclear who the acting MD was supposed to be. (This statement can be interpreted in two ways: either there were internal rivalries between the senior management or nobody wanted to take responsibility in a highly hierarchical organisation.) Consequently no decisions were made by the management and the company drifted while its owners were fighting with each other. It can also be assumed that the involvement of the Russian investor and his public disagreements with the ÁPV Rt (or rather ÁV Rt as it was then called) did nothing to improve H6's reputation in the Western banking community or to encourage interest in potential Western investors.

By 1995 at the latest, the battle and disagreements between the two main owners became the very much public knowledge and the fate of the company a question with political implications for the government. It was at this point that the Hungarian State Property Agency instituted a new MD against the resistance of the Russian investor.[22] According to an off-the record comment by an interview partner (not necessarily from within H6 itself) 'this person was a well-known political figure from the "old" system. In the economic sphere, his main qualification was that he had totally ruined the Hungarian shipbuilding industry in the 1980s by dubious deals to Russia.'

The new MD's plan was that the company was to be prepared for public tender so that it could be acquired by a foreign direct investor from the same industry. This would have meant that the advocates of finding a privatisation strategy which maintains the production of buses in Hungary would have lost. It was expected that the acquisition by a foreign direct investor would have almost certainly entailed that the company would have become a components manufacturer for the investor. Apparently the Russian minority owner was not at all in favour of this renewed effort at privatisation.[23] Since it was planned however that 80 per cent of the shares of the company should be offered, the cooperation of the Russian consortium was necessary.

> It is claimed that [the MD] had the lion's share in 'convincing' the Russian investor: apparently he recommended the rather risky strategy, according to which if H6 is allowed to drift towards bankruptcy, then [the Russian investor] will understand that he will loose more during bankruptcy proceedings [than if he offers his shares for sale] ...[24]

It is true that the Russian investor would have lost his initial 50 million US $ investment during bankruptcy agreements. It is also true however, that bankruptcy proceedings would have also meant that the company would have been broken up into several pieces with the aim of selling whatever is possible before the unsellable rest would have been closed down. Bankruptcy proceedings would have hence been very much in the interest of a foreign direct investor, who was only interested in acquiring parts of H6: they would have enabled him to acquire the attractive pieces, without having to take on the risks and costs associated with restructuring the entire company.[25] Investors typically only showed interested in the factory in which the mass production of the lower quality models takes place rather the factory which produces the latest and more upmarket models in smaller batches and engages in the company's R&D.

Whatever the true motivation of the new MD might have been, during his one and a half years at the company, H6 did indeed almost go bankrupt: the fall in its sales accelerated, the company suffered record losses and debt levels. The public tender came about, but straight from the beginning there were claims that 'the conception of the tender has not been thought through and there is a great ex ante probability that it is going to be unsuccessful'.[26] The tender did indeed end very quickly in a fiasco and not a single share was sold to a foreign investor.[27]

During this time the management of the company was slowly waking up to the fact that a) the MD was indeed driving the company bankrupt and b) if the company goes bankrupt they will all loose their jobs. Nevertheless it was not resistance on the side of the management which ultimately lead to the dismissal of the MD but the involvement of the workforce and the Russian investor. The trade union representative stated that:

> the workers resisted the liquidation of the company. Every two months we had a general meeting in which the union told the employees about each and every decision the management had taken or was planning. We disseminated every piece of information available to us. This information contra-acted the worker's fear and totally eroded the credibility of the management. In December 1995 we had a three day general strike because the employees were not getting paid and they no longer trusted the management. The ÁPV Rt wanted the employees to publicly discredit the MD, but we refused to do this because those who put him in charge in the first place, that is the Minister of Industry and the Prime Minister, they should also take the responsibility and blame.

In their attempts to get rid of the MD the management and workforce were joined by the Russian investor and apparently this 'lobby' won over the support of the then minister in charge of privatisation and related questions.[28] The idea of replacing the MD by a well-known entrepreneur, who is also the president of the independent association of manufacturing employers, was first leaked to the press and then put into action on a general meeting in July 1996.

The new MD has a programme which is radically different from the strategy endorsed by his predecessor. In his opinion not a single production site belonging to H6 needs to be closed and he views the company's sales prospects as so positive that he expects the output levels of the company to stabilise around 3,500 buses per annum in the medium term. Although he is universally seen as a large improvement upon the last MD, the opinions on the new MD diverge: in the interviews I conducted in 1997, the head of corporate strategy stated that 'the new MD is celebrated for 'saving' company X.[29] But today they do not produce a finished product there any more, just components which nobody wanted to produce in Asia.' A young engineer who recently joined H6 stated his personal opinion about company X: 'Engineers like me who can design and build entire finished products are just sticking cables together. He has saved and created jobs, but they are further down the value added chain than the ones which were there originally.' What worries the head of strategy in particular is that in his opinion:

> the new MD does not have the know-how needed for H6 and he is keen in quantity but neglects quality.[30] However, he had got a good reputation, good connections to the banking sector and is the darling of the Western media.

In the opinion of the trade union representative, the new MD is:

> the countries best entrepreneur. He is the head of the industry lobby and he has very good private sector experiences. I am sure he means his promises and that he is sincerely interested in continuing the operations of the company and in making us profitable again.

The new MD has kept his promise to increase production, which to a large extent have been made possible by World Bank loans to customers. The personnel manager stated that:

> in each and every sale we make to countries in the former eastern block there is some World Bank involvement down the line. There has always been demand for our products, our customers just could not pay.

For the first time since the late 1980s, the company was making a small profit in 1997.

I was told that the next planned step is to have a management buy-out of the company, which would also greatly reduce the stake of the Russian investor. This buy-out would effectively see the new MD acquiring 51 per cent of the company and a further 5 per cent and 10 per cent of the shares going to the employees and the management of the company respectively. The new MD does not exclude the possibility of selling the remaining shares to Western investors, but claims that this would, as in the case of company X, only happen in the context of a holding company.[31] The trade union representative thinks that this MBO would be highly beneficial for the company, since like this the property rights in the company would be acquired by its real stakeholders. I asked him what in his opinion will stop the new MD from selling on his 51 per cent stake to a Western investor after he has achieved a consolidation of the company's debts and an improvement in its prospects. The trade union representative looked at me with some alarm and said after a moment's pause: 'You are right, nothing stops him. When it comes down to it, we just trust him.'

Intriguingly, in early autumn 1997 with 1,800–2,000 buses having been sold and the company making profits again that year, 53.9 per cent of H6 was offered for public tender.[32] A public tender to a Western foreign director had not been mentioned to me in any way when I visited the company in May. In the same article in the *Financial Times* we can also read that the parties interested in acquiring this stake did not only include a Malaysian, German and Swedish bus manufacturer but also that the MD 'expressed an interest in bidding for the stake'. However already six weeks later we can read in the *FT* that the main bidder, who had tried to acquire the company already once previously, 'withdrew due to (H6's) deceptive financial position and difficulties in fulfilling the severe condition of the bid'.[33]

Company H7: U-turn to Success

Company H7 used to produce lamp equipment, lamps, electronic tools and robotics. After its privatisation in 1990 H7 concentrated on its core business, acting as a vertically integrated lamp manufacturer. Vertical integration has increased since the export of components has increased. The production of electronic tools, robotics and plastics has been closed down. Consequently, of H7's 10 factories acquired by the investor six are still operative in 1997. Accumulative investment into the remaining production sites has amounted to over 650 million US $ between 1990 and 1997. This investment has been mainly into physical capital, the working and natural environment and infrastructural needs, new products (mainly the new Genura lamp) and improving the telecommunications facilities in the company.

Both nationally and internationally Company H7 is widely regarded as 'one of the flagships of Hungarian industry, which was privatised in an exemplary way ... Its existence and activities are proof of how valuable and valued Hungarian brain-power is.'[34] The acquisition of company H7 by its investor in 1989/90 'represented the largest post-WWII investment in Eastern Europe by a Western company'. Which lead to 'the eyes of the world watching us (H7 and its investor) with great interest'.[35] The investor purchased 51 per cent of H7's shares in 1990. By 1993 he increased his stake in the company to 99 per cent.

If one visits the company today, then one can very easily gain the impression that the relationship between H7 and its investor was always a harmonious and exemplary one. When asking more probing questions however, one soon discovers that this relationship underwent two distinct phases: In the first phase from 1989 to the end of 1992 the relationship between H7 and its investor was increasingly strained. According to the trade union representative, in 1992 things got so bad that it almost came to a general strike and a negative publicity campaign in the press against the investor. The reason for this discontent was that the company's employees reached the conviction 'with 75 per cent certainty' (trade union representative) that the investor had only been really interested in gaining market share for himself by acquiring H7 and was now systematically working towards H7's closure.

For example, H7 had a 7 per cent market share in Western Europe in its main product lines in 1989. By 1992 this percentage had almost halved due to 'the investor's insistence of introducing American methods into the European market leading to a total disorganisation in H7's sales and marketing activities'[36] (trade union representative). Furthermore the investor did not realise the international strength of H7's brand name and insisted on H7's brand being replaced by the investor's brand on all of H7's products from one day to the next. 'Our sales people had to pick up the phone and introduce themselves as employees of our investor. We literally had buyers calling up and responding "Sorry, I misdialled. I wanted to speak to company H7" and hanging up.'[37]

At the same time it was widely reported in the *Economist*, *FT* and *Wall Street Journal* in March 1992 that H7's investor was cutting investment from the agreed 40 million US $ in 1992 to 30 million US $, cutting employment by 25 per cent and introducing production stoppages. The move was justified with the company suffering three years of successive losses and increasing costs due to the insufficient devaluation of the HUF. It is only an article in the Wall Street Journal which mentions that 'by US accounting methods (H7) was profitable in 1992. The reported loss is due to the fact that Hungarian accounting methods do not allow restructuring costs to be spread over several years as US methods do.'[38] It was furthermore not reported that H7's output had been growing both in value and volume from year to year in this period even though its Eastern markets collapsed.[39]

As part of the restructuring process in this early phase about 2,000 employees were transferred to ancillary service companies which were separated out of H7. The trade union representative saw it as a further indication that the investor was intending to bankrupt the company that:

> the union had co-operated in the dismissal of 6,000 people between 1990 and the end of 1991. However in 1992 the investor suddenly reduced the workforce from 11,600 to 9,300 people and announced that he wished to reduce the workforce by another 25 per cent. They were sending people away although nobody could operate the new machines. In order to try and justify the bad results the company was suffering, the American side was also spreading lies in the press about Hungarian workers.[40] At this point the employees of the company decided to blow the whistle. Even though they were afraid they presented a united front behind the union because the union knew the value of the company and its potential. We also got hold of a copy of the investor's 1989 contract with the government and publicly attacked the government. For an investor who had come here as the messiah of democracy to be contradicted by his own actions is very embarrassing. Things were getting out of hand for the investor and in order to avoid the scandal gaining momentum and harming his international brand image, he introduced a few changes. These changes had almost immediate and highly positive results. It was a heaven sent that at this moment in time the few people the investor had forgotten to sack from our R&D department came up with a ground breaking invention. With our crippled R&D department solving problems the pampered US facilities had been incapable of solving and minute organisational changes bringing such large results, the investor made a U-turn in his policies towards us.

The U-turn which took place in the end of 1992 was reported in the Western press as 'a shake up in [H7's investor] aimed at integrating [H7] with [the investor's UK] business ...'.[41] The same article reports that the investor moved four out of nine of its European lighting research centres to H7. There is only a vague indication in the article of what lead to these developments, when in an interview the Hungarian head of R&D states that 'up to now the Westerners gave the instructions'.

The clearest statement of what had concerned the employees of H7 and of the investor's changed attitude is the contractual agreement which the management of H7 and the trade union representatives signed concerning 'the present and future situation of H7' on the 7 December 1992. The first point made after the introduction is that 'the management [of the investor] assures the trade union and the collective of H7 that they do not intend to liquidate H7'. Assurances also include that:

- H7 will continue to produce modern products;
- it will receive machines which fit into its existing profile;
- further capital investments are going to take place;
- there will be concentrated effort at increasing H7's output and market share; and
- there will be an effort to sell rather than liquidate all those activities which do not fit into H7's profile.

The management also commits itself to 'continue to honestly communicate those goals which affect the future of H7'. In return to union states that it 'does not wish to hinder the restructuring process nor the increase in production' while they expect that the management 'do everything to sell the additional output resulting from the increases in productivity'. The management commits itself to continue to employ in labour restructuring 'all those human methods[42] – early retirement, ... redundancy payments – which are worth considering' while the management 'continues to expect the participation and help of the trade union in these [restructuring] activities'. The unions agree to 'do every-thing in the interest of achieving an atmosphere of work peace and trust' while the management agree to give detailed information to the trade unions every two months. The management also agrees that only 'justified' reductions in employee numbers are going to take place and that at no point is the activity of H7 going to be endangered due to excessive reductions in employee numbers. The trade union only accepts those redundancies as justified which are the result of new capital goods investment, the introduction of new technologies or a consequence of technology based restructuring. Both sides express the wish for their 'cooperative partnership to become deeper and more lasting on all levels'. The document ends by asserting that 'both parties work towards maintaining and strengthening an atmosphere of mutual trust in each employee of H7, so that with united strength we can all create an H7 which is economically strong'.

The trade union representative states that in the beginning the Americans had claimed that the company's productivity was only one-seventh of Western levels. He says that this was never true, already because the investor was comparing a highly integrated company (H7) with many social and ancillary services with a company focusing only on production itself. In 1997 productivity in the company has reached Western levels, with some comparable Western companies being less productive than H7. These productivity levels have been reached via a succession of two digit growth levels over the past few years.

It is in keeping with the spirit of the 1992 agreement that the company still provides its employees with a wide range of social benefits. These include holiday camps, sport clubs, doctor's surgeries, legal aid, a swimming pool, kindergarten as well as loans for house buyers and house builders. The personnel manager says that these benefits were kept out of tradition and that a special effort was made to keep those benefits which benefited the low-paid workers. The aim was to improve the employee's loyalty to the company and their work motivation. The trade union representative stresses that the employees had to fight hard to keep these benefits. Their attitude was that these benefits could only be taken away from them if people earn so much that they can afford to buy these services outside. He also claimed that in his opinion 'the East Germans were only concerned with consumption, they had the utopian expectation that their rich brother will provide them with Western living standards over night.'

Since 1994 the company was making profits according to both the US and the Hungarian accounting systems and the number of employees was raised to 10,300 in 1994. Employee numbers have been stable at this level ever since and if anything, further increases are expected in the medium run, leaving the personnel manager to worry about a possible shortage in skilled labour.

The R&D[43] capacity of the company has been continuously increased since 1992, with the investor eventually transferring his entire worldwide lighting research capacity to the Hungarian site. H7 is now exporting 95 per cent of its output worldwide and has been described in a *Financial Times* article (1 October 1997) as a 'world-class company with at least half the advanced technology being done locally'.

Company H11: Politicking Most Horrid

Between 1990 and 1997 the company's core products and their relative importance has remained unchanged. H11's productive activities fall into two main groups: firstly the exploration of natural gas and production of gas product such a butane and propane and secondly the exploration (in Hungary mainly) and refining of crude oil into jet fuel, kerosene, diesel, gas oil, light fuel oil and heavy fuel oil. In 1996 the company's largest product groups in terms of their gross sales revenues contribution were motoric gasolines, gas and heating oils, fuel oils and lubricants.[44]

The company started updating its operation in 1985 when a World Bank loan it received was tied to the condition of restructuring. This early restructuring did not however effect employee numbers significantly. Consequently H11 still had 40,000 employees in 1990. Between 1985 and when the company was floated in 1991, 33 new companies with overall 17,000 employees were founded, leaving H11 to float with 22,000 employees. The company has a vertically integrated core business incorporating oil exploration and production on the one had and refining and marketing on the other. The 33 companies which have been separated out mainly consist of ancillary services outside this verticum.

Overall, H11's yearly investment has been between 45 and 60 bn HUF since 1990. Consequently, even on the most conservative estimate H11 had capital investments of at least 2.78 billion DM between 1990 and 1996.[45]

In 1997 the company had 14.500 employees. Consequently the overall number of redundancies in H11 itself between 1990 and 1997 is estimated to have been no more than 8,500 (trade union representative). According to the personnel manager there were many people who went voluntarily in the beginning, either because they thought they could do better outside or because they could not cope with the uncertainty they were facing. He also complains about targeted head-hunting of their best employees by Western rivals entering the market. The company made extensive use of early retirement and gave redundancy payments which reflected the years of employment. The trade union representative points out that in 1992 an agreement was reached between the management and the trade union that it would be necessary to reduce the number of H11's employees to 12,000 people by 1997 in order to maintain the company's long-run international competitiveness. He states that these redundancies are still necessary to reduce the relatively high costs of the company and blames this 'restructuring backlog' on the distraction provided by the political struggles in the top management in the first half of the 1990s.

Company H11 is one of the largest Hungarian companies. Although it has been floated in the stock exchange in 1991, it has continued to receive a lot of political attention since the state has maintained a majority stake in what is viewed as a company of strategic importance (about 60 per cent in 1997, reduced to 45 per cent in 1997). Rumours about the company are abound and regularly make their appearances in the press.[46] They range from oil smuggling to Serbia during the embargo to the whole impenetrable web of interwoven political interests in the company termed 'Oilgate' by one of the interviewees (who was not necessarily from H11 itself).

The interview partner referring to smuggling operations to Serbia stated:

> It was a highly organised operation through which oil was smuggled from the Ukraine to Serbia via Hungary, fetching prices three times the world price during the embargo. One can safely assume that one of the agents involved in this on the Hungarian side was H11. We had instances where 20 wagons of crude oil were parked in a small station near the Russian border over night, ostensibly for administrative reasons. By the morning the content of all these wagons had vanished. Nobody had heard or seen anything.

Why this operation went 'undetected' and unexamined for years is indicated by the 'Oilgate' scandal of 1994–summer 1995.

An informal but illustrative summary was given to me by another interview partner:

> It was simple really. One group of politicians was making money out of the storage operations of H11. Another group was making money out of refining. As part of restructuring, it was proposed that H11 should reduce its storage facilities.[47] This would have meant losses for the guys making money out of storage, so they then dished the dirt on those making money out of refining, accusing them of corruption. These predictably retaliated by throwing the mud at those who make money out of storage and the nation was watching in amazement as the scandal unfolded and started implicating the son of the then Minister of Industry, high ranking officials in this ministry and members of the MSZP [the successor to the Communist Party].

Apparently in 1997 it is still a political question as to who should gain control over the company. An indication of the extent of political involvement in the company is that regular changes in its top management not only reflect government changes but also political struggles within the ruling political party. One contestor for control is 'the Russian lobby'. According to one source this lobby 'attempted a coup' in 1994 when a group internal to the company rumoured to have had close associations with the then minister for industry, who incidentally studied in Russia and has a Russian wife, 'tried to buy the company on their behalf'.[48] This attempt was apparently stopped because 'the head offices of H11 blew the whistle' (trade union representative of H11) and 'the then American ambassador got involved' (another interview partner). The minister of trade and industry was sacked over this affair. The *Financial Times*, noting his resistance against privatising the electricity and oil sector to foreign investors, commented that his dismissal was 'a victory for reformers who considered [him] an obstacle to the rapid sale of the state electricity company and other utilities ...'.[49] Not much later the MD of H11, who was a chief agent in making public the scandal surrounding the activities of the 'Russian lobby' in the company and the former minister of trade was sacked as well.[50] He was replaced by the very same former minister of industry to whose dismissal he had contributed. The former minister has held to post of MD for several years to come. An employee stated (anonymously) about the new MD towards the researchers conducting a study for ÁPV Rt:

> He was unsuitable for being a minister [of trade and industry] ... Horn [the Prime Minister] behaves like a feudal lord who fist punishes his servant and then gives him a new turf ... They put people in our neck who are clueless about economics ...[51]

An alternative scenario would be for a company like Schell to buy H11, that is for a majority stake in it to be acquired by a direct foreign investor.

One does not have to, however, resort to rather murky rumours to gain an indication of the extent to which the operations of this company are politicised. H11 still has a state monopoly in gas wholesaling, but at the same time until recently it had to effectively sell the gas it imports to the domestic market below costs.[52] The company has greatly benefited from import taxes on fuel hitting its competitors, while at the same time it had to provide an effective cross subsidy to company H5 between 1992 and 1996.[53] In a contract made in December 1992 the obligation to pay the majority of a lease taken up in 1992 by H5 in order to finance the construction of a polyethylene and of a polypropylene plant was transferred to H11. In May 1996 the ÁPV Rt decided to settle the transaction between the two companies by having H5 pay H11 HUF 3.840 million in compensation for H11 involvement over the past four years in the leasing transaction. This is a rather small sum when considering that H11 paid H5 over 2.5 billion HUF between 1992 and 1996.

For quite some time it did not seem that there were intentions of reducing the level of political interference in H11. In the 1997 company report to the stock market we could read, for example, that:

> In the course of H11's history the Hungarian state has exercised an important supervisory function over H11's strategy, performance and leadership. After

> the most recent sale of shares 45 per cent of the company's shares stay in the property of the Hungarian state, ... as does the golden share and thus [the state] will continue to be able to exercise an important supervisory function over H11.

Although with the change in government by 1999 the previously declared goal[54] of reducing the state's share in H11 to 25 per cent has been achieved, the government still holds considerable power at shareholder meetings.

An Ex-pat Manager's View: Interview with the President and Managing Director of Douwe Egberts Hungaria

The interview with the President and Managing Director of Douwe Egberts Hungaria provides us with the viewpoint of a Western expat manager. He stated that when he came to Hungary he found that the acquired company employed 'too many people and had a far to fragmented internal organisation. Many seemed to view the office as an extension of their living-room'. He saw a particular problem with the ethical and moral attitudes of the 'older' generation (that is people who are over 35 years old).

In his judgement labour productivity in Hungary is generally below Western levels, but 'has the potential to be above Western levels because people are better skilled here. People are used to studying and learning, many have two degrees.' The main problems are in his opinion with a lack of motivation and experience. 'People have to get used to the idea that they need to perform rather than just work.' The company has introduced a flat internal organisational form which is supposed to force employees to take responsibility and make decisions, something that the older generation apparently finds difficult. Training in the company thus also aims at enhancing employee's creativity and negotiation and communication skills, which the MD sees as being important enabling factors for taking responsibility. Unemployment is a big consideration for employees in the Eastern parts of Hungary, but it constitutes not threat or disciplining factor to people in Budapest and the surrounding area. To motivate their employees and to attract a high quality workforce multinationals tend to pay wages which are about 20–25 per cent above the local market rate.

My interview partner did not have good experiences with the trade union in the acquired company. 'They have been completely destructive and were only in it for the money. They had no sense of Western business.' There were no strikes however, even though they were threatened. 'They never followed their threats up. One gains the impression that the threat is an objective in itself rather than that it serves an objective.' He states that:

> the trade union is not professional, it does not have a good knowledge of the company and the management, they only know how to demand by not how to negotiate, they do not know how Western managers are likely to react and how to handle them.

The company employs no 'old' managers but has aimed at replacing them by young Hungarians, with a few ex-pats being present in the top and middle management. Indeed the MD himself came to Hungary in 1994 to replace an 'old' local MD, who was caught manipulating the assets and asset value of the company as well as spiriting away funds via a shady Russian investment fund.

In the interview the MD complained about an opportunistic mentality in parts of the workforce, the government and Hungarian business partners. He stated the neither the government (irrespective of which political party is in power) nor business partners are fully reliable.

> They do not stick to deals. Once the investment is in the country or resources have been sunk into a deal they do not care about their commitments ... There is a lot of bribery and they do not care about any code of conduct ... Even simple employees frequently have second jobs which provide them with conflicting interests.

Notes

1 All the write-ups in this chapter are based on the interviews conducted in each company, as well as the archival material collected. The data collected for each company is described in detail in the Introduction.

2 I will quote here at length because it is rare that tensions with the investor are so explicitly delineated and so freely discussed.

3 This includes state subsidies which H8 received.

4 Company prospectus, 1996: (in 1996, 80 per cent of employees have got university degrees at the MSc level, and 4 per cent of employees have got a Book).

5 Here again the claim was made that the investor is trying to clutter product space through brand proliferation.

6 Apparently, only two people (the general manager of H2's Budapest factory and the MD of H3) remain in the top management of all of what used to be the Budapest sweets' industry before 1990. In the top and upper middle management local managers were replaced almost entirely by ex-pat managers in H2. Middle managers tended to be replaced

by young Hungarians who 'have the language and computing skills but lack the knowledge which based on experience'.

7 When asked to give an example, the personnel manager claimed that a difference is, that in Germany there is more of a command tradition than in Hungary. At another point he added that 'we are a fairly decentralised company and not full of guidelines as in a German company'.

8 All its plants, even the oldest one dating from 1970, use Western technology from companies such as ICI, Linde, Sumitomo, Philipps, BASF and Himont.

9 Accumulative investment data is not available for H5. Furthermore, H5 has a multitude of financial activities which belong under the heading of 'investments' including investments in bonds and into subsidiaries. Major capital investments since 1995 included a revamp of the Olefin plant, the building of a very modern and environmentally friendly waste incinerator (costing 423 million HUF, that is 3.74 million DM), the upgrading of the packaging facilities and a restructuring of plastics processing (an area of anticipated expansion). The company's expected total capital expenditure for 1997 was 7,404 million HUF (65.5 million DM) and 7,547 million HUF for 1996 . For 1997/98 the company was focusing on revamping its cracker facilities and expanding its capacity in this area, launching metallocene/PE wax projects and further investments into plastic processing and environmental protection. (This data comes from H5's annual report for 1996 and the PR script for a presentation by the manager in charge of investor relations in May 1997.)

10 Source: script for presentation by the manager in charge of investor relations.

11 Between 1989 and 1995 H5 had five MDs. It has been suggested that all these appointments were due to political struggles within the state property agency (ÁPV Rt) or within the government itself (*HVG*, 1996, July 13).

12 Source: script of a presentation by the manager in charge of investor relations in May 1997.

13 PR information provided by company H6.

14 From the case study written by T. Calamita.

15 *HVG*, 1996 October 12.

16 Interview with the TUR.

17 'Kiemelt Ipari Nagyvállalatok', study conducted in 1995 for the ÁPV Rt on the fate of the 49 large companies which had been given special emphasis in the old economic system.

18 *HVG*, 1994 October 1.

19 *HVG* 1995 June 10 and 1995 November 25.

20 I would like to emphasise that this does not imply that the management consisted of drunkards. There are generally many anecdotes about the generosity with which Russian business partners dish out vodka before and during business meetings.

21 For an example where a pro-active management managed to realise its own privatisation strategy against the actions and interests of the ÁPV Rt see the case of the pharmaceutical company EGIS as written up in 'Nagyvállalatok a gyógyszeriparban', Antalóczy Katalin, Társadalmi Szemle, 1994.

22 *HVG*, 1995 June 10.

23 As explained below, this privatisation would have had the very likely consequence that bus production in the company would have ceased. This was not at all in the interest of the Russian investor, who is a major (even if illiquid) customer and would have had to

either resort to buying buses of far inferior quality from India, China, Poland, etc. or to buying far more expensive buses from Western companies.

24 *HVG* 1995 November 25.

25 It is due to this logic that it is still rumoured in opposition circles that the then MD of H6 might have been in the pocket of an interested potential foreign investor. These rumours, although persistent, are entirely unsubstantiated.

26 *HVG* 1995 November 25.

27 *HVG* 1996 October 12.

28 *HVG* 1996 October 12.

29 The company in question used to be a large electronics company producing TVs and other electrical products. His success in turning this company around although it was standing shortly before liquidation in the early 1990s and the success of the computer components company founded by him is what the reputation of the new MD is built on.

30 It is impossible to obtain a consistent picture on whether the rapid increase in production after the rapid decline which took place is going to adversely affect quality: The head of logistics, for example, claimed that there are such large unexploited economies of scale at these 'low' production levels, that an increase in production actually leads to quality improvements. The TUR does not think that quality is neglected because 'that would be catastrophic for us since we depend on repeat purchases.'

31 *HVG* 1996 October 12.

32 *Financial Times*, 11 September 1997.

33 *Financial Times*, 30 October 1997.

34 Minister Szabolcs Farkas, quoted in an article in *Ipari Szemle*, February 1997.

35 Letter by the Vice President of H7's parent company in a special edition of the employees' magazine of H7, published in 1996 to mark H7's 100 year anniversary.

36 H7 was very unusual in the fact that ever since 1957 it (rather than a central government agency) was in charge of its own export activities and had a very high proportion of its output being exported into Western countries.

37 Interview with the trade union representative.

38 *Wall Street Journal*, 1992, March 27.

39 Statement in the contractual agreement reached between the management and workforce of the company on 7 December 1992.

40 In an informal talk with an employee over lunch I was told that it had been suggested in this context that 'Hungarian employees even steal the newly installed loo-roll holders'. Whether a claim to this effect has been made or not is not as important as the fact that the workforce was left with the impression that this was the investor's opinion of them. As one can imagine, such accusations are not easily forgotten.

41 *Financial Times*, December 1992.

42 The personnel manager stressed that although very large mass redundancies occurred, the company had been concerned about their social impact. Of the overall 7,000 or so people who were dismissed in the end, 2,500 went into early retirement. He claims that of the remaining people about 60–70 per cent found new jobs with external companies with the help of H7. This help apparently involved retraining, legal information, consultations, etc.

43 It should be noted that H7 has a very long and famous tradition into lighting research. H7 was one of the first European companies to establish an R&D department in the late 1920s. The researchers employed by the company were world-class scientists and the

company achieved many R&D breakthroughs in its history, including a world patent for incandescent lamps using tungsten filament (1904) and the world patent for the krypton lamp (1931). The company also started producing energy saving compact fluorescent lamps in 1986. In this area the company had significant R&D advancements in recent years, leading to the production of a compact fluorescent lamp marketed under the name of Genura, which according to the investor's 1997 company profile is a 'revolutionary lamp ... [which] combines the energy efficiency and long life of a compact fluorescent wit the aesthetic qualities of a standards incandescent reflector lamp'. The research underlying the development of this lamp had been done in H7 in the late 1980s and early 1990s. The company had however lacked the material means for translating the research results into a product. It was decided in 1992–93 to start the production of this lamp, which has developed into one of the most advanced lamps on the market. Between 1993 and 1996 the R&D department of H7 produced 70–80 patents which have been registered in the US and EU (sources: company publication celebrating its 100 year anniversary and Interview with the head of R&D, Népsabadság, 1996, November 11).

44 H11's stock market report for February 1997.

45 Data from the interview with the vice-president of the finance department and the company's investors' report for February 1997.

46 I would like to emphasise that I do not claim that any of these rumours are true. I merely relay what has been recounted to me. Although these rumours are common currency in informed circles and the people who made these claims would without doubt stand by them, I do not wish to mention their names. Newspaper articles dealing (rather cautiously) with H11 in this period are, for example: *HVG*, 1994, October 8; 1995, January 28; 1995, June 24; 1995, December 9; 1996, January 6; 1996, March 30; 1996, July 13.

47 By 1997 the company has ceased to operate any significant storage facilities.

48 The TUR of H11 refers to this incident in the following passage: 'In the first few years [after 1990] the company was highly disorganised. There were several spontaneous activities [this is in common parlance a code for the former nomenclature trying to gain ownership of the company]. An internal grouping was trying to acquire the company for themselves. These activities were stopped by our Head Office who blew the whistle on this group.'

49 *FT*, 23 June 1995.

50 H11's employee magazine, October 1995: '[At the meeting] the small shareholders were primarily expecting that they would be given a reason by the majority shareholder [the Hungarian state] why he had initiated the restructuring of the board. They waited in vain.'

51 From: 'Kiemelt Ipari Nagyvállalatok', study conducted in 1995 for the ÁPV Rt on the fate of the 49 large companies which had been given special emphasis in the old economic system.

52 According to the law regulating the gas sector, from 1997 onwards the company is allowed to earn an 8 per cent profit on these operations. This is open to interpretation since there are the usual problems faced by rate of return regulation, such as the precise measurement of costs and of the relevant capital base as well as the determination of the appropriate depreciation rate.

53 Company H5 has an entire page in the financial statements section of its 1996 company report devoted to this issue. See also the employee's magazine of H11, December 1992.

54 See, for example, *FT*, 1995, 8 December.

3 Restructuring the Boundaries of the Firm: Changes in Vertical Integration

This chapter examines the way in which previously highly integrated enterprises have restructured their vertical boundaries, both with respect to the internal production of inputs and their functional integration. Empirical hypotheses derived from the literature on enterprise restructuring and on transaction costs are examined both qualitatively and statistically. In particular I ask whether, as suggested by the literature on enterprise restructuring, vertical disintegration leads to transaction cost savings and efficiency gains. I find a startling difference: in East Germany restructuring measures resulting in less vertical integration are associated with higher profitability while in the Hungarian data the opposite holds. It is argued that in the Hungarian context the lack of a well established background industry and the relatively high degree of economic, political and legal uncertainty strongly favour vertical integration. These environmental factors even dominate hypotheses based on opportunism and asset specificity, which are generally supported by my data. Foreign direct investors tend to fail to appreciate country specific factors and as a consequence tend to endorse restructuring measures which are performance enhancing in the East German context but not in the Hungarian one.

Introduction

Most formerly state owned companies in the transition economies of Central and Eastern Europe have inherited a highly integrated vertical structure. Using a transaction cost framework this chapter examines two questions which can be derived from the literature on enterprise restructuring, namely:

- whether a reduction in vertical integration unambiguously leads to transaction cost savings and efficiency improvements;[1]

- and whether companies with foreign direct investors are 'better' able to implement the required vertical disintegration[2] and to restructure the their supply arrangements.[3]

This chapter examines the validity of these contentions. Explicit reference is made to the restructuring of both physical and functional vertical inputs. When a company reduces its vertical integration by stopping the production of physical inputs, then I will refer to this as the company experiencing the closure of vertical product lines and hence reducing the *physical vertical integration* of its product range. I interpret 'functions' as ancillary services or activities which are an input into the productive process and can be potentially separated out in the process of reducing the company's *functional vertical integration.* The chapter proceeds as follows: section 1 provides a survey of the literature; section 2 derives empirical hypotheses; section 3 presents the empirical evidence found in my case studies and derives statistical variables; section 4 confronts the hypotheses. Section 5 concludes by interpreting the statistical evidence found.

1 Literature Survey: Advocating a Reduction in Vertical Integration[4]

The Situation Before 1990

Before 1990 East German and Hungarian companies operated in an economy characterised by bottlenecks. Consequently companies developed a desire for 'reproductive self-containment' (Grabher, 1996) which led them to produce as many inputs internally as possible. In addition planners in both countries tended to have a preference for monopolising industrial sectors as it was deemed that larger but fewer enterprises would be easier to control than many small ones (Kornai, 1992). The creation of autarchic mass producers was also hoped to achieve greater efficiency by making widespread use of the principles of concentration and specialisation (Grabher, 1996).

These two forces frequently resulted in the creation of highly vertically integrated local monopolies whose boundaries had been determined by non-market based considerations. One result was that in any given sector individual firm size tended to be a lot larger in Central and Eastern Europe. To illustrate this point Kornai (1992, Table 17.4) suggests that in 1988 in the chemical industry, for example, the mean number employees was 1,419 in an East German company and 296 in a West German one. In addition Amsden et al.

(1994, Table 4.3) point out that not only were individual companies larger and more integrated, but that the size distribution of companies on an economy-wide level was skewed in favour of very large ones. For example, in the late 1980s 90.8 per cent and 75.3 per cent of the East German and Hungarian workforce respectively were employed in companies counting more than 1,000 employees. In contrast only 31.2 per cent of the Austrian and 49.8 per cent of West German employees worked in such companies.

Advocating a Reduction in Integration on Efficiency Grounds

The unbundling of these 'excessively' integrated enterprises (Estrin, 1994, p.15) and the demonopolisation of the industrial sectors they operate in are generally regarded as central to improving efficiency in the enterprise sector of transition economies. Privatisation is frequently seen as a prime way of achieving the former objective and trade liberalisation as a crucial contributor to the latter (see, for example: Gros and Steinherr, 1995, p. 285). The contention that on the enterprise level a reduction in vertical integration is needed to increase productive efficiency and a reduction in horizontal integration is a prerequisite for greater allocative efficiency is so widespread that it is rarely discussed in depth in the enterprise restructuring literature. Authors also do not tend to differentiate between functional and physical vertical integration. Carlin (1994, p. 40), for example, states with reference to East Germany that:

> The motivation for breaking up the Kombinates and for splitting up enterprises was to increase efficiency. Allocative efficiency requirements to reduce horizontal integration have played a relatively limited role in East Germany in the light of the strength of competition in the product market coming from West German suppliers ... The need to improve private productive efficiency has dominated the splitting up process.

The general tendency is to simply include a call for a reduction in vertical integration in a general list of urgent restructuring measures required as part of the process of 'the closure of non-viable units' and the 'separation of core from non-core activities' (see, for example, Aghion, Blanchard and Carlin, W 1994, p. 2; Dobrinsky, 1996, p. 402; Meyer and Moller, 1998, p. 412; Ericson, 1998, p. 108).

It is sometimes implied that companies with FDI will be able to better restructure their vertical structure because investors can break the power of insiders who might form coalitions to oppose such restructuring measures (see, for example, the implications of the Aghion, Blanchard and Burgess,

1994 model). An alternative possible reason for companies with FDI being better able to restructure their supply arrangements is that investors might facilitate a reduction in vertical integration by giving their subsidiaries access to international supplier networks as well as to marketing, R&D and other facilities at the head offices.

A strand of literature which cautions against endorsing reduced vertical integration simply because firms are more integrated than their Western counterparts can be found with authors of a more evolutionary and network based focus. Grabher and Stark (1996), for example, provide evolutionary arguments in favour of organisation diversity and against adopting winning models from the west. On this account some redundancy and slack and hence a reduction point optimality might be required to preserve adaptability and dynamic efficiency. They view the persistence of organisational forms and social relationships from the old system not so much as a signal for incomplete change as an option for the future.

The Question of Holding Companies and Imperfect Vertical Disintegration

It is generally not discussed whether companies should preferably reduce their vertical integration by selling off their input producing facilities or by closing them. The creation of structures in which the parent company maintains an ownership stake in its (separated out) supplier tends to be classified as 'ambiguous restructuring' (Carlin, Van Reenen and Wolfe, 1995, pp. 442 ff.; Grosfeld and Roland, 1995, p. 9). Ambiguous restructuring is generally defined as restructuring measures which are not clearly motivated by market based and efficiency considerations. The alternative is that they aimed at 'building up different protections from pressures to change' (Grosfeld and Roland, 1995, p. 9). Grosfeld and Roland (ibid.) state that in their judgement:

> another form of rent-seeking behaviour is the creation of cross-ownership or of holding companies retaining stakes in their subsidiaries in order to shelter insiders from outsider control and securing monopoly power for the firm.

Carlin, Van Reenen and Wolfe (1995, pp. 442 ff.) are more differentiated in their assessment of the motivation for creating holding companies which retain ownership stakes in separated out suppliers and suggest (p. 444) that, although it is unclear whether this practice will actually hinder or help the subsequent sale of these suppliers to outsiders, 'stakes for suppliers ... may enable the enterprise to guarantee secure suppliers in an uncertain market'.

The network literature elaborates on the risk hedging implications of the creation of holding companies with ownership stakes in separated-out suppliers. Stark (1996) argues that such practices create networks which can reduce risk and offer hedging strategies under conditions of extreme market volatility and in some instances might even lead to supply arrangements which are conducive towards innovation. This statement leads us directly to an argument why the separating out (whether by sale or by the creation of a holding company) rather than liquidation of non-core activities might be preferable in a transition context: In a situation where the principle of 'reproductive self-containment' lead to underdeveloped networks of external suppliers companies which separate out units are actually creating their own background industry. This is such a central observation that it is worth elaborating with a quote from Auerbach (1993, p. 145) made when discussing the general relationship between planning and the market:

> Firms have been at the same time devices for the avoidance of the market mechanism as well as for its extension. The option of avoiding internal organisation by the use of the market is only possible if *other* entities, such as firms, have been organised in sufficient depth for a 'market' to appear for the service at hand ... a presupposition of the existence of markets and the failure to see the role of firms in the *making* of markets informs Coase's analysis ...

I would like to add that this presupposition seems to also inform some of the literature on enterprise restructuring and, as we will see from my Hungarian case studies, the policies of many investors.

Can one Assume that all the Determinants of 'Optimal' Vertical Integration are Moving in the Same Direction in all Transition Economies?

Another presupposition which needs to be made explicit underlies the general claim that a reduction in vertical integration should increase productive efficiency in *all* transition economies.[5] Underlying such a notion is the implicit assumption that all the theoretical and empirical determinants of vertical integration are moving in the same direction in all transition economies. This is not trivial. Should I find contrary to what the literature leads us to expect that the efficiency implications of differing degrees of vertical integration do indeed differ across countries, then these basic determinants of the 'optimal' degree of vertical integration will have to be referred back to.

On the basis of the transactions cost literature one should only expect companies in different economies to exhibit the same degree of vertical integration if in each case this particular degree of vertical integration happens to be the transaction cost minimising corporate configuration. This is a direct result of what Williamson (1998) calls the discriminating-alignment hypothesis underlying the predictions of transaction cost economics, namely that (p. 76) 'transactions, which differ in their attributes, are aligned with governance structures, which differ in their cost competence, so as to effect a (mainly) transaction cost economising result'.[6]

The major premise of transaction cost theory is that the properties of transactions determine the contracting hazards involved and the response of agents to these hazards in turn determines the governance structure for that transaction. The magnitude of contracting hazards depends on the attributes of the assets and on the characteristics of the contracting relation (Williamson, 1985, p. 84). Factors producing contractual hazards and hence transaction costs are considered to be the crucial behavioural assumptions of bounded rationality and opportunism as well as situations characterised by small number bargaining and asymmetric information. Transaction costs are traditionally assumed to increase with the asset specificity and uncertainty involved in a transaction as well as its infrequency (Reve, 1990; Masten, 1996; Williamson, 1996, p. 59).

Bounded rationality relates to the impossibility of writing complete contracts which cover all possible future contingencies. Such incompleteness gives rise to residual rights of control, that is a situation where it is no longer the case that any rights conferred by ownership can be contracted away (Hart, 1993).[7] Kreps (1986) extends the notion of residual rights of control by stating that party A to a transaction will only be willing to give to party B such residual rights if party B has a reputation for sticking to an implicit contract concerning the adjudication processes that meet unforeseen contingencies. Such a 'culture' characterising the implicit rules of the game and the private norms and sanctions applicable becomes all the more important the more complex and uncertain a transaction is, that is the more incomplete explicit contracting is.

Informational asymmetries can be expected to confound the problems caused by bounded rationality and to increase the costs associated with writing, monitoring and enforcing contracts (Joskow, 1993, p. 125). Similar costs are associated with opportunism. Opportunism is generally aimed at obtaining a higher share of the benefits of trade for oneself than the other party has agreed to a priori. Masten (1996, p. 7) distinguishes between two types of opportunism: Firstly actions aimed at a redistribution of the gains from trade within the terms of an existing agreement (a moral hazard problem) and secondly actions aimed at forcing renegotiation (the hold up problem). He claims that opportunism is costly not only because efforts to constrain opportunism directly consume resources and place additional demands on bounded rationality, but also because it can cause a failure to reach agreement and to realise potential gains from trade.

A lot of attention has focused on how asset specificity increases transaction costs. Asset specificity or a lock-in effect is generally assumed to be caused by relationship-specific investment undertaken by one party to a transaction. For this party a 'fundamental transformation' (Williamson, 1993, p. 97) occurs as a consequence of which a situation of ex ante competition turns to one of small number bargaining ex post, thus greatly increasing the scope for opportunism by the other party. Williamson (1985, p.95) distinguishes between four types of asset specificity: physical, site or location and human asset specificity as well as the presence of dedicated assets. He argues for a common ownership of core activities for which asset specificity is high (1985, p. 98).[8] Both uncertainty and infrequency increase transaction costs by increasing the informational requirements on and the demands on the bounded rationality of contracting parties. A particular problem with infrequent transactions is that agents cannot acquire reputations, which would have tempered their propensity to behave opportunistically (Masten, 1996, p. 150).

Contracting hazards do not, however, only occur due to the characteristics of a given transaction and of the contracting agents, but also due to the characteristics of the wider economic, political and social system within which a transaction is located. In his later writings Williamson (1998) increasingly takes account of this 'embeddedness' of transactions, claiming that additional contracting hazards might arise from systemic features such as weak property rights and a general weakness in the institutional environment. Similarly Coase (1998, p. 73) states that 'the costs of exchange depend on the institutions of a country: its legal system, its political system ... its culture and so on'. If two economies systematically differ along these dimensions, then one would expect their organisational structures to reflect these differences, even if in both instances a given transaction is characterised by the same degree of, for example, asset specificity and infrequency.

When contracting hazards are severe then vertical integration provides an alternative way of organising a given transaction. Grossman and Hart (1986) interpret vertical integration as the unified ownership of the physical assets involved in successive stages of production. They interpret ownership over an asset to entail the purchase of all the residual rights of control over that asset. On this account in an externality-free world the person whose actions determine the profitability of an asset would also own it (Hart, 1993, p. 114).[9] Grossman and Hart's (1986) approach to vertical integration differs from that of Williamson and Coase. Instead of emphasising changes in the ownership of physical assets Williamson and Coase tend to mainly associate vertical integration with changes in incentives and control mechanisms caused by the substitution of an ordinary contractual relationship with a relationship of hierarchically organised authority. Such an interpretation of the main features of integration leads to definitions which defined integration in terms of the *organisation* (rather than ownership) of two successive processes by a single firm (Riordan, 1990).[10]

The potential benefits of integration can be directly derived from a consideration of the contractual hazards it tries to mitigate.[11] Asset specificity and the increased danger of opportunism it entails are frequently seen as and found to be the single most important motivating factor favouring vertical integration (Williamson, 1985, p. 86; Lieberman (1991). Integration can avoid hold-up problems by eliminating the second transactor (Grossman and Hart, 1986; Masten, 1996). Alternatively it could be argued (Williamson, 1985) that a reduced probability of opportunism in an integrated supplier is due to feelings of loyalty which might result from integration. The aim of avoiding opportunism becomes all the more important the higher the fraction of total costs accounted for by a given input (Lieberman, 1991). Klein (1988) argues that the reduced likelihood of opportunistic hold-up is the principal transaction cost saved by vertical integration.

Whyte (1994) suggest that an alternative reason why high asset specificity is associated with integration is the 'sunk cost effect' according to which people take into account the sunk costs they have incurred when deciding how much use to make of, e.g. a facility. A consequence of this effect is a tendency to escalate commitment (by, for example, integrating) to a previously chosen course of action to a greater degree than is justified by the objective facts of the situation. On this account there is no reason why one should expect greater vertical integration motivated by such sunk cost consideration to be positively associated with profitability.

An improved information flow to the integrating customer can help mitigate the informational problems inherent to bounded rationality, asymmetric information and the infrequency of transactions. It is argued that employees have a greater duty to disclose information to employers than suppliers have to customers (Masten, 1996; Riordan, 1990). Williamson (1985, p. 154) also argues that by integrating companies gain better information through an increased ability to control their subsidiary's accounting procedures.

The decision to vertically integrate not only affects the information available to a company but also the risks it faces: Hanson (1995) argues that the choice of ownership involves a trade-off between minimising hold-up risk and spreading natural risk. Ownership under one party increases exposure to environmental uncertainty while reducing hold-up risk. He arrives at the empirical prediction that a manufacturer will subcontract a high share of production where demand is highly variable and a low share where they make large relationship-specific investments. The possible risk hedging properties of vertical integration are supported by Lieberman (1991) who found in a study of 34 companies that firms appear to have integrated backward to avoid variability in the input market that was independent of fluctuations in their downstream market.

Although this is disputed by Alchian and Demsetz (1972) it is also argued that vertical integration gives a customer greater flexibility and adaptability to changing circumstances, since he can now resolve disputes in the supply relationship by administrative fiat rather than having to appeal to courts (Masten, 1996; Williamson, 1996; Dow, 1993). It is important to distinguish two types of flexibility, however. To the extent that private ordering does away with the need to determine a wide range of possible future contingencies in advance (since they can be dealt with internally when they arise) it is likely to be associated with transaction cost savings as well as greater flexibility in responding to unforeseen eventualities. Vertical integration, however, causes a company also have the reduced flexibility in *choosing* a new supplier. The greater the competitiveness of a company's background industry the more likely it is that a company's adaptability is better preserved by maintaining choice rather than integrating with any individual supplier.

Considering the competition in a company's background industry leads us to two further factors favouring integration which are not directly related to transaction costs. Firstly one can expect companies whose competitors have monopoly power to consider integrating with the aim of avoiding the negative externality effect which a double marginalisation has on their final demand (Waterson, 1993). Secondly because they will be better able to realise economies of scale one can expect larger firms to be more integrated into components than will be smaller ones, ceteris paribus (Williamson, 1985, p. 94).

Vertical integration is not without costs, however, otherwise there would be no limit on firm size. The costs associated with integration are mainly incentive type costs, usually implying a reduced incentive for costs savings and productivity improvements in the subsidiary (Waterson, 1993) as well as increased monitoring and bureaucratic costs for the parent (Dow, 1993), Williamson (1985, ch. 6). The main factor driving the result that managers in a subsidiary will have lower effort incentives ex ante is the fact that upon integration the principal obtains better information upon the upstream manager's ex post rent (Olsen, 1996). Since a commitment to selective intervention by the principal is not credible, the agent, who is no longer the holder of the residual rights of control, becomes vulnerable to the principal's opportunism. The agent's reaction is to reduce his effort. Grossman and Hart (1986) analyse the resulting countervailing incentive effect: integration is only beneficial if firm 1's (the purchaser's) control increase the productivity of its management more than the loss of control decreases the productivity of firm 2's management.[12] They conclude that non-integration is desirable if both firms' relationship specific investments are important to the final outcome. Williamson (1985, pp. 279 ff.) and Kay (1993) suggest that m-form companies, where inter-function coordination is carried out by divisions, can at least partially mitigate the incentive and control-loss problems associated with vertical integration.

To conclude this discussion I can state that the widespread notion that a reduction in vertical integration is going to unambiguously have positive efficiency effects in the form of improved incentives and transaction cost savings in *all* transition economies presupposes that in all these countries:

- contracting hazards and uncertainty arising from the characteristics of the wider economic, political and legal system are moving in the same direction;
- pre-existing background industries are developed and competitive to a similar extent;
- agents are characterised by similar levels of opportunism;
- pre-existing internal supply arrangements are characterised by a similar degree of asset specificity and the effort exerted by suppliers of valuable inputs is equally important in both contexts.

2 The Empirical Hypotheses

The foremost question this chapter examines is whether a reduction in both physical and functional vertical integration unambiguously leads to transaction cost savings and increased cost efficiency in both East Germany and Hungary. Accordingly Hypothesis 1 formulates this question by suggesting that less integrated companies should have a higher likelihood of being profitable in both countries. Hypothesis 2 suggests that in this context reducing vertical integration by the creation of holding companies is likely to have ambiguous profitability implications. According to Hypothesis 3 foreign direct investors were better able to accomplish reductions in vertical integration. Hypothesis 4 combines Hypotheses 1 and 3 by concluding that companies with FDI should perform better than those without. The remaining hypotheses relate directly to the implications of the transaction costs literature. To the extent that I find on the basis of these secondary hypotheses that Hungarian and German companies systematically differ along the dimensions favouring vertical (dis)integration I will be better able to interpret the findings for Hypothesis 1.

2.1 Hypotheses Relating to the Profitability Implications of Vertical Disintegration and to the Role of Foreign Direct Investors

HYPOTHESIS 1:

- *a negative association between profitability (as a proxy for cost efficiency and transaction cost savings) and vertical integration for both Hungarian and East German companies* (Carlin, 1994, p. 285; Aghion, Blanchard and Carlin, 1994, p. 2; Dobrinsky, 1996, p. 402; Meyer and Moller, 1998, p. 412; Ericson, 1998, p. 108).

HYPOTHESIS 2:

- *an ambiguous association between profitability and the creation of holding companies by separating out ancillary units.* (To the extent that such measures are aimed at insulating insiders against outside pressures, they will be negatively associated with profitability (Grosfeld and Roland, 1995, p. 9). On the other hand they might guarantee secure supply channels Carlin, Van Reenen and Wolfe, 1995, pp. 442 ff.).)

HYPOTHESIS 3:

- *a positive association between FDI and reductions in vertical integration.* (The Aghion, Blanchard and Burgess (1994) model can be interpreted in this way if an insufficient reduction in vertical integration is due to insider power. Alternatively investors might reduce their subsidiaries' integration because they can use alternative suppliers from pre-existing worldwide supply networks. This is implied by Grabher's (1996, p. 181) discussion of 'cathedrals in the desert' being created by investors with globally focused supply strategies.)

HYPOTHESIS 4:

- *a positive association between FDI and profitability.* (This is a logical conclusion from Hypotheses 1 and 3. No causation is implied.)

2.2 Secondary Hypotheses Relating to the Implications of the Transaction Costs Literature

HYPOTHESIS 5:

- *positive association between opportunistic suppliers and vertical integration* (Masten, 1996, p. 7), implication of Grossman and Hart, 1986; Klein, 1988, p. 166).

HYPOTHESIS 6:

- *positive association between reductions in vertical integration and companies procuring mainly standardised products (that is products involving a low asset specificity)* (Winger, 1994, p. 10), implication of Williamson, 1985, pp. 86, 94; Lieberman, 1991).

HYPOTHESIS 7:

- *positive association between company size (proxied by the number of employees) and vertical integration.* (Larger companies are more likely to remain vertically integrated into components because they will be able to make better use of scale economies than smaller companies (Williamson, 1985, p. 94[13]).)

2.3 Explanatory Hypotheses which are not going to be Confronted Statistically

HYPOTHESIS 8:

- *companies operating in an environment characterised by greater economic, legal and political uncertainty are likely to remain more integrated* (Coase, 1998, p. 73; Williamson, 1998).

HYPOTHESIS 9:

- *companies with a less developed background industry are more likely to remain integrated.* (The motivation for this is that they are more likely to face a double marginalisation problem if they turn to external suppliers.)

3 Variables and Case Study Evidence[14]

The aim of this section is to present the case study evidence on which the statistical variables capturing changes in the companies' physical and functional vertical integration are based. Case study evidence is presented concerning the relative advantages of different degrees of integration.

3.1 Variables Capturing and Examining Changes in the Companies' Physical and Functional Vertical Integration[15]

Variables capturing changes in the companies' physical integration In each company I obtained information in the number of vertical product lines which were closed and newly introduced, making it possible to capture the overall net change in the companies' physical integration. The means reported in Tables 3.4a and b suggest that in my data set 33 per cent of the East German companies closed an important input producing facility and none introduced new vertical products. In Hungary on the other hand only one company closed down a vertical product line and 25 per cent of companies actually started producing new inputs internally. The net effect is a mean decline of 0.33 vertical product lines in East Germany and a small mean increase in the Hungarian companies' physical vertical integration. These differences are statistically significant. The notion that in both countries companies are adjusting their (physical) vertical integration in the same direction can be clearly rejected at this stage already: The claims that the mean East German company is closing down more input producing facilities and introducing fewer new ones are both significant at the 10 per cent level, while the observation that Hungarian companies have been experiencing much smaller declines in their integration is significant at the 1 per cent level.[16]

Variables capturing changes in the companies' functional integration I asked each company which functional inputs were catered for internally, by other companies in the Kombinat and by entirely external suppliers in 1990 and, similarly, internally, by the investor and by external suppliers in 1996(7). For 1990 the functions considered were:

- *Bilanzierung*, that is, checking whether production in the company is running according to the plan given from the central authorities;
- investment planning;
- personnel;
- product development;
- process development;
- input procurement;
- maintenance;
- distribution; and
- transportation.

In reflection of the fact that the functional inputs required for production and administration have changed 11 categories were considered for 1996(7):

- personnel;
- design;
- quality control;
- R&D;
- procurement;
- maintenance;
- sales;
- transportation;
- marketing;
- customer services; and
- computer facilities.[17]

I find that in 1990 the Hungarian companies in my data set made more use of suppliers which were entirely external to the company and the conglomerate it belonged to. One in six Hungarian companies used such external suppliers, while no German company reports such arrangements. This difference is an indicator of the overall greater (micro)economic decentralisation and liberalisation which existed in Hungary by the late 1980s as a result of the reform period in the 1980s. By 1997, however, the Hungarian companies tend to be more functionally integrated than their East German counterparts, with the Hungarian companies tending to cater internally for 8.18 functions out of a maximum of 11 and the average German company catering for only

7.[18] A major reason for why the Hungarian companies are more functionally integrated is that there are far more R&D (significant at the 10 per cent level) and customer service departments (significant at the 1 per cent level) in the Hungarian data set than in the German one. The overall trend has been, however, for functional vertical integration to decline in both countries, by a mean value of 17.2 percentage points in the Hungarian data set and of 22.5 in the East German one. The Hungarian companies tend to rely to a relatively greater extent on suppliers which have been separated out of the parent company, while East German companies make greater use of entirely external suppliers.[19]

I asked several interview partners in each company to explain the main advantages and disadvantages of having a more integrated structure. The arguments given by Hungarian and East German managers for and against integration are largely the same and reflect many of the theoretical considerations raised by the transaction cost literature. Hungarian and East German managers seem to have arrived at different conclusions concerning the 'optimal' degree of vertical integration from similar starting points. Companies name as the major *advantages of having an overall less integrated structure*:

- *cost savings* due to the use of external subcontractors (D7, D1) who, for example, can pass on gains due to scale economies. On a similar note the production manager in H6 claimed that by separating out ancillary units capacity utilisation has increased, because outsiders are also using these facilities;
- *flexibility:* an ability to react faster to changes in the competitive environment by having direct information about local demand conditions, having direct access to local networks and being able to reorganise the company's operations faster[20] (H5, H10, D1);
- a *reduction in the internal bureaucracy* of the company (D9, H3).[21]

Perceived disadvantages of having a less integrated structure and *advantages of greater integration* are:

- *autonomy has the advantage of the company not having to rely on a nonexistent or highly unstable background industry* (H1, H6, H8, D5: Input procurement from the investor can serve to smooth production runs and capacity utilisation);[22]
- control loss by less integration is mitigated resulting in *greater flexibility and faster decision making in more integrated structures* (D8, D9, H3).[23]

Furthermore *quality control problems* with external suppliers can be mitigated by internal production;

- the *use of synergies* between different vertical stages enables the company to, for example, secure optimal delivery conditions and smoother operations (H11);[24]
- the company is better able keep high quality workers (H11, H6).

The case studies showed[25] that a major way of reducing the internal provision of functions in companies was to obtain them from their investor instead, effectively causing functional integration of the subsidiary with the investor. Entirely external or separated out suppliers tend to be predominantly used for transportation and maintenance, with the remaining reduction in functional integration being accounted for by investors. Companies cite as the *main advantages of being functionally more integrated with the investor*:

- *integration of the local company with the investor's worldwide procurement activities leads to cost savings* (H4, H7, H9);[26]
- if the investor provides computing facilities, this can lead to *knowledge transfer* (H4);
- *integration of the marketing functions can open up new trade channels to the Hungarian subsidiary* (H4);[27]
- functional integration with the investors enables the subsidiary to make use of *synergies* (D4, D5, D8, D9).[28]

Companies cite as the *main disadvantages of being functionally more integrated with the investor*:

- *some investors try to import practices and policies which are ill-adjusted to the subsidiaries' environment* (H2, H3, H7, D7);[29]
- *a reduction in the subsidiaries' flexibility* (H3, D8).[30]

3.3 'Explanatory' Variables

- *Dummies to capture whether the company is profitable in 1995, 1996 or 1997* (Hypotheses 1, 2, 4): interview partners were simply asked whether their company was profitable or not. In 1995 44 per cent of the companies in my East German data were profitable rising to 77 per cent in 1997. In 1996 54 per cent of the Hungarian companies were profitable and all expected to at least break even by 1999.

- *A variable to capture whether the company has separated out ancillary units or not* (Hypothesis 2): although 66 per cent of the East German companies and 75 per cent of Hungarian ones created new companies by splitting off previously integrated units, there are very important qualitative differences between the two countries. In Hungary this was a very common practice affecting a large number of employees in service as well as production units. In East Germany separated out units only tended to be small and with hindsight not viable companies with typically under 50 employees who provide maintenance, transportation, cleaning and guarding services. In contrast to Hungary it was entirely uncommon for East German companies to maintain an ownership stake in these small new companies.
- *A dummy to capture whether the company has a foreign direct investor or not*[31] *and one relating to the influence on the restructuring of the product range that the foreign direct investor has had* (Hypotheses 3 and 4): in the East German data 77 per cent of companies had foreign, including West German, investors in 1996. The two companies which at this time did not fall into this category were both up for resale after failed privatisations. The privatisation of D6 failed because the investor ended up asset stripping until the company's board intervened and initiated a repurchase by the Treuhand. When I called in 1998, D6 had been reprivatised to a UK company. The case of D7 is very unusual in that this is a company which is very successful in spite of its investor who went bankrupt. D7 was the only company in a large conglomerate which did not go down with its Austrian investor.

  In Hungary the picture is more varied. Sixty-three per cent of the companies visited have a foreign direct investor, H5 and H11 have floated on the Budapest stock exchange after prolonged government involvement (some would say interference), H6 has been going from one crisis and government intervention to the next and H8 has an institutional investor who does not interfere in the day-to-day running of the company. Only in four of the East German and five Hungarian companies did the investor have a determining influence on the restructuring of the product range.
- *A variable to capture the extent to which a company is facing opportunistic suppliers* (Hypothesis 5):[32] Hungarian interview partners tended to view their suppliers as slightly more opportunistic, but this was not a statistically significant difference.
- *A variable capturing the extent to which a company's inputs are standardised* and hence characterised by a low asset specificity (Hypothesis 6): the case studies suggest that for East German companies 65 per cent of their inputs tend to be standardised, while the mean value for Hungary is

85 per cent. This difference is significant at the at the 10 per cent level. Consequently on the basis of Hypothesis 6 one should expect the Hungarian companies to have a tendency to be *less* integrated into input production than their East German counterparts.

- *Variables capturing the size, that is number of employees, of a company in 1990 and 1996/7* (Hypothesis 7): in the East German companies the mean number of employees fell from 4,150 to 577, while in Hungary there was a much smaller decline from 4,430 to 2,270.

4 Confronting the Hypotheses

This section presents the statistical evidence obtained with respect to Hypotheses 1–7. Tables 3.5a and 3.5b in Appendix C summarise the associations found for the variables introduced.

4.1 Hypotheses Relating to the Profitability Implications of Vertical Disintegration and to the Role of Foreign Direct Investors

HYPOTHESIS 1:

- *a negative association between profitability (as a proxy for cost efficiency and transaction cost savings) and vertical integration.*
  Summary: this hypothesis is supported by the East German data both with respect to functional and physical vertical integration. In the Hungarian data, however, higher functional and physical integration are both associated with a higher probability of being profitable, not a lower one as Hypothesis 1 suggests.

In the East German data there is clear evidence that companies which procure a larger share of their functional inputs from outside agents in 1996 have a higher than average probability of being profitable (0.64, 5 per cent).[33] In addition I observe positive but overall insignificant associations between net reductions in physical and functional vertical integration and profitability.

I find that companies which have been particularly effective in reducing their physical integration also tend to have reduced their functional integration (0.76, 1 per cent).[34] East German companies which have greatly reduced their functional integration tend to heavily rely on entirely external suppliers (0.62, 5 per cent).[35]

Table 3.1 Summary of the main statistical findings

Hypothesis	East Germany	Hungary
1	YES	NO – on the contrary – Hungarian data higher functional and physical integration are both associated with a higher probability of being profitable, not a lower one as Hypothesis 1 suggests.
2	YES – separating out ancillary units is associated with other restructuring measures, which in turn are profitable – in the East German data these other restructuring measures include reductions in physical and functional integration	YES – separating out ancillary units is associated with other restructuring measures, which in turn are profitable – in the Hungarian data companies which separate out ancillary units tend to maintain a high degree of vertical integration
3 and 4	WEAKLY YES for Hypothesis 4 only	NO – all relevant associations are insignificant
5	YES – companies with opportunistic suppliers remain more integrated	NO – all relevant associations are insignificant
6	YES – companies with standardised inputs have less opportunistic suppliers and reduce their integration more	YES
7	NO – on the contrary – larger companies have reduced their integration more	NO – all relevant associations are insignificant

In the Hungarian data the opposite profitability trends prevail. Companies which have experienced below average reductions (or even an increase) in their vertical integration are more likely to be profitable than average (0.43, 10 per cent). In addition there is consistent evidence that reductions in and a smaller degree of functional integration affect a company's performance negatively: companies which have an above average degree of functional integration in 1997 are likely to be profitable (0.49, 10 per cent).[36] Similarly using agents external to the companies as suppliers of functional inputs is negatively associated with profitability in both 1997 and 1990 (-0.49, 10 per cent in both cases). In particular entirely external suppliers, that is those without historic or ownership ties with the company, are associated with reduced profitability in 1996 (-0.42, 10 per cent). The negative association between procuring inputs from the investor and profitability is noticeable but insignificant.

In the Hungarian data there is no evidence that the companies reducing their physical integration have also reduced their functional integration. I do find, however, that companies which close down input production tend to end up relying on entirely external suppliers (0.77, 1 per cent). Similarly reductions in functional integration are associated with a reliance on the investor (0.53, 5 per cent) and on entirely external suppliers (0.64, 5 per cent) rather than on suppliers with whom the company has historic ties. There is strong evidence that functional integration with the investor is the predominant way in which companies achieve a low on-site integration in 1997 (0.89, 1 per cent).

HYPOTHESIS 2:

- *an ambiguous association between profitability and the creation of holding companies by separating out ancillary units.*
  Summary: separating out ancillary units is clearly associated with other[37] *restructuring measures which in turn have been shown to be associated with better performance (see Hypothesis 1). Consequently separating out ancillary units is unambiguously associated with higher profitability in both countries.*

By 1997/6 a policy of separating out ancillary units is strongly associated with a higher probability of being profitable in both the East German (0.76, 5 per cent) and Hungarian (0.67, 5 per cent) data sets. Interestingly in Germany separating out ancillary units seems to have been a concomitant of high reductions in physical integration (0.50, 10 per cent) and of obtaining a low level of functional vertical integration by 1996 (0.73, 5 per cent). In Hungary on the other hand a policy of separating out ancillary units seems to be a partial substitute for closures: Companies which have separated out ancillary services have overall closed a below average number of input producing facilities (-0.52, 5 per cent), remain more functionally integrated (0.43, 10 per cent) and use fewer than average subcontractors with whom they have no historical or ownership ties (-0.59, 5 per cent). I can conclude that in both countries separating out ancillary units is associated with other -and on the country level diametrically opposed- restructuring measures which in turn have been shown to be associated with better performance (see Hypothesis 1).

In addition there is evidence in both data sets that companies separating out ancillary units are actually creating their own background industry because they continue using these newly founded companies as subcontractors (0.49, 10 per cent for Germany; 0.59, 5 per cent for Hungary). This clearly indicates that one should interpret the policy of separating out units with reference to a country's background industry, that is the availability of alternative, entirely external suppliers (Hypothesis 9).

HYPOTHESIS 3:

- *a positive association between FDI and reductions in vertical integration.*

HYPOTHESIS 4:

- *a positive association between FDI and profitability.*
  Summary: in neither country data set is there evidence that companies with FDI have experienced above average reductions in their physical and functional integration. There is evidence, however, that they arrange their new supply arrangements in contrast to other companies. There is a tendency to rely on functional inputs from the investor and in Hungary an above average propensity to use entirely external suppliers. There is very weak evidence that in the German context such new supply arrangements are profit enhancing but not in the Hungarian one.

In the East German data there is no evidence that companies with FDI have reduced their integration more than average. There is clear support, however, for the contention that investors give their subsidiaries access to functional inputs from the head offices. Companies with an investor who was the main force in the restructuring of the product range are very likely to be functionally integrated with their investor (0.78, 1 per cent) and FDI in general is associated with a smaller than average propensity to use entirely external suppliers (-0.49, 10 per cent). These observations can either be interpreted as evidence for extensive knowledge transfer to the subsidiary or as the creation of 'cathedrals in the desert'. Only qualitative case study evidence can help to distinguish between these two interpretations. The associations between the investor related dummies and profitability in 1997 are positive but insignificant.

In Hungary investors seem to have had a propensity to endorse restructuring measures which in the Hungarian context tend to be associated with lower profitability (see Hypothesis 1).[38] Investors, especially those who took an active interest in the restructuring of the product range, tend to be less likely to separate out ancillary units (-0.77, 5 per cent), tending to prefer liquidating non-core activities. Consequently they are also unlikely to be using subcontractors with whom the company has historic ties (-0.78, 1 per cent) and they have an above average propensity to use entirely external suppliers (0.42, 10 per cent). FDI in general is also associated with functional integration with the investor (0.54, 5 per cent) and a below average degree of on-site functional integration in 1997 (-0.45, 10 per cent). There is no evidence, however, that companies with FDI have actually experienced greater overall reductions in physical and functional integration rather than investors being attracted to companies which were less integrated a priori.

4.2 Secondary Hypotheses Relating to the Implications of the Transaction Costs Literature

HYPOTHESIS 5:

- *positive association between opportunistic suppliers and vertical integration.*
  Summary: support in the East German data, none in the Hungarian one.

In accordance with Hypothesis 5 I find that East German companies with opportunistic suppliers tend to not only remain functionally more integrated in 1996 (0.49, 10 per cent) but have also experienced smaller reductions in this respect (-0.60, 5 per cent). As would be expected on the basis of the transaction cost literature opportunistic suppliers are associated with a lower probability of being profitable, especially in 1995 (-0.60, 5 per cent). The associations found in the Hungarian data set are generally insignificant with respect to opportunism.

HYPOTHESIS 6:

- *positive association between reductions in vertical integration and companies procuring mainly standardised products (that is products involving a low asset specificity).*
  Summary: support in both the East German data and Hungarian.

The East German data suggests that companies with more standardised inputs have less opportunistic suppliers (0.84, 1 per cent). This strongly supports the suggestion that more standardised products involve a lower asset specificity and hence a lower risk of lock-in and opportunism. In accordance with Hypothesis 6 companies procuring more standardised products are also found to have more strongly reduced their physical and functional integration (0.48, 10 per cent in both instances). In the Hungarian data as well I find that companies procuring standardised inputs have experienced above average net decreases in their physical integration (-0.54, 5 per cent).

HYPOTHESIS 7:

- *positive association between company size (proxied by the number of employees) and vertical integration.*
  Summary: no support in the Hungarian data and the opposite trend holds in the east German context.

In the East German data the general impression is that larger companies have reduced their vertical integration more than average. I find that both companies which were large in 1990 and are so in 1996 have closed an above average number of input producing facilities (0.56, 10 per cent and 0.77, 1 per cent respectively) and have also experienced above average reductions in their functional vertical integration (0.48, 10 per cent). In addition they have had an above average propensity to reduce their integration by separating out ancillary units (0.84, 1 per cent). The data suggests that companies which were large in 1990 have mainly reduced their functional integration by obtaining inputs from their investor instead in 1996 (0.54, 10 per cent).[39] In the Hungarian data both size variables are entirely insignificant and there is no support whatsoever for Hypothesis 7.

5 Conclusions and Interpretations[40]

I have found evidence of a startling difference with respect to the restructuring of enterprise boundaries. In East Germany restructuring measures resulting in lower vertical integration are associated with higher profitability. In the Hungarian context, however, the opposite trend holds. Since managers in both Hungary and East Germany refer to similar considerations when discussing their company's vertical integration, one has to examine how differences between the two countries affect the importance of the theoretical and empirical arguments for and against vertical integration.

The very first point to emerge from the case studies in this context is that no East German company endorsed a high degree of vertical integration because of a nonexistent or unstable background industry, while this was a commonly cited reason in Hungary. Through reunification East German companies were able to access pre-existing and stable West German suppliers, effectively giving them a ready-made background industry in relatively close proximity. In addition these well-established and large suppliers made scale economy arguments in favour of internal input production in large East German companies irrelevant. These considerations explain why East German companies only separated out, if at all, service providers whom it was advantageous to have in immediate proximity, while Hungarian companies engaged in measures aimed at creating their own background industry on a much larger scale.

My data clearly suggests that far from being an instance of 'ambiguous restructuring' creating your own background industry by separating out units is a profitable strategy. This is especially the case in an economy such as Hungary which characterised by a limited choice of suppliers and a high degree of supply uncertainty which is not necessarily related to variability in output markets. In this context the creation of holding companies with ownership stakes in these separated out units can reinforce and formalise the overall risk-hedging effect: the holding company benefits from an m-form organisation giving its subsidiaries a high degree of flexibility but at the same time the flow of information from below and the shared company culture and identity are preserved. The desire to obtain cost savings, increased flexibility in choosing suppliers and a reduction in the internal bureaucracy in the company was shared by both East German and Hungarian companies, but only the East German companies had immediate access to suitable pre-existing supplier networks.

Hungarian companies not only faced greater uncertainty in their dealings with potential external suppliers because these were likely to face strong economic and quality problems themselves but also because of a higher level of uncertainty in the wider framework within which the transactions are located.[41] The optimal degree of vertical integration can be assumed to also depend on environmental factors such as the overall economic, legal and political uncertainty.

- When a country is characterised by relatively low levels of *economic uncertainty*, it is easier to negotiate longer-term contracts as one can assume that price and demand fluctuations as well as bankruptcy rates will be low enough not to entail prohibitively frequent renegotiations.

- Low *legal uncertainty* in the form of a well-established legal framework and a sufficient number of precedents entails that, should problems in the interpretation of contracts arise in the future, it is predictable how these will be resolved by a recourse to the law.
- Low levels of *political uncertainty* mean that, firstly, independently of which political party or social grouping gains power, parties to a contract can reasonably expect that the overall economic, legal and political framework within which they operate is not going to be substantially changed (by, for example, the introduction of nationalisation programmes) and, secondly, that changes in government are not going to entail changes in the two companies' management due to political appointments.

The transaction costs involved in the negotiation and implementation of contracts increase with all three forms of uncertainty (see also Williamson, 1998; Coase, 1998). In this situation vertical integration has distinct advantages:

- the parent does not face the uncertainty of the supplier's unexpected bankruptcy;
- it can resolve problems arising from demand and price fluctuations without having to renegotiate any supply contracts (resulting in greater flexibility and faster decision making in more integrated structures);
- these resolutions are unlikely to lead to court cases with an uncertain outcome; and
- to the extent that political uncertainty is likely to affect the integrated supplier, the parent is going to have more information on the nature of this political uncertainty than if it did not have ownership ties with the supplier.

If, however, a company operates in an environment such as East Germany where the overall level of political and economic uncertainty is low, then the uncertainty and transaction costs involved in contractual relationships is likely to be outweighed by the benefits of using contractual rather than hierarchical control mechanisms. Since Hungary is arguably characterised by higher levels of economic, legal and political uncertainty than is East Germany, one would, on the basis of the above arguments, expect a higher degree of vertical integration to be profitable in Hungary and a lower one in East Germany. Indeed this reasoning, together with the absence of a well-developed background industry in Hungary, seems to be driving our results. The questions whether a) there are suitable external suppliers and b) whether the degree of environmental uncertainty can be satisfactorily resolved by contractual means are logically prior to considerations based on opportunism and asset specificity.

It is these two considerations which best explain my results. The implications of transaction cost theory concerning opportunistic suppliers and standardised products are generally borne out but are arguably not determining the difference in the relative degree of 'optimal' vertical integration in the two countries. There is strong evidence that East German companies with more opportunistic suppliers do indeed exhibit a higher degree of vertical integration, but opportunism does not even enter into the consideration of Hungarian companies because their supply arrangements are dominated by a need to deal with a lacking background industry and a large amount of environmental uncertainty. This is so even though the mean value for opportunism is even higher in Hungary (but not significantly so) than it is in East Germany.

Considerations based on the degree of asset specificity in a company's inputs are even more clearly dominated by environmental factors in the Hungarian context. In both Hungary and especially East Germany I find that companies with more standardised products will reduce both their functional and physical integration. Since the companies in the Hungarian data set procured standardised products to a higher extent this effect should lead to *less* vertical integration in Hungary than East Germany. I observe the opposite and environmental consideration are clearly dominating the Hungarian companies' vertical integration decision.

Many investors do not seem to understand these important differences between the country-specific factors determining the profitability of vertical integration in the East German and Hungarian contexts. There has been a general tendency to try to impose a lower degree of vertical integration as found in their Western subsidiaries, but there is no evidence that the overall degree of vertical disintegration is greater in companies with FDI.[42] What differentiates companies with FDI, however, is their reliance on entirely external suppliers and a usually high degree of functional integration with the investor. Especially in Hungary investors seem to have been unwilling to actively contribute to the development of a local background industry by separating out ancillary units. The preferred method of dealing with non-core units has been their liquidation, with the intention of buying these inputs from external suppliers. In the East German context these policies tended to work well especially since the pre-existing supply network tend to be the investor's. In the Hungarian data set, however, after closing down non-core vertical units many investors ended up having to choose between incurring high transportation costs by importing inputs from non-local suppliers (other companies in their conglomerate, for example) or having to rely on embryonic and unstable local companies. In this context they frequently found that the most effective local suppliers were those which had been separated out from their Hungarian rivals.

Functional integration with the investor is a two-edged sword. On the one hand it can lead to genuine knowledge transfer and an opening of marketing and supply channels for the subsidiary. On the other hand, however, it can amount to a situation where the investor tries to transfer knowledge and impose practices which do not work well in the context of local idiosyncrasies. Furthermore functional integration can lead to increased bureaucracy, reducing the subsidiary's flexibility in responding to local conditions. Since East and West Germany share the same laws, regulations, competitors and many cultural factors, one can expect most of the functional knowledge and practices which are transferred by West German investors to be appropriate. The possible negative effects of functional integration with the investor are more likely to be of importance in the Hungarian context.

Overall foreign investors seem to have a tendency to try to achieve vertical disintegration by liquidating non-core activities and as a consequence tend to endorse new supply arrangements which are performance enhancing in the East German context but not in the Hungarian one. This can be traced back to a failure to fully appreciate the importance of the absence of a well-developed background industry and the impact of the relatively high degree of economic, legal and political uncertainty in Hungary.

Notes

1 See, for example, Carlin, 1994, p. 285; Aghion, Blanchard and Carlin, 1994, p. 2; Dobrinsky, 1996, p. 402; Meyer and Moller, 1998, p. 412; Ericson, 1998, p. 108.

2 See, for example, the implications of Aghion, Blanchard and Burgess, 1994.

3 See, for example, the implications of the literature on 'deep restructuring', Carlin, Van Reenen and Wolfe, 1995.

4 This literature survey will serve as the basis for the derivation of the empirical hypotheses in section 2 and in section 5 it will constitute the framework for interpreting the evidence found. Consequently this survey is more detailed than would be required if the sole objective was to give a simple overview.

5 Since none of the authors surveyed distinguish between different countries in this respect it is reasonable to infer that they intend their conclusions to hold for transition economies in general.

6 In Williamson, 1996, p. 95 the same idea is referred to as 'discriminating match'.

7 Bernheim and Whinston (1998) argue that bounded rationality and transaction costs are not sufficient to explain why contracts sometimes make actions less sensitive the verifiable events than would appear optimal or even fail to specify verifiable obligations of the

parties. They suggest that once some aspects are unverifiable, then it is often optimal to leave other verifiable aspects of performance unspecified. Such purposeful incompleteness can help contracting parties sustain cooperation by allowing them to create more severe history-dependent punishments and they argue that many best-response functions may be achievable only through the use of an incomplete contract that leaves the alter-moving player with discretion.

8 Similarly Hart (1989, p. 209) argues that with extreme complementarity between assets- that is if no transacting party can benefits from any increase in his marginal productivity unless he has access to both sets of assets- assets should be owned in common, which may provide a minimum size of the firm. From a rather different starting point and without making clear how codification costs relate to transaction costs Casson and Wadeson (1998) suggest that the boundaries of the firm should lie where information is most easily codified and where communication can therefore take a relatively impersonal form.

9 Dow (1993) claims that it is sufficient for essential input suppliers, who have large sunk costs before production and are indispensable in the production process, to be able to appropriate large ex-post quasi-rent streams. Rajan and Zingales (1998) suggest that giving them access to critical resources is an alternative to giving ownership to motivate agents to make relationship specific investments.

10 These two types of definitions are not mutually exclusive. For the purposes of this chapter I will define vertical integration in organisational terms, including the degree of control exercised over the subsidiary's operations. In the context of examining the organisational and efficiency issues arising in the subsidiaries of foreign direct investors and in Hungarian holding companies this is far more fruitful than sticking to ownership relations as such.

11 It should be noted that the decision to remain vertically integrated, which is what I am are dealing with in this chapter, is intellectually analogous to the decision to become more vertically integrated.

12 In contrast to Grossman and Hart Chiu (1998) suggests that the loss of ownership of an asset may actually increase the assets loser's investment incentive. This result is based on a different interpretation of the role of the threat point and outside options in bargaining.

13 A counterargument is that smaller companies might still be able to realise sufficient scale economies by selling internally produced components to external agents.

14 The case study evidence not only serves as a basis for the statistical variables used, but will also help to interpret the statistical results obtained.

15 Tables 3.1 and 2 summarise the changes in the companies' functional integration. Table 3.3 describes the variables which were used to examine the changes in the companies' integration. Tables 3.4a and b summarise the data. Tables 3.5a and b show the correlation matrices obtained. All tables can be found in Appendix C.

16 At this point I am testing for homogeneity between Hungary and East Germany. Unless it is otherwise stated the null cannot be rejected for the variables used in my case studies. Testing the hypothesis of homogeneity for two country-specific dummies involves using the chi-square test of independence. In the case of continuous variables a t-test on their means was used. If the null hypothesis of homogeneity cannot be rejected, then the two country specific variables can be pooled. Correlation matrices were obtained for the pooled data but did generally not contradict previous findings or add something new.

17 See Tables 3.1a, b and 3.2a, b for details.

18 All these mean values can be found in Tables 3.4a and b.

19 These differences are noticeable but not statistically significant.

20 For example an interview partner in H10 claimed that less integrated structures increase flexibility and ease information flow problems: 'We have a very small centre and most day-to-day decisions are made on the building site or in the factory where they arise. These local units are only accountable for their profitability but are not asked to justify each and every decision made. This increases our flexibility and makes us responsive to local demands. Furthermore, like this we are better able to tap into local networks, which is important in gaining jobs.'

21 'When we have to ask for permission from the head offices to do something, then this costs time and increases the administrative burden on us' (H3's managing director).

22 'Vertical integration reduces our dependency on others. The infrastructure is not sufficiently developed to subcontract more functions out. The aim is to maintain this level of integration in the medium-run as well' (H1's managing director).

23 The managing director of H3 cites of the main advantages of generally having internal departments, rather than using the investor that it gives the local company flexibility, local information and cost advantages. He adds that: 'When we have to ask for permission from the head offices to do something, then this costs time and increases the administrative burden on us.'

24 In H11 both upstream (due to temperature changes) and downstream activities (due to tourism) are highly seasonal, but their seasonal fluctuations cancel each other.

25 See Tables 3.2a and b.

26 H3's managing director: 'The advantages of the investor conducting part of our procurement is that we can save costs due to bargaining with larger orders. We can also save time by using the expertise of procurement managers in the Head Offices. However we expect this division of labour to stay constant in the medium-run, since it makes no sense for the head offices, which are far away in Cologne, to take on more functions' (also H9).

27 H4 benefits from the investor's trade channels and experience in the West and the investor from H4's in the East. Similar synergies can be achieved in R&D, where both the investor and the subsidiary provide R&D services (H4, H7).

28 This is especially the case with R&D activities.

29 For example H2 is highly integrated with its investor and the production manager interviewed made the following comments: '[Our parent company] tries to have a coherent organisational methods on a worldwide level. This results in very hierarchical structures and in methods which in their uniformity do not always adjust well to local conditions. In particular, the Hungarian subsidiary suffers from information flow problems. This is particularly true for the investor's marketing department, which seems to be unable to get to grips with Hungarian idiosyncrasies because they are unable to take in information from the Hungarian subsidiary. The overall consequence is that H2 is very slow in reacting to market developments.'

30 For example the change manager in D8 complains that if D8 wants to introduce changes, the interests and position of other companies within the investor's conglomerate (some of its suppliers belong to the same investor) have to be taken into consideration.

31 By 1997 all the companies with FDI are fully owned subsidiaries, that is we are dealing with acquisitions rather than joint ventures.

32 This variable was obtained from interviews with the procurement manager in each company.

33 The numbers in parentheses indicate the association found and its statistical significance. Statements along the lines of 'companies with a higher than average functional integration

have a higher than average probability of being profitable' are meant to indicate that in the case studies there is, for example, a significant positive association between functional integration and the profit dummy.

34 From a historical perspective I find that companies which were more functionally integrated in 1990 tend to have experienced above average subsequent reductions in their integration (0.62, 5 per cent).

35 Companies which relied on other companies in the same Kombinat in 1990 (that is they were less than average functionally integrated) tend to have a strong propensity to use separated out suppliers with whom they have historic ties (0.70, 5 per cent) rather than entirely external ones. This might suggest the persistence of a 'relying on local networks' attitude.

36 In addition companies which were highly functionally integrated in 1990 already have above average profit prospects in 1996 (0.55, 5 per cent).

37 – and on the country level diametrically opposed.

38 The associations between the investor dummies and profitability are negative but insignificant.

39 Both in the East German and Hungarian data there is some indication that investors have been deterred from investing into large companies which presumably offered a bigger restructuring challenge. A company's size in 1990 is negatively associated with FDI at the 10 per cent level in both countries.

40 This section is best started by a caveat: all my conclusions relate only to the 20 companies studied. Although I am hence unable to make statements about trends pertaining to Hungarian and East German companies in general, my case studies nevertheless are well suited to show the degree of support found for the hypotheses studied and to indicate avenues for future research.

41 Lyons (1996) gives a review of the theoretical arguments and empirical evidence relating to how environmental and behavioural risk are likely to affect inter-firm contracting.

42 This might be partly due to the fact that investors tended to be attracted to companies which were smaller and less integrated to start off with.

References

Aghion, P., Blanchard, O. and Burgess, R. (1994), 'The behaviour of state firms in Eastern Europe, pre-privatisation', *European Economic Review*, Vol. 38 (6).

Aghion, P., Blanchard, O. and Carlin, W. (1994), 'The economics of enterprise restructuring in Central and Eastern Europe', *CEPR, Discussion Chapter No. 1058*.

Alchian, A. and Demsetz, H. (1972), 'Production, information and economic organisation', *American Economic Review*, Vol. 62.

Amsden, A., Kochanowicz, J. and Taylor, L. (1994), *The market meets its match: Restructuring the economies of Eastern Europe*, Harvard University Press.

Auerbach, P. (1993), 'Vertical integration, planning and the market', in Arestis, P. and Chick, V. (eds), *Recent developments in post-Keynesian economics*, Elgar.

Bernheim, B. and Whinston, M. (1998), 'Incomplete contracts and strategic ambiguity', *The American Economic Review*, September.

Carlin, W. (1994), 'Privatisation and deindustrialisation in East Germany', in Estrin, S. (ed.), *Privatisation in Central and Eastern Europe*, Longman.

Carlin, W., Van Reenen, J. and Wolfe, T. (1995), 'Enterprise restructuring in early transition: the case study evidence from Central and eastern Europe', *Economics of Transition*, Vol. 3 (4).

Casson, M. and Wadeson, N. (1998), 'Communication costs and the boundaries of the firm', *International Journal of the Economics of Business*, February.

Chiu, S. (1998), 'Noncooperative bargaining, hostages and optimal asset ownership', *American Economic Review*, September.

Coase, R. (1998), 'The new institutional economics', *AEA Chapters and Proceedings*, May.

Dobrinsky, R. (1996), 'Enterprise restructuring and adjustment in the transition to market economy', *Economics of Transition*, Vol. 4 (2).

Dow, G. (1993), 'The appropriability critique of transaction cost economics', in Pitelis, C. (ed.), *Transaction costs, markets and hierarchies*, Blackwell.

Ericson, R. (1998), 'Restructuring in transition: Conception and measurement', *Comparative Economic Studies*, Summer.

Estrin, S. (1994), *Privatisation in Central and Eastern Europe*, Longman.

Grabher, G. (1996), 'Adaptation at the cost of adaptability? Restructuring the East German regional economy', in Grabher, G. and Stark, D. (eds), *Restructuring networks in postsocialism*, Oxford University Press.

Grabher, G. and Stark, D. (1996), 'Organising diversity: Evolutionary theory, network analysis and postsocialist transformations', in Grabher, G. and Stark, D. (eds), *Restructuring networks in postsocialism*, Oxford University Press.

Gros, D. and Steinherr, A. (1995), *Winds of change*, Longman.

Grosfeld, I. and Roland, G. (1995), 'Defensive and strategic restructuring in Central European enterprises' *CEPR, Discussion Chapter No. 1135.*

Grossman, S. and Hart, O. (1986), 'The costs and benefits of ownership: a theory of vertical and lateral integration', *Journal of Political Economy*, Vol. 94 (4).

Hanson, G. (1995), 'Incomplete contracts, risk and ownership', *International Economic Review*, Vol. 36 (2).

Hart, O. (1993), 'Incomplete contracts and the theory of the firm', in Williamson, O. and Winter, S. (eds), *The nature of the firm*, Oxford University Press.

Hart, O. (1989), 'An economist's perspective on the theory of the firm', *Columbia Law Review*, Vol. 89; reprinted in Buckley, P. and Michie, J. (eds), *Firms, organisations and contracts*, Oxford University Press.

Joskow, P. (1993), 'Asset specificity and the structure of vertical relationships', in Williamson, O. and Winter, S. (eds), *The nature of the firm*, Oxford University Press.

Kay, N. (1993), 'Corporate governance and transaction costs', in McCahery, J., Picciotto, S. and Scott, C. (eds), *Corporate control and accountability*, Oxford University Press.

Klein, B. (1988), 'Vertical integration as organisational ownership: the Fisher Body–General Motors relationship revisited' *Journal of Law, Economics and Organisation*, Vol. 4 (1); reprinted in *Case studies in contracting and organisation*, Oxford University Press.

Kornai, J. (1992), *The political economy of communism*, Clarendon Press.

Kreps, D. (1986), 'Corporate culture and economic theory'; reprinted in Buckley, P. and Michie, J. (eds) (1996), *Firms, organisation and contracts*, Oxford University Press.

Lieberman, M. (1991), 'Determinants of vertical integration: an empirical test', *Journal of Industrial Economics*, September.

Lyons, B. (1996), 'Empirical evidence of efficient contract theory: Inter-firm contracts', *Oxford Review of Economic Policy*, Vol. 12 (4).

Masten, S. (1996), 'Introduction', *Case studies in contracting and organisation*, Oxford University Press.

Meyer, K. and Moller, I. (1998), 'Managing deep restructuring: Danish experiences in Eastern Germany', *European Management Journal*, Vol. 16 (4).
Olsen, T. (1996), 'Agency costs and the limits of integration', *Rand Journal of Economics*, Vol. 27.
Rajan, R. and Zingales, L. (1998), 'Power in a theory of the firm', *Quarterly Journal of Economics*, May.
Reve, T. (1990), 'The firm as a nexus of internal and external contracts', in Aoki, M., Gustafsson, B. and Williamson, O. (eds), *The firms as a nexus of treaties*, Sage Publications.
Riordan, M. (1990), 'What is vertical integration?', in Aoki, M., Gustafsson, B. and Williamson, O. (eds), *The firms as a nexus of treaties*, Sage Publications.
Stark, D. (1996), 'Recombinant networks: Property transformation and restructuring of large firms', in Grabher, G. and Stark, D. (eds), *Restructuring networks in postsocialism*, Oxford University Press.
Waterson, M. (1993), 'Vertical integration and vertical restraints', *Oxford Review of Economic Policy*, Vol. 9 (2).
Whyte, G. (1994), 'The role of asset specificity in the vertical integration decision', *Journal of Economic behaviour and Organisation*, Vol. 23.
Williamson, O. (1998), 'The institutions of governance', *The American Economic Review*, May.
Williamson, O. (1996), *The mechanisms of governance*, Oxford University Press.
Williamson, O. (1993), 'The logic of economic organisation', in Williamson,O. and Winter, S. (eds), *The nature of the firm*, Oxford University Press.
Williamson, O. (1985), *The economic institutions of capitalism*, The Free Press.
Winger, A. (1994), 'Is big really bad?', *Business Economics*, July.

4 Social Disintegration? Changes in the Internal Provision of Social Services

This chapter examines the way in which enterprises have restructured the extensive social services they used to provide internally, changing the company's degree of vertical integration. Empirical hypotheses derived from the literature on enterprise restructuring are examined both qualitatively and statistically. I find that although the economic literature captures important aspects of social service restructuring in East Germany, developments in Hungary tend to be in stark contrast. There is strong evidence that companies which maintain their internal social service provision and shed less employees actually outperform other companies. This outperformance can be measured in terms of profits, domestic market share and exports. Surprisingly Hungarian companies with FDI show just as strong a persistence in social service provision as those run by local managers. Nor has it been, as generally suggested, a question of time until Hungarian companies follow East German trends and shed their social services. It is not that Hungarian companies are laggards in restructuring social service provision, it is that they have chosen a different restructuring path. Instead of admonishing Hungarian companies for their lack of restructuring we should turn our attention to examining the efficiency rationale behind the choices they have made. Companies which maintain social service provision and maintain historically accepted social responsibility norms tend to benefit from a highly cooperative trade union and workforce. This is an important and overlooked factor enhancing their ability to meet the challenges posed by transition.

Introduction

In the early literature[1] the issue as to how enterprises should deal with nonproductive social facilities and activities aroused little controversy. Their divestment was recommended to reduce vertical integration and improve efficiency. This chapter examines:

- the extent of social service shedding[2] by different sized companies;
- the impact of social service shedding on a company's performance;
- whether management style affects the degree of shedding; and
- differences in the experiences of East German and Hungarian companies.

These issues are examined from a comparative perspective using extensive qualitative and quantitative case study evidence from 20 newly privatised and state owned East German and Hungarian enterprises. The chapter proceeds as follows: section 1 provides a survey of the literature; section 2 derives empirical hypotheses; section 3 presents the empirical evidence found in my case studies and derives statistical variables; section 4 confronts the hypotheses. Section 5 concludes.

1 Literature Survey

Before 1990 East German and Hungarian companies operated in an economy characterised by bottlenecks. Consequently companies developed a desire for 'reproductive self-containment' (Grabher, 1996) which led them to produce as many inputs internally as possible. In addition planners in both countries tended to have a preference for monopolising industrial sectors as it was deemed that larger but fewer enterprises would be easier to control than many small ones. These two forces frequently resulted in the creation of highly vertically integrated local monopolies whose boundaries had been determined by non-market based considerations. Consequently the unbundling of these 'excessively' integrated enterprises (Estrin, 1994, p. 15) and the demonopolisation of the industrial sectors they operate in are generally regarded as central to improving efficiency in the enterprise sector of transition economies. Privatisation is frequently seen as a prime way of achieving the former objective and trade liberalisation as a crucial contributor to the latter (see, for example, Gros and Steinherr, 1995, p. 285).

This chapter focuses on the social aspects of the unbundling of former state-owned enterprises. This social question derives from the fact that as part of their high vertical integration enterprises were not only engaged in the internal production of physical inputs, but also provided their employees with a wide range of social services, such as crèches, doctors' surgeries, canteens, holiday camps, sports' facilities and the like. Consequently enterprises in Central and Eastern Europe provided a large range of social services to their employees which in Western economies are more commonly provided by local governments or non-profit organisations. At the same time social protection benefits,[3] a common feature of non-wage benefits in many Western economies, tended to be the task of the government (Friedman and Wörgötter, 1997).

In the early literature the issue as to how enterprises should deal with these nonproductive social facilities aroused little controversy. They were either not mentioned explicitly and implicitly included in the general recommendation for the need to reduce vertical integration (see, for example, Fisher and Gelb, 1991; Dhanji, 1991) or it was, for example, briefly stated that:

> State-owned enterprises are typically collections of both production and on-production activities. The reasons which led to such an organisation are gone. Non-production activities, schools, housing, hospitals and the like should be operated independently (Aghion, Blanchard and Burgess, 1994, p. 4).

Similarly Carlin, Van Reenen and Wolfe (1995, p. 428) state that: 'undertaking restructuring generally entails cuts in employment and the shedding of social assets by the enterprise'. The almost unanimous recommendation was divestiture to the local government or, should no alternative operator be found, their ultimate closure.

The reasoning behind this recommendation focused on the efficiency implications of a continued internal provision. Since these social services are nonproductive activities they reduce per capita productivity in the company. Estrin, Schaffer and Sing (1997) have also suggested that overextensive social provision might not only raise the costs of enterprise restructuring but also deter potential foreign direct investors. One reason for this is suggested by the Aghion, Blanchard and Burgess (1994) model of restructuring: at any point in time the closure of social services creates groups of 'losers' who will have an incentive to form a coalition against the proposed restructuring measures, thus complicating restructuring. If a company has not shed its social service provision prior to its acquisition by a foreign investor, then an investor will anticipate the future complications which would arise as a consequence of an attempt to implement restructuring measures and might be therefore deterred from investing in the first place. A further concern is the possibility that a persistence of social service provision in former state-owned enterprises would raise the effective wage paid by the state sector and lead to increased set-up costs for new companies, thus distorting their relative efficiency and stifling the growth of a dynamic private sector (Commander and Schankerman, 1997). Commander and Schankerman as well as Estrin, Schaffer and Sing (1997) are also concerned about the possibility that social services might create attachment in workers and retard their mobility, thus preventing them from moving to more productive sectors.[4]

Based on these cost and efficiency considerations an expectation of rapid restructuring in the provision of social services developed. Since internal provision was primarily associated with negative consequences for the enterprise and economy overall, it was reasonable to expect that not only would enterprises seek to rid themselves of these nonproductive units as quickly as possible, but that they would also be encouraged to do so by the government. Indeed in my interviews I found that most managers in state-owned or privatised enterprises were relatively quick to learn the language of free-market entrepreneurs, stressing the need to focus on core activities and improving efficiency by shedding all nonproductive social activities and eliminating the slack induced by overstaffing (see Clark and Soulsby (1998) for a similar finding in Czech enterprises).

Nevertheless over time increasing case study evidence emerged that this expectation of speed has not generally materialised (see, for example, Carlin, Van Reenen and Wolfe, 1995; Friedman and Wörgötter, 1997). Not only do most companies in Central and Eastern Europe continue to provide social services, but furthermore there is evidence that governments continue to subsidise their provision. There is a discernible tendency in the literature to equate a continuing internal provision of social services with a failure to restructure sufficiently the enterprise's operations. Dobrinsky (1996, p. 402), for example, states that:

> The enterprises' responsiveness to the new environment and the changes in their behaviour and performance are the most important indicators of adjustment at the micro level. Enterprise adjustment shows up in changes such as ... restructuring of costs aimed at their reduction by eliminating non-essential and non-productive expenses (for example, the maintenance of social assets) ...

Since most of the studies finding a continuity of social service provision tend to only cover data up to 1993 and many of the pressures to restructure can be expected to intensify over time with the progress of, for example, privatisation, FDI and trade liberalisation, Rein and Friedman (1997, p. 147) express a general sentiment when they state that: 'The finding of stability in overall benefits is probably a result of the [shortness of the] time period [studied].'

Explanations for the persistence of internal social service provision tend to focus on the power of insiders and the lack of alternative sources of supply, heightening the resistance against their divestiture.[5] When trying to explain the fact that in a survey of overall 117 case studies of Polish, Hungarian and Czech companies they find no examples of companies which have got rid of all or nearly all their social assets Carlin, Van Reenen and Wolfe (1995) put forward the hypothesis that this was due to the continuing power of the companies' insiders, that is the employees and local managers. They summarise their findings by stating that the majority of restructuring efforts undertaken in the initial years of transition were not threatening to insiders and did not require much cash, thus resulting in a general lack of 'deep' restructuring.

Commander and Schankerman (1997, p. 3) also blame the 'continuing dominance of insiders in decision-making and control in privatised as well as state firms' and add that managers consider social services to be a necessary 'social burden' which is not primarily kept in order to ensure worker attachment but out of a sense of 'social responsibility'. Overall they conclude (p. 11) that 'from the perspective of firms, these choices (to maintain the internal provision of social services) seem difficult to explain.' Based on three case studies in the Czech Republic Clark and Soulsby (1998) give an explanation for the persistence of social services which ties in with the notion of 'social responsibility': on their account the nature of the inherited enterprise-community relationship, that is of the social embeddedness of the company, impacts on restructuring decisions to reduce overstaffing and to unburden the enterprise of its social and welfare assets. A logical conclusion from all this is that companies will only be able to improve their efficiency by fully shedding their social service provision once the power of insiders and of historically inherited norms is broken by, for example, sale to a foreign direct investor.

2 The Empirical Hypotheses

From the literature surveyed four main empirical questions arise:

- do large companies continue to provide an above average number of benefits;
- do companies which provide many benefits underperform those which have shed them more effectively;
- does management style affect the number of benefits a company provides;
- have East German and Hungarian companies chosen the same approach to restructuring their social services?

This section explores answers to these questions suggested by the literature surveyed and formulates them in the form of testable empirical hypotheses.

2.1 Hypothesis Relating the Number of Benefits Provided to Company Size

HYPOTHESIS 1:

- *positive association between firm size (proxied by the number of employees) and number of benefits provided.* (See, for example, Commander and Schankerman (1997, p. 5) for empirical findings to this effect with respect to Russian and Ukrainian firms and Estrin, Schaffer and Singh (1997, p. 26) for Polish ones.)

Companies which were larger than average in 1990 can be expected to have exhibited higher than average vertical integration. As part of this greater integration I would expect larger companies to have provided a greater number of social services in 1990. To the extent that there is a persistence of historical trends both with respect to firm size and benefit provision, I would expect the same to hold in 1996.

HYPOTHESIS 2:

- *positive association between monopoly power (proxied by market share) and number of benefits provided.* (Carlin, Van Reenen and Wolfe (1995, pp. 440–2), for example, give the favourable financial position associated with a monopoly as a reason for a general lack of restructuring. Others, such as Grosfeld and Roland (1995, p. 21), formulate the same idea by stressing the positive incentive effect of demonopolisation.)

Companies with greater than average monopoly power in 1996 can be expected to have experienced fewer pressures to restructure in general and hence to have maintained a larger number of internally provided social services.

2.2 Hypotheses Relating the Number of Benefits Provided to Performance

The hypotheses in this section are all deduced from the suggestion that a continued social service provision will have negative efficiency implications on the enterprise level: see, for example, Commander and Schankerman (1997, pp. 2–11), Estrin, Schaffer and Singh (1997, p. 25), Dobrinsky (1996, p. 402). A company's 'future decline' is also an implied consequence of delaying restructuring in the Aghion, Blanchard and Burgess (1994) model. I examine whether these negative efficiency implications can be seen in terms of a company's profitability, market share and export performance.

HYPOTHESIS 3:

- *negative association between profits and number of benefits provided.*[6]

Due to the negative efficiency implications of a continued internal social service provision I would expect firms which maintain an above average number of internal social services to be less profitable than average.

HYPOTHESIS 4:

- *negative association between market share (as an indication of a company's competitiveness) and number of benefits provided.*

HYPOTHESIS 5:

- *negative association between export performance and number of benefits provided.*

To the extent that a continued social service provision is an indication of a general failure to restructure sufficiently the firm's operations (see, for example, Dobrinsky, 1996, p. 402; Aghion, Blanchard and Burgess, 1994, p. 4; Carlin, Van Reenen and Wolfe, 1995, p. 439) I would expect companies with numerous social services to have a below average market share in 1996[7] and, because they are less internationally competitive, to achieve few exports to the EU and worldwide markets.

2.3 Hypotheses Relating to Management Style, that is to the Role of Insiders and Foreign Direct Investors

HYPOTHESIS 6:

- *a negative association between FDI and the number of social services provided.* (This is an implication of the suggestion that a general lack of 'deep restructuring' and the concomitant persistence of social service provision is largely due to a prevalence of privatisation measures which leave insiders in charge: see, for example, Carlin, Van Reenen and Wolfe (1995, p 441) and Carlin and Aghion (1996, p. 374). See also comments on the general role of foreign direct investors: Estrin, Brada, Gelb and Singh (1995, p. 23), Grosfeld and Roland (1995, p. 10), for example.)

HYPOTHESIS 7:

- *a positive association between insider power and the number of benefits provided.* (This is merely another way of expressing the ideas underlying Hypothesis 6.)

HYPOTHESIS 8:

- *local managers who, deriving from the previous economic order, have a moral conviction that they have a 'social responsibility' are less likely to shed both superfluous employees and the internal provision of social services.* (Clark and Soulsby (1998) find support for a variant of this hypothesis in three Czech companies. Commander and Schankerman (1997, pp. 4 and 13) mention social responsibility and consider the case of company towns. Estrin, Schaffer and Singh (1997, p. 37) mention the role of 'historically accepted norms'. Usually such factors are merely reported or mentioned but not discussed in detail.)

To the extent that companies do not engage in an efficiency enhancing restructuring of their social services as a result of insider power or due to the historically determined ethical values of local managers, I would expect to find a) a persistence of social service provision in companies in which local managers are in charge and b) that the companies with FDI provide almost no social services internally.

2. 4 Hypotheses Relating to a Comparison between Developments in East Germany and Hungary

Both East German and Hungarian companies tended to provide social services internally which in Western market based economies are typically provided by agents external to the company. In both countries companies are in a process of transition to a market based economy. Consequently one can expect that:

HYPOTHESIS 9:

- *Both East German and Hungarian companies should show an unambiguous trend towards shedding the internal provision of social services.* (The expectation that this trend should hold in all transition economies is evident in the entire literature surveyed.)

The finding of relative stability in internal social service provision tended to be made in studies including only data up to 1993[8] and there was a general expectation that this stability would not last (Rein and Friedman, 1997, p. 147). Even if Hungarian companies had weaker incentives to restructure in an environment characterised by a much more gradualist approach to transition, by 1997 one can expect that Hungarian companies should be starting to catch up with their East German counterparts.

3 Variables and Case Study Evidence

The aim of this section is to present the empirical evidence which can then be used to confront Hypotheses 1–9. The case study evidence not only serves as a basis for the statistical variables used in section 4, but will also help to interpret the statistical results obtained. It is for this reason that this section goes into some detail. section 3.1 presents the case study evidence on which the statistical variables capturing changes in the provision of social services are based. The reasons given by managers for their continued provision are explored and changes in the provision of individual benefit types are discussed. Section 3.2 presents the 'explanatory' variables which relate to the companies' size and performance. In section 3.3 I explore the case study evidence pertaining to the role of foreign direct investors, insider power and different management styles in the restructuring process. Tables 4.1, 4.2, 4.3a and 4.3b in Appendix D explain and list all the variables.

3.1 Social Service Variables

- *Variables capturing changes in the number of social services provided internally*

These include variables capturing the number of benefits provided in 1990 and 1996/7 as well as the change in the number of benefits over this time period. I had seven categories into which benefits could fall and counted the number of categories covered by a given company. These categories were:

1 food related benefits: canteens or food-tokens;
2 childcare: kindergartens and crèches;
3 medical services: on-site doctor's surgeries;
4 holiday services: hotels, children's camps, financial contributions to holidays;
5 non-food commodity benefits and presents: subsidies for school books, transportation, Easter and Christmas presents, subsidised on-site shops;
6 housing: housebuyers and -builders loans, provision of dormitories, provision of apartments;
7 cultural, sports and community activities as well as recreational facilities: libraries, cultural centres, swimming pools, sponsorship of sports' clubs.

This list also provides an indication of the wide range of social services which these companies have historical provided to their employees.[9] My average *German* company provided 4.2 social services in 1990 out of which at most a canteen was left in 1996. Foreign direct investors usually made it a condition of their acquisition that the company sheds all its social services and a certain number of employees first. In this process canteens were kept or upgraded by 'socially minded' investors as 'sweeteners'.[10] Only the two enterprises without FDI (D6, D7) have kept any benefits at all. D7, for example, the holiday camp for children, presents for anniversaries and activities centred at over 1,200 former employees who are now retired, such as company fetes with special emphasis on the elderly and young. The personnel manager points out that D7 is the only company in the entire building sector which has kept such services. He attributes this fact to D7 still having a different management culture in this respect than other companies where investors are in the driving seat. D6 as well has kept similar benefits which are all relatively cheap and have a motivational and community-building role.

In *Hungary* the decline in social service provision was much smaller, from an average of 5.7 services in 1990 to 5 in 1997.[11] I asked both managers and trade union representatives why their company had maintained the internal provision of social services.[12] The answers obtained can be grouped into to following categories:

- *they increase productivity by improving loyalty, morale and work motivation*;[13]

- *tradition and company culture*;[14]
- *'humane' company philosophy* of the investor/local management;[15]
- *maintaining social peace, management's fear of the trade union*/the trade union fought hard to keep the benefits;[16]
- they *constitute a compensation for being paid lower monetary wages*;[17]
- *tax savings* when compared with providing monetary wage increases.[18]

Interestingly only one personnel manager (in H11, incidentally the company which was in state ownership the longest) claims that providing social services is not the task of the company in the first place. Furthermore it is stated in only one company (H5) that many of the extensive social activities this particular company engages in detract from its profitability, but the company would not even consider abolishing them because they are so essential for maintaining morale. No company has the medium-run aim of winding its internal provision of social services down, the general aim seems to be to fine-tune existing arrangements.

This overall stability in the number of social services provided by Hungarian companies, does not mean that there have been no changes within individual benefit types. In accordance with other authors Table 4.2 suggests that there has been a shift away from in-kind benefits towards monetary benefits (vouchers) especially in the area of *food* provision (see Rein and Friedman, 1997, p. 145; Fajth and Lakatos, 1997, p. 183: both chapters also discuss the other types of benefits). Only the two smallest enterprises have dropped food provision altogether and two companies, H8 and H2, have even built a new canteen. Eighty-one per cent of the Hungarian enterprises provide food benefits in one form or the other. The popularity of food vouchers was explained by several interview partners in terms of the tax advantages they incur.

Childcare has been generally separated out and given to the local government, but in only one case, H3, was the facility closed down altogether. Separating-out childcare facilities seems to have caused little overall controversy, possibly because already historically there were numerous alternative suppliers in this area and employees have generally retained access to their old facilities even after restructuring.

No company with pre-existing *medical services* has scrapped them. Overall 81 per cent of the Hungarian companies in my data provide on-site medical facilities. Employees value the ready access they have to medical care if they can use facilities at work rather than having to go through the GP (rationing) system introduced in 1995. In favour of keeping medical facilities employers give paternalistic as well as efficiency reasons, such as reduced sick leave.

Astonishingly, all of the companies in my Hungarian data set continue to provide *holiday facilities* to their employees. Rein and Friedman (1997, p. 154) suggested that enterprises might be prevented from selling these assets by there being an oversupply of such properties on the market, but I encountered no enterprise which had even tried to sell its holiday facilities all together. As Fajth and Lakatos (1997, p. 181) concluded: 'It is the general experience that enterprises sell their holiday homes only when they are in extreme difficulties.' I gained the impression from interview partners that selling holiday facilities would be a certain way to create demotivation and industrial unrest unless the situation was so bad that 'employees had to accept that we have to sell our silver in order to survive'.[19] In addition, although holidays are usually accessible to all, they tend to be disproportionately used by better-off employees (managers), since companies only tend to provide a contribution rather than providing their holiday facilities free of charge. It should be noted that this is the only benefit requiring a physical infrastructure which has been kept by the two East German companies still providing some old-style benefits.

The category of *commodity benefits* includes, for example, presents, money towards school books and transportation but also on-site shops selling items at a reduced rate.[20] Presents are small bonuses in kind while the other benefits in this category are effective wage subsidies which, as in the case of food vouchers, incur tax advantages both for the employer and the employees because they are not subject to generally high social insurance and income taxes. The importance of the benefits seems to be declining with only 63 per cent of companies using them in 1997. Since economic theory suggests that outright wage increases would be preferred by employees I would expect a decline in commodity benefits as inflationary pressures subside and as the tax rules which made their provision advantageous change.

Community benefits such as sporting facilities, libraries and cultural clubs are again an area where no company has scrapped its pre-existing facilities, although only 63 per cent of companies provided such facilities in the first place. The finding of stability in this area is in contradiction with suggestions made by other authors that enterprises are showing a tendency to divest themselves of these facilities (Rein, Friedman and Wörgötter, 1997, p. 7). This is possibly the area where it is hardest to give an economic rationale for a continued provision of such facilities by enterprises and where a wider analytical approach is warranted which takes into account a given enterprises' role and 'embeddedness' in the local community and economy.

Housing benefits have generally been restructured, with companies selling their apartments and closing the dormitories which used to house (now sacked) migrant rural workers. Low interest loans for housebuyers and -builders, aimed mainly at better-off employees in managerial and administrative ranks, still enjoy great popularity and are provided by 72 per cent of companies. This overall trend has also been found by Rein and Friedman (1997, p. 154) and Fajth and Lakatos (1997, p. 183). This is the clearest example where social services are restructured in such a way that they prime objective is no longer redistributional, but rather they are aimed at attracting and keeping the 'right' type of workers.

- *Variables capturing qualitative changes in social service provision*

Simply counting of the number of benefits provided does not give us important information concerning changes in their extent and in the organisation of their provision. For this reason I introduced three state variables to capture a) whether the real value of the overall social services provided by the company has at least stayed constant, b) whether it has increased and c) whether the provision of the remaining social services has been reorganised, by, for example, shifting from and an internal canteen to giving employees food-tokens of equivalent value. Table 4.3b shows that 72 per cent of companies in the Hungarian data maintained the real value of their social services and 27 per cent even increased it. Only 27 per cent of companies reorganised the provision of their remaining services.

3.2 'Explanatory' Variables Relating to the Companies' Size and Performance

- *Variables capturing the size, that is number of employees, of a company in 1990 and 1996/7* (Hypothesis 1): in the East German companies the mean number of employees fell from 4150 to 577, while in Hungary there was a much smaller decline from 4430 to 3173.
- *Variables capturing the domestic market share of a company in 1990 and in 1996/7* (Hypothesis 2, Hypothesis 4): there have been radical changes in the market share[21] of the East German companies: a fall from a mean value of 89 per cent in 1990 to only 15.5 per cent in 1996. It should be noted that only has the share of the domestic market decreased, but frequently the size of the domestic market itself has shrunk rapidly. Many East German companies are obtaining a smaller slice in a smaller domestic pie, making it a matter of survival to achieve high sales outside East Germany. Hungarian companies have benefited from much more stable

demand patterns and fewer new entrants.[22] From the starting point of a relatively less monopolised overall industrial structure the Hungarian companies market share only fell from a mean value of 60 per cent to 56 per cent between 1990 and 1997.

- *Dummies to capture whether the company is profitable in 1995, 1996 or 1997* (Hypothesis 3): in 1995 44 per cent of the companies in my East German data were profitable rising to 77 per cent in 1997. In 1996 54 per cent of the Hungarian companies were profitable and all expected to at least break even by 1999.
- *The percentage of total output sold in worldwide and EU markets* (Hypothesis 5): in 1996 the East German companies tended to sell about 33 per cent of their total output in these markets, while the mean for the Hungarian companies was only 20 per cent.
- *The percentage of original employees shed and the percentage of employees made unemployed* have been included as further indicators of restructuring in the enterprise. I find that the East German companies tended to shed about 76 per cent of their workforce, making 54 per cent directly unemployed. The mean values for Hungary are 57 per cent and 38 per cent. Employees who were shed but not made directly unemployed either went into state-run employment programmes (Germany) or are employed by separated out non-core units which are now operating as independent companies. It should be noted that these shedding figures are well in excess of estimates (Estrin, 1994, p. 15) to the effect that labour hoarding before 1990 might have amounted to about 25 per cent of the workforce.

3.3 Variables Capturing the Role of Foreign Direct Investors, Insider Power and Different Management Styles

- *A dummy to capture whether the company has a foreign direct investor or not* (Hypothesis 6):[23] in the East German data 77 per cent of companies had foreign, including West German, investors in 1996. The two companies which at this time did not fall into this category were both up for resale after failed privatisations. The privatisation of D6 failed because the investor ended up asset stripping until the company's board intervened and initiated a repurchase by the Treuhand. When I called in 1998, D6 had been re-privatised to a UK company. The case of D7 is very unusual in that this is a company which is very successful in spite of its investor who went bankrupt. D7 was the only company in a large conglomerate which did not go down with its Austrian investor. It is currently up for resale but I gained the impression that it is not particularly keen on being sold.

In Hungary the picture is more varied. 63 per cent of the companies visited have a foreign direct investor, H5 and H11 have floated on the Budapest stock exchange after prolonged government involvement (some would say interference), H6 has been going from one crisis and government intervention to the next and H8 has an institutional investor who does not interfere in the day-to-day running of the company.

- (Hypotheses 7 and 8): lastly I have included two dummies which are aimed at examining the issue of *insider power* and to capture the extent to which *ethical and social values derived from the past* influence restructuring in the company.

  The first dummy captures whether the trade union cooperated in the restructuring process of the company[24] and the second whether the management is deemed to be and thinks of itself as 'socially responsible' or, to use the Hungarian expression, 'humane'. These variables warrant some explanation, especially since they are likely to effect not only the restructuring of social services but the restructuring process in general. They not only relate to the notion of insider power, but also the notion of the social embeddedness of economic activity.[25] Case study evidence is particularly useful in illustrating the rationale behind the persistence of attitudes and social norms for the provision of social services.

Interview partners frequently used the terms 'socially responsible' (Germany) and 'humane' (Hungary)[26] in order to describe a managerial approach to restructuring which takes into account how restructuring decisions are going to affect employees and which tries to cushion the adverse social effects this restructuring process entails. Put differently, 'socially responsible' managers placed themselves into their employees' shoes when making decisions and took their needs and worries into consideration. It is for this reason that 'socially responsible' is an indication of the 'power' of employees to influence decision-making: their concerns are being heard and taken into account.

Fifty-five per cent[27] of the German[28] and 45 per cent of the Hungarian companies[29] examined explicitly refer to such considerations. Measures which are considered to be humane or socially responsible include an extensive use of early retirement, providing employees with retraining and help in finding new jobs, making an effort not to sack all the members of a family employed by the company, paying redundancy payments which are higher than the legally required minimum and generally treating employees as individuals rather than faceless numbers. A socially responsible management will also have a predisposition towards separating out rather than liquidating non-core units in order to limit the unemployment impact of restructuring. It is also generally implied that a humane management involves employees and their representatives in designing the details of restructuring and stick to agreements once they are made. I asked both the personnel manager and trade union representative to explain the reasons for managers endorsing a 'humane' or 'socially responsible' approach to restructuring. Their answers can be grouped under the headings:

- a humane approach *maintains the motivation of the remaining workforce* by reducing the employees' fears concerning their future;[30]
- the desire to keep *social peace in the company*[31] *and its wider community*
- *the philosophy of the investor*[32]*/of the Treuhand representative;*[33]
- *empathy with the employees being made redundant* and *personal ethical motives.*[34]

Since in Hungary maintaining the internal provision of social services is frequently associated with a humane management, it should not be surprising that the reasons for maintaining social services are very similar to those given in favour of a humane approach to restructuring in general.

In 61 per cent of the East German companies and 54 per cent of the Hungarian ones the trade union cooperated in the restructuring process. These high percentages confirm an early finding obtained by Svejnar (1991, p. 128) who stated that trade unions 'have generally co-operated with (or at least tolerated) the transition process'. Cooperation by the unions consists in:

- *loyalty to the company: keeping back with their wage and non-wage demands;*[35]
- *refraining from strikes* and strike threats;[36]
- *providing employees with information* concerning retraining and job hunting opportunities and *encouraging employees to have a constructive input into workplace innovations;*[37]
- in East Germany there are many examples of employees *working unpaid overtime* and doing further training on the weekends.[38]

Cooperation by the trade union is only sustained in the long run if the management is perceived to be sticking to its side of the deal. In East Germany the implicit contract[39] implies that the workers contribute all they can by restraining their demands concerning wages and the work load until the company is doing well enough to meet them while the management pays

Tarif wages[40] and makes every effort not to have further redundancies. The basic idea that loyalty, restraint and cooperativeness by the union should be met by the management ensuring the company's long-run success and increasing wages and benefits in line with profits was also widespread in Hungary.[41] A management worth cooperating with is also expected to avoid 'unnecessary' redundancies,[42] to communicate honestly about the company's situation and plans for the future[43] and to generally stick to agreements reached with the union.

Cooperation by the trade union usually only breaks down when local managers or the investor renege on agreements made concerning investment or restructuring plans.[44] Such managerial behaviour is extremely damaging to industrial relations and in Germany usually results in employees resorting to the courts against the management while in Hungary strike threats and strike threats are more common. Both types of responses cause internal friction and wasting managerial time and effort.

4 Confronting the Hypotheses

This section presents the statistical evidence obtained with respect to Hypotheses 1–9 in my data set. Tables 4.4a and 4.4b in Appendix C list the associations found.

4.1 Confronting the Hypothesis Relating the Number of Benefits Provided to Company Size

HYPOTHESIS 1:

- *positive association between firm size and number of benefits provided. Summary: support in both the East German and Hungarian data.*

In the East German data companies which were relatively large in terms of their employee numbers in 1990 tend to provide an above average number of benefits in 1996 (0.62, 5 per cent).[45] Interestingly the company's current size is entirely insignificant, clearly indicating that it is historical factors which are important in explaining the persistence of benefits rather than the company's current number of employees.

In Hungary I also find support for Hypothesis 1. Companies which were relatively large in 1990 tended to provide numerous benefits already then

Table 4.1 Summary of the main statistical findings

Hypothesis	East Germany	Hungary
1	YES – historically larger companies still tend to provide more benefits in 1996	YES – strong persistence in trends for size and number of benefits provided – no evidence for the hypothesis of Estrin et al (1997) that larger firms experience larger declines
2	NOT APPLICABLE – large losses in market share for all companies, no East German companies with monopoly power in data	YES (?) – strong positive relationship between market share and social service provision: result of insufficient restructuring pressures due to lack of competition? – strong persistence of historical trends
3	WEAKLY YES – it is not clear whether companies are less profitable because of continued provision or whether social services are a compensation for lower wages in less profitable companies – companies which provided more social services in 1990 seem to have faced a greater restructuring challenge overall and were less profitable than average in 1995 but no longer in 1997	NO – on the contrary – companies which have at least maintained the real value of their social services are more likely to be profitable in 1996
4	NO – all relevant associations are insignificant	NO (?) – strong positive relationship between market share and social service provision: does maintaining the latter have a positive net effect on efficiency?
5	WEAKLY YES – companies which have achieved high exports in 1996 have shed an above average number of benefits	NO – on the contrary – companies with a good export performance provide many benefits – they shed fewer than average employees – they are larger than average – they tend to have a humane management – they are more likely to be profitable

Table 4.1 cont'd

Hypo-thesis	East Germany	Hungary
6	STRONGLY YES	NO
7 and 8	YES – BUT UNEXPECTED EFFICIENCY IMPLICATIONS – socially responsible management makes fewer than average employees unemployed – results in co-operative trade union BUT far from this insider involvement and these inherited social norms being efficiency reducing we find that: – these companies are more likely to be profitable	YES – BUT UNEXPECTED EFFICIENCY IMPLICATIONS – humane management sheds fewer than average employees – keeps the real value of social services at least constant – results in co-operative trade union BUT far from this insider involvement and these inherited social norms being efficiency reducing we find that: – these companies are more likely to be profitable – have higher than average market shares – better than average export performance – tend to be bigger than average – high levels of labour shedding likely to be due to bad business prospects rather than due to insufficient restructuring
9	NO – the differences in the trends are significant. There is no indication that the Hungarian companies are aiming following the West German trends by significantly reducing their social service provision rather than just fine tuning existing arrangements.	

(0.51, 10 per cent) and continue to do so in 1997 (0.53, 5 per cent). In Hungary there has been a strong persistence of historical trends with respect to firm size (0.98, 1 per cent) and with respect to the relative number of benefits provided (0.81, 1 per cent). Consequently I also find that companies which are large in 1997 behave similarly to and tend to be identical to the companies which were large in 1990. Furthermore I find that companies which have at least maintained the real value of their social services provided an above average number of benefits in 1990 (0.42, 10 per cent) and do so in 1997 (0.56, 5 per cent). These observations support statistically the general picture of stability and only gradual change in the provision of social services found by other authors.[46]

Estrin, Schaffer and Sing (1997)[47] not only also find evidence for a significant size effect in social service provision (p. 37) but they also suggest that larger Polish firms have experienced a greater decline than small firms (p. 46). I find little evidence of such a relationship in East Germany or Hungary. In East Germany the relevant association is very close to zero, probably because the decline in social service provision was so universal, with companies scrapping a greater number of services the more they had to start off with (-0.77, 1 per cent). In Hungary the negative association between a decline in the number of social services and the firm's size in 1990 is almost significant at the 10 per cent level, suggesting, if anything, that historically larger companies have experienced smaller than average declines in the number of benefits provided. In contrast to East Germany, the Hungarian companies showed no universal decline in the number of benefits provided. Most companies have kept the level of provision constant and some companies have even increased the number of their benefits. This is reflected in the strong positive association between the current number of benefits and changes in benefit provision (0.72, 1 per cent).[48]

HYPOTHESIS 2:

- *positive association between monopoly power (proxied by market share) and number of benefits provided.*

In East Germany all the companies have suffered such large losses in their market share and such intense competition that the idea that they might have retained any degree of monopoly power is highly unrealistic. Accordingly all associations which might be relevant to Hypothesis 2 are insignificant. In Hungary on the other hand I find a strong relationship between market share and the number of social services provided for both 1990 and 1997 (0.72,0.70, 1 per cent). The interpretation of this finding is not, however, straightforward. This will be discussed in greater detail with reference to Hypothesis 4.

4.2 Hypotheses Relating the Number of Benefits Provided to Performance

HYPOTHESIS 3:

- *negative association between profits and number of benefits provided. Summary: I find weak support in the East German data and the opposite trend in Hungary.*

In East Germany there is some evidence that, as the literature suggests, the efficiency implications of abandoning social service provision are favourable: Companies with a good export performance and hence high international competitiveness have shed a relatively high number of benefits (-0.68, 5 per cent). Furthermore companies who are not profitable in 1995 are more likely to have maintained some social services (-0.50, 10 per cent),[49] although it is not a priori clear whether the social services are dragging their profitability down or whether benefits are being kept as a compensation for lower wages in these companies.

In Hungary there is absolutely no support for Hypothesis 3. I find that the profit dummy is insignificant with respect to all the benefit variables, suggesting that there is no evidence that companies which provide a greater number of benefits than others are less profitable than average. What is more, I find that companies which have kept the real value of their social services at least constant are more likely than average to be profitable (0.67, 5 per cent). Only case study evidence can, however, shed light on the causality involved, that is on whether companies maintain their services because they can afford to do so, or whether they are profitable because of the positive effects of social service provision.[50]

HYPOTHESIS 4:

- *negative association between market share (as an indication of a company's competitiveness) and number of benefits provided.*
  Summary: in Hungary there is a strong positive relationship between market share and social service provision, but it is unclear whether continued social service provision is a consequence of an insufficient pressure to restructure or whether internal provision has positive net efficiency effects, giving these companies a competitive advantage.

Hypotheses 2 and 4 try to disentangle the effect market share is likely to have on restructuring. In doing so I am plagued by an age-old problem: does a high market share indicate monopoly power and hence an insufficient incentive to restructure (Hypothesis 2) or superior efficiency (Hypothesis 4)? In the East German data this problem is resolved by the fact that no company has sufficient market share for the monopoly power hypothesis to bear any relationship to reality whatsoever and all the associations pertaining to Hypotheses 2 and 4 are insignificant.

In Hungary on the other hand I not only find a strong relationship between market share and the number of social services provided for both 1990 and 1997 (0.72, 0.70, 1 per cent) [51] but my data even provides a weak indication that companies which have a high market share in 1997 have tended to either keep their benefits constant or to even increase them (0.44, 10 per cent). There is no obvious way of deciding whether these social services constitute a form of rent dispersion by companies with monopoly power, or whether highly efficient companies maintain them because their net efficiency implications are positive. The fact that a higher market share is associated with higher profits in both 1990 (0.49, 10 per cent) and 1997 (0.48, 10 per cent) is consistent with both the monopoly power and efficiency interpretation of a high market share.

HYPOTHESIS 5:

- *negative association between export performance and number of benefits provided.*
  Summary: I find weak support in the East German data and the opposite trend in Hungary.

In the East German data I find no significant associations which might shed light on Hypothesis 5, except that companies which have shed a large number of benefits have also achieved high exports in 1996 (-0.68, 5 per cent), suggesting that shedding benefits might have been efficiency improving for these companies.

In Hungary the picture is again radically different. The overall impression is that maintaining social services constitutes some form of competitive advantage in Hungary: not only are these companies more likely to be profitable, but companies which provide an above average number of benefits in 1997 also tend to have a good export performance (0.43, 10 per cent). What is more, I find than companies which have high exports tend to also have shed fewer than average employees (-0.64, 5 per cent), made a smaller proportion of their employees unemployed (-0.54, 5 per cent), are larger than average both in 1990 (0.84, 1 per cent) and 1997 (0.61, 5 per cent) and tend to have a humane management (0.48, 10 per cent). They exhibit all the signs of 'insufficient restructuring', 'continued adherence to historically accepted norms' and an 'excessive size'. They seem to be doing very well by doing the opposite of what the literature suggests they should be doing.

4.3 Hypotheses Relating to Management Style, that is to the Role of Insiders and Foreign Direct Investors

HYPOTHESIS 6:

- *a negative association between FDI and the number of social services provided.*
  Summary: strong for this hypothesis in the East German data, no such trend in Hungary.

As Hypothesis 6 suggests, in East Germany the arrival of a powerful outsider in the form of a foreign direct investor is strongly negatively associated with continued social service provision (-0.93, 1 per cent). The finding that in Hungary companies with FDI are no more likely to scrap social services than those without is rather perplexing in this context,[52] especially since one can expect foreign direct investors to have initially exactly the same attitudes as they would in East Germany. What exactly happens in the interactions between investors and the local workforce is best resolved by case study evidence.

HYPOTHESIS 7:

- *a positive association between insider power and the number of benefits provided.*

HYPOTHESIS 8:

- *local managers who, deriving from the previous economic order, have a moral conviction that they have a 'social responsibility' are less likely to shed both superfluous employees and the internal provision of social services.*
  Summary: I find the associations suggested by Hypotheses 7 and 8, but in both East Germany and Hungary the efficiency implications of restructuring measures based on notions of social responsibility are entirely unexpected.

When delving more deeply into the issues surrounding 'insider power' and 'historically accepted norms' my data hold some more surprises. The expectation that a management ascribing to historically accepted norms which effectively make them highly aware of the enterprises' social embeddedness generates the associations suggested by Hypotheses 7 and 8. Indeed I find that a humane management sheds fewer than average employees (-0.53, 5 per cent), tends to provide a relatively high number of benefits in 1990 (0.67 and respectively, 5 per cent) and in 1997 (0.84, 1 per cent and 0.67, 5 per cent respectively) and keeps the real value of social services at least constant (0.52, 5 per cent).[53] In East Germany socially responsible managers make fewer than average employees unemployed (-0.76, 1 per cent).[54]

What is not borne out, however, is the expectation that such 'insufficient' labour and social service shedding as a consequence of humane attitudes is going to have negative profitability implications for the company. On the contrary, by 1996/7 these companies are more likely to be profitable both in East Germany and Hungary (0.60 and 0.47 respectively, 10 per cent).

The crucially missing link is that humane managers and socially responsible managers tend to be rewarded by a cooperative trade union (0.71, 5 per cent and 0.83, 1 per cent respectively), which the case study evidence suggests can greatly facilitate overall restructuring. By 1997 German companies with a cooperative trade union are very likely to be profitable (0.71, 5 per cent) while Hungarian companies with a cooperative trade union are likely to have a higher than average market share in 1990 (0.71, 1 per cent) and 1997 (0.670, 5 per cent) as well as an above average export performance (0.49, 10 per cent). Far from keeping companies from adapting effectively to their changing environment and restructuring, some of the historically accepted norms seem to be actually conducive to efficiency enhancing behaviour.

The reduced labour shedding I observe in companies with a humane management can be an indication of two things: firstly of insufficient restructuring on the labour side or secondly of the fact that the company is doing well and has enough orders to continue to employ a relatively high proportion of its original workforce. The second interpretation finds support in the fact that high labour shedding and unemployment figures are both associated with lower probability of being profitable in 1996 (-0.57 and -0.59 respectively, 5 per cent). It seems that companies with high labour shedding rates are not shedding labour because they are restructuring their workforce especially effectively but because they have below average business prospects.[55]

4. 4 Hypotheses Relating to a Comparison between Developments in East Germany and Hungary

HYPOTHESIS 9:

- *both East German and Hungarian companies should show an unambiguous trend towards shedding the internal provision of social services.*
  Summary: the differences in trends are significant. With respect to the provision of social services formerly state owned Hungarian companies seem to have tended to chose a different restructuring altogether.

It is quite clear that my data provides no support whatsoever for shared trends between East Germany and Hungary. The assumption that the Hungarian and East German observations were generated by the same underlying process, that is that they come from a homogenous population, can be rejected at least at the 10 per cent level for all benefit related variables, the market share variables, the export variable, the labour shedding variable as well as the variable capturing the enterprises' size in 1996/7.[56] Although previously state owned East German and Hungarian companies started at historically similar starting points, they have embarked on very different trajectories with respect to the internal provision of social services and the Hungarian companies are showing no signs of catching the German trend after some delay.

5 Conclusions

The economic literature on enterprise restructuring strongly suggests that maintaining the internal provision of social services complicates the general restructuring process and reduces per capita productivity. Insider power and historically accepted norms concerning the management's social responsibility are usually cited as the main reasons for delaying crucial efficiency-enhancing restructuring. The general expectation is, however, that once the general transition process gains momentum and companies are sufficiently subject to market pressures, the insiders and their now outdated norms will have to give way. Consequently it can be only a question of time until the shedding of social services will take place in all transition economies.

In examining these questions there is a typical chicken and egg problem: do companies keep their social services because they can afford to do so (they are doing well enough to engage in rent dispersion) or are they doing well because they have maintained some social service provision? Correlations do not indicate causation. However, I did not encounter any managers who said that they kept social services because they had enough profits to disperse. Under transition every company's survival was under threat at some point and managers generally kept social service provision *in spite of* these pressures. At the very least my data suggests that alternative explanations and interpretations cannot be discounted.

Although the East German data provides weak support for some of the contentions found in the literature surveyed, surprisingly few of these expectations find empirical support in the Hungarian context.

There is evidence that companies which maintain their internal social service provision and shed less employees actually outperform other companies. This outperformance can be measured in terms of profits, domestic market share and exports. The surprising fact that Hungarian companies with FDI show just as strong a persistence in social service provision as those run by local managers and that several investors explicitly endorse a humane restructuring philosophy suggests that we have to search for explanations other than the persistence of insider power and outdated norms.

The differential behaviour of investors in the Hungarian and East German companies was generally not due to different initial restructuring approaches. In Hungary investors tend to arrive with preconceived ideas and a desire to more or less transplant structures and practices which work well or are commonly accepted in the West. They tend to realise soon that they have not acquired a clean slate but a company with its own traditions and culture which are ignored at the cost of demotivating the workforce, generating industrial unrest or at least apathy, creating distrust in the local management as well as a general lack of communication and cooperation. Since all of this is not conducive to an acquisition's success, investors tend to accept after some initial clashes that they have to work with these traditions rather than against them. In this context maintaining the internal provision of social services is a highly symbolic and effective gesture. By recognising the historically grown social role of the enterprise an investor signals that he is humane and worth cooperating with.

In East Germany the situation was different: In the process of reunification East Germany became fully integrated into the West German system of social benefit provision. Since East German companies generally needed to find an investor very quickly in order to survive, shedding all forms of traditional social services had to be accepted as one price one paid for having an investor. This shedding was all the easier to accept than in Hungary since East German employees were anticipating wage increases and the fast emergence alternative sources of social service provision. Nevertheless there were investors who were keen to signal that they were socially responsible in their attitudes to general restructuring, even if this did not include preserving the provision of social services: These investors tended to abolish services with 'sweeteners' such as upgraded canteens, changing areas and a generally improved working environment.

I find that historically determined attitudes towards restructuring have been adopted by some investors and, far from being an atavism, have surprisingly strong positive efficiency implications in terms of the companies' overall performance. Even in East Germany, where companies have been subject to very strong transition pressures, this unexpected relationship holds. My data suggests a reason for this which goes beyond the effects of social service provision on the individual worker's productivity and which has commonly been overlooked: Companies which ascribe to historically accepted norms tend to benefit form a highly cooperative trade union and workforce, a factor which greatly enhances their ability to meet the challenges posed by transition.[57]

I find little support for the hypotheses relating social service provision and management styles to company performance. The hypotheses relating social service provision to company size fare better. Both in East Germany and Hungary there is strong evidence that larger companies do indeed provide an above number of benefits. What is somewhat unexpected are the efficiency implications of staying large: large Hungarian companies again tend to exhibit 'insufficient' social service and labour shedding, but they also have an above average market share and export performance.

The fact that seven years into transition I find few companies who are perturbed by the persistence of internal social service provision and none who want to shed rather than fine-tune their services suggests that it is not simply a question of time until Hungarian companies follow East German trends and shed their social services. Hungarian companies seem to have chosen a long-run position characterised by continuing social service provision. It is not that Hungarian companies are laggards in restructuring social service provision, it is that they have chosen a different restructuring path. Instead of admonishing Hungarian companies for their lack of restructuring we should turn our attention to examining the efficiency rationale behind the choices they have made.

My conclusions indicate that much of the literature on enterprise restructuring has failed to adequately capture developments in Hungary. In particular my results call for a re-examination of the efficiency implications of managers being guided by social considerations in designing and implementing restructuring measures. Such a re-examination is all the more pertinent because empirical evidence for the persistence of social service provision and of 'socially responsible' attitudes is mounting also for transition countries other than Hungary.[58] The importance of restructuring wage and non-wage costs has to be put into relationship with the other, more pressing, transition challenges a company faces, such as the challenge of finding a new market niche in a market that is frequently rapidly changing both on the demand and supply side, the restructuring of its product range and supplier networks, the upgrading of its technology and the need to find new marketing and sales channels, to name just a few. There are strands of literature which suggest that the importance of wage costs has been greatly overestimated in this context, as has been the contribution internally provided social services make to a company's total wage costs.[59]

It is important to note that my findings were made in a context where environmental pressures are so strong that both managers and employees cannot ignore the need engage in overall restructuring. In such a context a socially responsible management with progressive ideas concerning which overall direction the company should take is much better able to lead a company with a cooperative trade union than a management which excels at shedding employees and social services, but induces low productivity, demotivation, disillusionment and unrest in the process.

Notes

1 See, for example, Fisher and Gelb (1991), Dhanji (1991), Aghion, Blanchard and Burgess (1994).

2 Before 1990 East German and Hungarian companies used to internally provide a wide array of social services such as canteens, childcare facilities, medical surgeries, holiday camps etc. Section 3.1 deals with individual services in greater detail.

3 Benefits which protect employees from falls in income associated with eventualities such as unemployment, sickness and retirement would are generally termed social protection benefits.

4 In my case studies a lack of labour mobility was mentioned by several Hungarian interview partners as creating a problem for companies facing labour shortages in certain skill categories (mostly managerial and highly trained blue collar employees). However, nobody mentioned social service provision as being the cause of lack of mobility. It was the rigidities in the housing market which attracted universal blame.

5 The fact that a different provider is supplying the same level of services at an affordable price should not in itself lead to any resistance. Problems are likely to arise, however, when divestiture is a euphemism for closure or radically reduced access.

6 In contrast to their underlying expectations Commander and Schankerman (1997, p. 5) find that in their Russian data there was actually a *positive* association between profitability and benefit provision. They do not, however, explore the possible causalities involved.
7 It should be stated explicitly that in contrast to Hypothesis 2, Hypothesis 4 assumes that a high market share is an indication of a company's superior efficiency and competitiveness, rather than of its monopoly power.
8 See, for example, Carlin, Van Reenen and Wolfe (1995) and the contributions in Rein, Friedman and Wörgötter (1997).
9 See Table 4.2 for more details.
10 Expressions used by the personnel manager of D4. The impression that even in 1990 the East German companies tended to provide fewer benefits is probably less a reflection of reality than of what interview partners could remember. In East Germany the provision of social services is not an ongoing issue as it is in Hungary, consequently interview partners are less likely to remember precisely all the benefits which the companies used to historically provide.
11 All the data in this section are taken from Tables 4.3a and 4.3b.
12 PM = personnel manager, MD = managing director, TUR = trade union representative.
13 TUR and PM in H3, PM in D6, H5, H7, H8, MD in H1.
14 MD in H1, PM in H2, H6, H7, D7.
15 TUR in H2, H4, TUR and PM in H8.
16 TUR in H3, H4, H5, H7, PM in H6. The TUR of H4 states that in companies where the trade union is less organised and strong 'employees loose all these benefits without being compensated for this loss by higher wages'.
17 'They are a small compensation and sign of appreciation for the employees in a situation where the company cannot give them many of the financial fringe benefits which employees of West German companies receive' (TUR in D6). 'Making sure that employees are looked after socially is also in the management's interest in a country where wages are extremely low when compared to Western levels' (TUR in H5). 'The workers would be very annoyed if these things ceased to exist. The attitude is that only if you pay us market rate wages (that is Western level wages), can we be expected to pay a market rate for all these benefits' (TUR in H6). 'These benefits could only be taken away from them if people earn so much that they can afford to buy these services outside' (TUR in H7).
18 PM in H11.
19 Expression used by the TUR in H6.
20 For example, employees of H2 can purchase H2's products at a reduced rate in an on-site shop.
21 The market referred to is East Germany.
22 Hungarian companies are not only at times still protected by some remaining trade barriers but, more importantly, their very low wage costs and relatively high quality standards, idiosyncratic domestic demand characteristics as well as high transportation costs can deter foreign entrants in many sectors.
23 One could include dummies which try to capture the influence on decision-making that the foreign direct investor has. If dummies are included asking the local management whether the investor was the main force in the restructuring of the product range or the main force in managerial training, then for the questions at hand one obtains results which are very similar to those in the FDI columns.

24 Unionisation rates are only obtainable for Hungarian companies. When these were included in the analysis they proved entirely insignificant. A similar finding was made by Estrin, Schaffer and Sing (1997, p. 46).
25 See Granovetter (1985) for a central chapter on this topic.
26 The Hungarian expression locates the origins of 'humane' behaviour in 'recognising the other persons' humanity', while the German phrase locates the origins of this type of attitude in 'recognising the social responsibility entailed by a position of power'.
27 The percentages referred to in this section are all derived from the means of the D(H)scores and D(H)coop variables.
28 D1, D2, D4, D7, D9.
29 H1, H2, H4, H5, H7.
30 H4 and H5.
31 D9, D2, H1, H2 and, after the clash between the employees and the investor in 1992, H7.
32 H1, H2, H4 and D1.
33 D9. It should be noted that Hungarian companies who had a choice (e.g. H4) very consciously sought out investors who were perceived to have a 'European' (that is humane) rather than an 'Anglo-Saxon' approach to redundancies. The trade union representative stated that 'an American investor would have lead to a strong cultural mismatch'.
34 H5, D4, D1. The personal need and ability on the side of decision makers to consider the fate of employees facing redundancy is generally a result of interpersonal relationships which have evolved over a long time in the previous economic system where jobs for life were the norm and labour turnover in companies was low. Similar sentiments were reported by Major and Voszka (1995) in study conducted in 1995 for the ÁPV Rt on the fate of the 49 large companies which had been given special emphasis in the old economic system.
35 H1, H3, H4, D1, D4, D7, D8, D9.
36 H4, H5, H8. A strike only occurred in company H6, while threats of strikes are more common (H4, H6, H7). In some instances strikes and their threat were a consequence of the union gaining the conviction that the investor or management is in the process of liquidating the company (H6, H7, H4) while in other instances strikes were threatened because the employees are renouncing agreements reached with the management previously (H6).
37 D8, D9.
38 D1, D4, D7, D8, D9.
39 This was formulated explicitly by the trade union representatives in D1, D2 and D4.
40 Tarif wages are wages which have been agreed upon through centralised bargaining but which lie above the average because very few East German companies honour them.
41 H4, H6, H7, H8.
42 H5, H7, H8.
43 H7, H5.
44 Such incidences have happened in company H7, D2 (here the problem was solved by firing the managing director by the investor), D5, D6 and D3.
45 The numbers in parentheses indicate the association found and its statistical significance. Statements along the lines of 'larger than average companies provide a larger than average number of benefits' are meant to indicate that in the case studies there is, for example, a significant positive association between company size and number of benefits provided.
46 Almost all the contributions in Friedman and Wörgötter (1997) support this basic conclusion.
47 Commander and Schankerman (1997) find the same basic size effect for both Russia and the Ukraine.

48 My finding is similar to that made by Commander and Schankerman (1997, p. 7) who find that in their Russian data set larger firms were actually less likely to reduce the number of benefits.

49 At least in part the association above is likely to be reflecting omitted third variables. For example I find that companies which provided a large number of social services in 1990 were also less likely to have a socially responsible management (-0.53, 10 per cent) and more likely to shed a large percentage of their employees (0.66, 5 per cent). Both these factors are associated with a lower probability of being profitable, so that the impression emerges that a higher level of social benefit provision in 1990 is associated with greater overall restructuring challenges and for this reason with lower profitability in 1995. This interpretation is supported by the fact that in 1995 companies which, usually from a relatively high starting point, shed a large number of social services are less likely than average to be profitable (0.54, 10 per cent). By 1997 both these effects become insignificant, suggesting that although these companies might have faced a greater restructuring challenge initially they now have the same likelihood of being profitable than others.

50 Commander and Schankerman (1997) too find a positive relationship between profitability and the number of benefits provided in Russian firms but they do not explore the causality involved.

51 In both years companies with a high market share tended to be also large in terms of employee numbers (0.48,0.49, 10 per cent) Since there is a significant persistence of historical trends, this time with respect to market share (0.89, 1 per cent), I find that for any given company the situation looks very similar in 1990 and 1997.

52 I am not the first to have a data set suggesting this conclusion, but Carlin, Van Reenen and Wolfe (1995) do not explicitly discuss the rather intriguing implication of their Table 4 (p. 449) that only one Hungarian company with FDI has shed its social assets and no Polish or Check company with FDI has done so.

53 Keeping the real value of social services constant is in turn associated with lower labour shedding and unemployment figures in the company (-0.46 and -0.44 respectively, 10 per cent).

Due to the almost universal scrapping of social services in East Germany no such observations can be made for that data set, but it should be borne in mind that there is some anecdotal evidence (e.g. in D4) of socially responsible managers scrapping socially services with 'sweeteners' such as an improved canteen and working environment.

54 The spirit of these findings is in accord with Clark and Soulsby (1998).

55 Although the association between size in 1997 and profitability is only significant at the 15 per cent level, I also find that companies which are large in 1997 are so because they have shed less than average labour and made fewer employees unemployed (-0.53 and -0.58 respectively, 5 per cent). In accordance with this finding large companies are also associated with a co-operative trade union both in 1990 and in 1997 (0.58, 5 per cent in both cases).

56 In this instance I am effectively examining whether the Hungarian and East German data could be pooled. In the case of two dummies the appropriate test is a chi-square test of independence and in the case of two continuous variables a t-test for differences of means was used.

57 I am not the first to suggest that maintaining social benefits might have efficiency enhancing effects by improving individual employees' productivity. Those suggested by,

for example, Rein, Friedman and Wörgötter (1997) are that social services attract the desired kind of worker, increase the loyalty of existing workers and enhance productivity. Similarly to Aghion, Blanchard and Burgess (1994) they also suggest, however, that on the downside maintaining social service provision might complicate restructuring. The reasons given in my studies for maintaining the internal provision of social services support the hypothesis that social benefit provision increases productivity by improving loyalty, morale and work motivation of the remaining workforce. The handling of housing subsidies also suggests that some benefits are being restructured in such a way as to attract scarce middle-ranking and managerial employees. What is unusual is my finding that maintaining social services, which is a clear symptom of a humane management, not only improves the productivity of individual workers but also induces co-operation in the trade union which facilitates the whole process of overall restructuring.

58 See, for example, Clark and Soulsby (1998) for the Czech Republic, Commander and Schankerman (1997) for Russia and the Ukraine, Estrin et al. (1997) for Poland.

59 Amsden et al. (1994, pp. 81ff) emphasise, for example, that wages are estimated to constitute only 15 to 25 per cent of total costs in Eastern European companies. Schaffer (1995) suggests that the internal provision of social services is not a very pressing policy issue because the costs incurred are comparable to non-wage compensation in Western firms. He argues that differences between Eastern and Western firms relate to the ownership of the assets used for provision and the types of benefits on offer, but not to the cost of provision itself. Rein, Friedman and Wörgötter (1997) suggest that enterprise benefits exclusive of social protection, which is what enterprise benefits in the East should be compared with, amounted to 9.9 per cent of total labour costs in the US. With this figure in mind Fajth and Lakatos (1997) estimate that the percentage of social services in labour costs is 14 per cent in Hungary, while Rein and Friedman (1997) put this figure at 10 per cent. Against the argument that companies cannot be *efficiently* involved in the provision of social services stand suggestions that the economies of scale involved in these social services might be relatively small (Schaffer (1995)) and that competition between firms in their provision might lead to efficiency improvements (Jackman (1995)). On these accounts the whole debate surrounding the importance extensive of labour and social service shedding is somewhat irrelevant. This contention is strongly supported by my case studies. Many Hungarian companies suggested that although there is room for increases in productivity, their total wage costs are so low that they constitute a competitive advantage, rather than a major worry. Interview partners also estimated that wages would reach Western levels in about 10 years time, but no-one seemed particularly worried about this prospect. Worries about collapsed Russian markets, insufficient funds to obtain the newest production technology etc. were a lot more common than those related to wage costs.

References

Aghion, P., Blanchard, O. and Burgess, R. (1994), 'The behaviour of state firms in Eastern Europe, pre-privatisation', *European Economic Review*, Vol. 38 (6).

Amsden, A., Kochanowicz, J. and Taylor, L. (1994), *The market meets its match: Restructuring the economies of Eastern Europe*, Harvard University Press.

Carlin, W. and Aghion, P. (1996), 'Restructuring outcomes and the evolution of ownership patterns in Central and Eastern Europe', *Economics of Transition*, Vol. 4 (2).

Carlin, W., Van Reenen, J. and Wolfe, T. (1995), 'Enterprise restructuring in early transition: The case study evidence from Central and eastern Europe', *Economics of Transition*, Vol. 3,(4).

Clark, E. and Soulsby, A. (1998), 'Organisation-community embeddedness: The social impact of enterprise restructuring in the post-communist Czech Republic', *Human Relations*, Jan.

Commander, S. and Schankerman, M. (1997), 'Enterprise restructuring and social services', *Economics of Transition*, Vol. 5(1).

Dhanji, F. (1991), 'Transformation programs: content and sequencing', *AEA Chapters and Proceedings*, May.

Dobrinsky, R. (1996), 'Enterprise restructuring and adjustment in the transition to market economy', *Economics of Transition*, Vol. 4 (2).

Estrin, S. (1994), *Privatisation in Central and Eastern Europe*, Longman.

Estrin, S., Schaffer, M. and Sing, I. (1997), 'The provision of social services in state-owned, privatised and private firms in Poland', in *Enterprise and social services after communism*, Cambridge University Press.

Estrin, S., Brada, J., Gelb, A. and Singh, I. (1995), 'Introduction', in *Restructuring and privatisation in Central and Eastern Europe: Case studies of firms in transition*, Sharpe.

Fajth, G. and Lakatos, J. (1997), 'Fringe benefits in transition in Hungary', in *Enterprise and social services after communism*, Cambridge University Press.

Gelb, A. and Fisher, S. (1991), 'The process of socialist economic transformation', *Journal of Economic Perspectives*, Fall.

Grabher, G. (1996), 'Adaptation at the cost of adaptability? Restructuring the East German regional economy', in *Restructuring networks in postsocialism*, Oxford University Press.

Granovetter, M. (1985), 'Economic action and social structure: The problem of embeddedness', *American Journal of Sociology*, Vol. 91.

Gros, D. and Steinherr, A. (1995), *Winds of change*, Longman.

Grosfeld, I. and Roland, G. (1995), 'Defensive and strategic restructuring in Central European enterprises', *CEPR, Discussion Chapter No. 1135.*

Jackman, R. (1995), 'Efficiency consideration in enterprise provision of social services', *Economics of Transition*, Vol. 3 (2).

Major, I. and Voszka, É. (1995), 'Kiemelt ipari nagyvállalatok', study conducted for the ÁPV Rt.

Rein, M., Friedman, B. and Wörgötter, A. (1997), 'Introduction', in *Enterprise and social services after communism*, Cambridge University Press.

Rein, M. and Friedman, B. (1997), 'Enterprise social services in Hungary', in *Enterprise and social services after communism*, Cambridge University Press.

Schaffer, M. (1995), 'Divestiture of social services from state-owned enterprises', *Economics of Transition*, Vol. 3 (2).

Svejnar, J. (1991), 'Microeconomic issues in the transition to a market economy', *Journal of Economic Perspectives*, Fall.

5 Integration with the Investor: Strategic Restructuring, Knowledge Transfer, New Products and Production Methods

This chapter examines the role of foreign direct investors in the strategic restructuring of their subsidiaries. Strategic restructuring is interpreted as the development of new capabilities and final products, which improve a company's performance both in terms of profits and exports. The notion that companies with FDI will outperform their rivals because of knowledge transfer from their investor and his role in introducing new products and production methods is examined both qualitatively and statistically. This is generally supported in the East German data but not in the Hungarian one. It emerges that a) investors are frequently unaware of local idiosyncrasies and consequently endorse the same restructuring in both East Germany and Hungary and b) these strategies are proving successful in the East German context but not the Hungarian one. I argue that the East German context is sufficiently 'similar' to the Western one for managerial approaches which have been developed elsewhere to work well. In Hungary, however, a mutual learning process has to take place; a simple one-way diffusion process from the investor to the local management is not enough. I also find little evidence that the valuable knowledge transferred to East German subsidiaries is being diffused down a local supply chain, while in the Hungarian context it is not clear how valuable the knowledge being diffused really is.

Introduction

Under the previous economic order the horizontal product range[1] of most formerly state owned companies in the transition economies of Central and Eastern Europe tended to be determined on the basis of non-market considerations. The dictates of planners were frequently more important than the preferences of consumers. To the extent that in any given case this is true there is a need to change the composition of a company's product range, both to ensure its future competitiveness and in order to improve allocative efficiency on an economy-wide scale.

In addition frequently even companies producing goods which were previously attractive to consumers are facing problems. This could be due to factors such as shifts in demand patterns making 'old' products intrinsically less desirable or due to entrants offering attractive new substitutes. Alternatively consumers, especially in the case of many export goods to the former Soviet Union, may lack the purchasing power to continue buying the company's output. Whatever the cause for the frequently sharp fall in a company's demand, it will have to find ways to improve its performance by developing new products and capabilities. This chapter examines the contribution of foreign direct investors in this process of strategic restructuring. Two main questions are asked:

- do companies with FDI outperform their rivals because of the knowledge transfer from their investor and his role in introducing new products and production methods?[2] How important is the potential contribution of local managers in this context;
- do foreign direct investors contribute to transition by inducing a knowledge diffusion process down the local supply chain?[3]

The chapter proceeds as follows: section 1 provides a survey of the literature; section 2 derives empirical hypotheses; section 3 presents the empirical evidence found in my case studies and derives statistical variables; section 4 confronts the hypotheses. Section 5 concludes by interpreting the statistical evidence found.

1 Literature Survey: The Expected Contribution of Foreign Direct Investors

The claim is frequently made that 'strategic' or 'deep' restructuring as opposed to 'reactive' and 'ambiguous' behaviour is commonly only observed in companies with FDI (Grosfeld and Roland, 1995, p. 10; Carlin, Van Reenen and Wolfe, 1995, pp. 448 ff.; Carlin and Landesmann, 1997, p. 77; Meyerand Moller, 1998, p. 412). The whole notion that there are different types of restructuring developed as a result of the, for some, unexpected observation that, given sufficiently hard budget constraints and sufficient (potential) product market competition, managers in state-owned enterprises engaged in a wide variety in restructuring measures even before companies were privatised (Carlin and Landesmann, 1997). The restructuring measures which different authors list as evidence of deep or strategic restructuring vary over time and between authors, so that it is hard to avoid the impression that to some extent strategic restructuring is simply 'what local managers cannot do by definition'.

In essence reactive restructuring is generally seen as survival orientated behaviour which aims at maximising enterprise performance within the company's existing resources and capabilities. Grosfeld and Roland (1995, p 6) have a narrow definition of reactive restructuring, namely activities which seek to 'reduce costs and scale down enterprise activity: cutting obsolete production lines, shedding labour, getting rid of nonproductive assets'. On such an account reactive restructuring becomes indistinguishable from a managed winding-down of the firm. Estrin et al. (1995, p. 19 ff.), give a list of 'short-run' responses local managers actually engaged in:

> adjustments to the production process (closure of lines) changing the product mix toward more sellable goods, laying off workers, selling machines or even plants and reorganising production toward cheaper or higher quality inputs.

The key feature of all the definitions of strategic restructuring is the development of new capabilities and final products, which enable a company to be internationally competitive in the long-run. The contention is that although managers in companies without FDI might have had the incentives to engage in reactive restructuring, they lack the resources and know-how to restructure strategically. Investors are expected to contribute both (Meyer and Moller, 1998; Grosfeld and Roland, 1995). Particular importance is ascribed to investors providing substantial new investments and changes in technology, new products and management structures (Carlin and Aghion, 1996).

Skills which researchers detect shortages in and which are needed as a prerequisite of strategic restructuring include accountancy, financial control, organisational restructuring, marketing and sales, quality control and information systems (Estrin et al., 1995). It is also hoped that investors will aid restructuring by giving their subsidiaries access to Western supplier and marketing networks.

The extent to which companies with FDI use local suppliers is central in determining the degree to which the knowledge transferred from investors becomes diffused through the wider economy. In this context Grabher (1996, p. 181) claims that globally focused strategies which entail the total integration of the local company with the investor have 'culminated in the construction of cathedrals in the desert', while investors with multidomestic strategies have favoured the emergence of locally integrated production networks.

A question which is rarely asked is the extent to which the knowledge investors bring with them is relevant in the transition context in the first place. The greater the country specific idiosyncrasies, for example, the more important is the historical and cultural knowledge of local managers. Since this increases the importance of the local manager's relationship specific investment an implication of the Grossman and Hart (1986) model is that the greater the importance of local factors and knowledge the less tightly the subsidiary should be integrated with its investor, allowing local managers to retain a greater share of the residual rights of control.[4]

The potential contribution of local managers is, however, frequently downplayed. Dyck's (1997) model of managerial selection in transition provides an extreme example since it is based on the underlying assumptions that there is a need to sack all East German managers and that a manager's quality in the West German context translates one to one to his abilities in the East German one. On the basis of adverse selection problems faced by central privatisation agencies he advocates a rapid sale of companies to direct investors who can internally transfer managers of the 'right' quality. Dyck does point out that one needs to distinguish, however, between *functional skills*, such as marketing, sales and accounting and *restructuring skills* which refer to a manager's ability to implement a wide-ranging process of change.

Only in the specific West German–East German example can one assume that functional skills are fully transferable, since both countries have the same set of laws, regulations and competitors. In Hungary, however, where Western managers face different societal norms, traditions, a frequently idiosyncratic market and language problems, it is not at all clear that a manager who might have shown good restructuring skills in, say West Germany, will do well in

Hungary. Meyer and Moller (1998, p. 417), for example, observe that frequently 'Western managers apply concepts of management developed elsewhere and adapted insufficiently to the local conditions'.

Another question which needs to be considered is whether the 'reactive restructuring'–'deep restructuring' literature is not simply observing a natural progression of different phases of restructuring. Grosfeld and Roland (1995) argue that defensive restructuring must not necessarily precede strategic restructuring, since both could and should be done simultaneously. Such a point of view ignores two issues. Firstly there is the question as to how much genuine change an organisation and its employees can cope with and adjust to at any given time. It might well be that sequential and targeted change is more effective in the long run than 'revolutionary' programmes which try to change all aspects of a company's operation at once and put too pressure on the employees' ability to learn and adapt. Interviewees in my case studies regularly gave examples of the organisational chaos and individual bewilderment which resulted from having to cope with 'too much' change.[5]

The second argument against 'revolutionary' restructuring is the possibility that delaying some aspects of restructuring might preserve valuable options. Measures termed as 'defensive' increase the efficiency of a company's existing operations and maintain the option of branching out into new areas as opportunities emerge over time in a highly uncertain environment. As new information emerges, managers can implement 'strategic' restructuring measures with much greater confidence that their strategy is a good one. Ericson (1998) suggest that companies in transition economies have gone through 'noisy' and 'niche-discovery' (1990–94) and 'cost-reduction' phases (1995 onwards) which seem to reflect stages of learning as a prelude to real restructuring rather than restructuring itself.

2 The Empirical Hypotheses

The main hypothesis emerging from the literature survey is that companies with foreign direct investors will outperform their rivals because of the unique and positive contribution investors make to enterprise restructuring. Hypotheses 1a and b formulate this contention. Hypotheses 2–5 state specific contributions investors are supposed to make to strategic restructuring. Hypothesis 6 asks whether investors are merely creating 'cathedrals in the desert' or contributing to the dissemination of know-how down the supply chain.

HYPOTHESIS 1:

- *a positive association between profitability/ export performance to Western European markets (as proxies for successful restructuring) and functional integration with the investor/ companies in which the investor is the main force in managerial training (as proxies for knowledge transfer).* This hypothesis is deduced from the 'strategic' versus 'reactive' restructuring literature. (See, for example, Grosfeld and Roland, 1995, p. 10; Carlin, Van Reenen and Wolfe, 1995, pp. 448 ff.; Carlin and Landesmann, 1997, p. 77; Meyer and Moller, 1998, p. 412).

Background assumption:

- *the larger local idiosyncrasies are, the more important is the potential contribution of local managers.* (See in this context, Grossman and Hart, 1986; Dyck, 1997; Grabher and Stark,1996, pp. 18ff.)

Hypotheses 2–5 are secondary hypotheses which will help us interpret the findings for Hypothesis 1. Unless otherwise stated they as well originate directly from the 'strategic' versus 'reactive restructuring' literature surveyed.

HYPOTHESIS 2:

- *a positive association between the introduction of new products and the closure of old ones in companies with FDI only.* This hypothesis is introduced to distinguish between a controlled winding down of a company, when only closures occur, and a strategic reorientation in a company's product range.

HYPOTHESIS 3:

- *a positive association between FDI and the introduction of new products.*

HYPOTHESIS 4:

- *a positive association between FDI and the introduction of new production methods and forms of work organisation.* If the new products introduced by investors genuinely augment the core capabilities of the company and entail knowledge transfer from the investor, then the new products should be associated with new production methods and concomitant new forms of work organisation.

HYPOTHESIS 5:

- *a positive association between FDI and relative investment levels.*

Hypothesis 6 relates to the extent of knowledge diffusion from companies with FDI through the wider economy (see Grabher, 1996, pp. 181 ff. on the topic). Even is extensive knowledge transfer from the investor to his subsidiary is taking place, investors might still be creating 'cathedrals in the desert'. The hypothesis is formulated in accordance with this latter suggestion.

HYPOTHESIS 6:

- *a negative association between FDI and companies using local suppliers.*

The relative contribution of local managers (see Grossman and Hart, 1986 and Dyck, 1997 in this context) and the degree of loose coupling between the investor and its subsidiary (Grabher and Stark, 1996, pp. 18ff.) are captured by dummies which represent the relative influence the investor had on the restructuring of the product range, production methods and in determining managerial training respectively. These dummies are included in all the hypotheses involving a relationship between FDI and another variable. The background assumption is in this context that the larger local idiosyncrasies are, the more important is the potential contribution of local managers.

3 The Variables and Case Study Evidence[6]

This section serves two functions: firstly to introduce the variables used and secondly to present the case study evidence relating to each variable. The case study evidence is presented in two ways. Trends in the data can be seen from a discussion of the means of the variables. Valuable information is obtained from asking whether these means show statistically significant differences for the East German and Hungarian case studies. Excerpts from interviews provide qualitative illustrations of some of the issues which easily get lost in statistical discussions.

3.1 Investor Related Variables[7]

- *A variable capturing whether the company has a foreign direct investor or not: By 1996 companies with FDI are usually wholly owned subsidiaries*

In the East German data 77 per cent of companies had foreign, including West German, investors in 1996. The two companies which at this time did not fall into this category were both up for resale after failed privatisations. The privatisation of D6 failed because the investor ended up asset stripping until the company's board intervened and initiated a repurchase by the Treuhand. When I called in 1998, D6 had been re-privatised to a UK company. The case of D7 is very unusual in that this is a company which is very successful in spite of its investor who went bankrupt. D7 was the only company in a large conglomerate which did not go down with its Austrian investor. It is currently up for resale.

In Hungary the picture is more varied. Sixty-three per cent of the companies visited have a foreign direct investor, H5 and H11 have floated on the Budapest stock exchange after prolonged government involvement (some would say interference), H6 has been going from one crisis and government intervention to the next and H8 has an institutional investor who does not interfere in the day-to-day running of the company. Only in four of the East German and five Hungarian companies did the investor have a determining influence on the restructuring of the product range.

- *Variables capturing the relative influence of the investor in the restructuring of the product range and production methods*

In each company with FDI I asked East German and Hungarian general, production and personnel managers to assess the extent to which the investor, rather than they, was the determining force in the restructuring of the (horizontal) product range and production methods. These variables capture two things: firstly the potential knowledge transfer which has occurred from the investor and secondly the input which local managers had into the restructuring process. The fact that the investor was the main force in the restructuring of the company's operations does not necessarily entail that he has transferred any know-how to the local management, since the restructuring process might have been 'dictatorial' rather than consultative. In companies where the local management was consulted in the strategy formation and involved in the implementation stage but where the investor gave important impulses and had the last word, managers usually claimed that they had about equal influence. The claim that the investor had sole influence usually stood for 'authoritarian' investors. It was not uncommon for a dictatorial investor to face a highly antagonistic local management.

Overall, however, investors tended to have a relative hands off stance, with only about a third of the East German and Hungarian companies experiencing a strong involvement in the restructuring of their product range and production methods.

> The main determining force in the restructuring of H2's products and production processes was the investor. The Budapest factory's general manager claims that 'in theory market forces play an important role, but in practice H2 is not innovative or very aggressive. The market is saturated and all the players have a large excess capacity.' The 'old' management had a secondary influence on the restructuring process of production, but this was not for lack of trying. Apparently there were large clashes between the old management and ex-pat managers in the factory in northern Hungary. My interview partner described them as follows: 'Two internally closed groups were facing each other. My colleagues had to deal with ex-pats who had little understanding of our products. The ex-pats wanted to get rid of all local brands. Many local managers got sacked over this issue and the ex-pats got their way. But the introduction of the Western brands was a flop: There was a big price difference between the new brands and the local brands which had been scrapped and this price difference was, in the eyes of the Hungarian consumer, not justified by quality differences. Introducing new brands also entails large advertising costs etc. The ex-pats learned it the hard way that it is worth keeping local Hungarian brands and have reintroduced the very brands they had been so keen to scrap and replace by their own Western ones.'
>
> ***
>
> The investor 'got all these young, dynamic people from Austria in who did not understand the situation here and wanted to introduce revolutionary changes. However if a company has been run differently for 40 years, then one cannot expect that even after 2 years of schooling everybody will support the new measures, that even if we understand the theory, in practice everything will work as people in the head offices have thought it out ... The new people who were supposed to run the company from the top did not know the market and had no contact with the people here. This lead to arguments and disagreements with the 'old' management and workforce.'[8]

- *A variable capturing whether the investor was the main force in managerial training*

Managerial training usually encompasses sector specific training in sales, marketing, communication, accounting and finance. In particular the following training needs were identified by interview partners:[9]

1 English language courses;[10]
2 quality control measures;[11]
3 computing/computer related skills;[12]
4 general management skills (e.g. the ability to take responsibility and make decisions, cost consciousness);[13]
5 commercial law, book-keeping, accounting, financial analysis;[14]
6 logistics, procurement, sales and marketing.[15]

Investors have overall been a lot more active in providing managerial training than in their direct involvement with the restructuring of the product range and production methods. The company's investor was the main force in managerial training in 55 per cent of the East German companies and 36 per cent of the Hungarian ones.[16] In companies with a foreign direct investor these managerial skills are typically transferred in two different phases: in the first phase the investor tends to put managers from Western subsidiaries into the top positions. Furthermore there is a tendency to send the remaining local managers on training and exchange programmes. Ex-pat managers can provide further on-the-job training.[17] In the second stage the number of ex-pat managers is reduced and they are replaced by newly hired young local employees or old managers who are thought to have now acquired the necessary skills. Clear evidence for knowledge transfer only occurs when the investor phases his direct presence out as soon as he feels that the subsidiary can run itself on its own.[18]

H2 provides an extreme example of a strong reliance on ex-pat managers and a lack of knowledge transfer. Only two people (the general manager of H2's Budapest factory and the MD of H3) remain in the top management of all of what used to be the Budapest sweets' industry before 1990. In H2's top and upper middle management local managers were replaced almost entirely by ex-pat managers. Middle managers tended to be replaced by young Hungarians who 'have the language and computing skills but lack the knowledge which based on experience. The ex-pat managers have learnt some Hungarian, but nevertheless it still has great problems in picking up information from the surroundings in which H2 operates. This is a particular problem for the marketing department.'[19]

***

In addition sacking local managers can have a very de-motivating affect on the workforce. 'Some "old" managers were simply untenable, everybody knew who they were. But with every competent and respected old manager the investor sacked, the investor signalled to the workforce that they were regarded as useless as well, the workforce identifies with these managers and thus is demotivated with every further manager being sacked.'[20]

Companies without FDI buy training courses on a steadily growing market and focus on hiring young employees with the requisite skills. This process, however, requires the incumbent management to realise out of their own volition that they need training.

- *A variable capturing the extent of functional integration with the investor*

Table 5.2 summarises the case study evidence on the type and extent of functional integration companies have with their investor. In four out of nine of the East German companies with FDI the investor provides design as well as R&D facilities. The provision of computing facilities by the investor plays a role in one third of the companies and in only one company does the investor provide the subsidiary with centralised procurement. All the East German companies are responsible for organising their personnel, quality control, maintenance, sales, transportation, marketing and customer service needs.

In Hungary the picture as to what types of functions are typically provided by investors is less clear. Rather companies tend to fall into two camps, that is those which are closely integrated with their investor and those which are not. In addition I find that investors tend to concentrate on different types of functions in the Hungarian companies than in the East German ones. In the Hungarian companies there is more involvement in sales, marketing and procurement and less in the areas of R&D, design and computing facilities. In strong contrast to the East German ones the most commonly provided functions in the Hungarian companies are procurement and marketing (in four out of nine companies), followed by cooperation in R&D, sales and design (in one third of the companies). In two out of eleven companies is the investor involved in quality control and computing facilities, while in only one company each does the investor concern himself with personnel and customer services. The only area experiencing no involvement by the investor in all cases is maintenance.

Companies cite as the main advantages of being functionally more integrated with the investor:

- integration of the local company with the investor's worldwide procurement activities leads to cost savings;[21]
- if the investor provides computing facilities, this can lead to an knowledge transfer;[22]
- integration of the marketing functions can open up new trade channels to the Hungarian subsidiary;[23]
- functional integration with the investors enables the subsidiary to make use of synergies, especially in R&D.[24]

Companies cite as the main disadvantages of being functionally more integrated with the investor:

- some investors try to import practices and policies which are ill-adjusted to the subsidiaries' environment;[25]

> H2 is highly integrated with its investor and the production manager interviewed made the following comments: '[Our parent company] tries to have a coherent organisational methods on a worldwide level. This results in very hierarchical structures and in methods which in their uniformity do not always adjust well to local conditions. In particular, the Hungarian subsidiary suffers from information flow problems. This is particularly true for the investor's marketing department, which seems to be unable to get to grips with Hungarian idiosyncrasies because they are unable to take in information from the Hungarian subsidiary. The overall consequence is that H2 is very slow in reacting to market developments.'
>
> ***
>
> H7 is very successful and has a good relationship with its investor. This has not always been the case. Around 1992 the company's employees reached the conviction 'with 75 per cent certainty' that the investor had only been really interested in gaining market share for himself by acquiring H7 and was now systematically working towards H7's closure. For example, H7 had a 7 per cent market share in Western Europe in its main product lines in 1989. By 1992 this percentage had almost halved due to 'the investor's insistence of introducing American methods into the European market leading to a total disorganisation in H7's sales and marketing activities'.[26] The investor did furthermore not realise the international strength of H7's brandname and insisted on H7's brand being replaced by the investor's brand on all of H7's products from one day to the next. 'Our sales people had to pick up the phone and introduce themselves as employees of our investor. We literally had buyers calling up and responding "Sorry, I misdialled. I wanted to speak to company H7" and hanging up.'[27]

- a general reduction in the subsidiaries' flexibility;[28]

> For example the change manager in D8 complains that if D8 wants to introduce changes, the interests and position of other companies within the investor's conglomerate [some of its suppliers belong to the same investor] have to be taken into consideration.

3.2 Variables Capturing Changes in the Companies' Product Range

- *Variables capturing the total number of restructuring measures affecting both the company's vertical and horizontal product range, the number of horizontal products closed and newly introduced as well as the net change in horizontal integration* (Hypotheses 2, 3 and 4)

In both the East German and Hungarian companies net horizontal integration has declined only marginally. This process of changing the composition of a company's horizontal product range tends to take place in three steps:

- firstly all companies have closed down some lines of production which were not inputs to other activities nor used internally produced products as inputs;
- secondly companies intensify their activities (that is further specialise within the core and increase the proportion of physical and human capital used in production) on the smaller section of the value added chain that has been defined by the reduction in vertical and horizontal product range. The newly defined core activity always closely relates to a line of production which the company has previously engaged in, even if not focused on;
- once this new core has been established, companies tend to partially reverse the reduction in horizontal product range they have experienced by introducing new products. These tend to aim at market niches which are new but closely related to the company's perceived core competency. To the extent that these new horizontal products entail more complex production processes their introduction can have adverse effects on the company's productivity.

> 'In the West one factory produces one product. Before privatisation, different factories in the food industry specialised as well. Now these factories have been privatised to different investors and all the new companies want to produce everything, reversing the previously existing division of labour within the food industry. This leads to a very high degree of complexity in each factory and when you compare such a factory to a specialised Western factory, you are not comparing like with like. Our one factory which is specialising in one product almost fulfils Western standards.'[29]

3.3 Further Variables

- *Dummies to capture whether the company is profitable in 1995, 1996 or 1997* (Hypotheses 1a and b)

In 1995 44 per cent of the companies in my East German data were profitable, rising to 77 per cent in 1997. In 1996 54 per cent of the Hungarian companies were profitable and all expected to at least break even by 1999. In each case interview partners were simply asked whether or not the company was making profits. Absolute profit levels were not explicitly sought because of the measurement problems entailed.

- *Variables capturing a company's export performance to the EU, including West Germany* (Hypothesis 1a)

Since the East German companies suffered particularly strong declines in their domestic demand, breaking into the West German market was a matter of survival in most cases. It is a reflection of this fact that they tend to sell 33 per cent of their output in the EU, which is significantly higher (at the 5 per cent level) than the 12 per cent typically obtained by the Hungarian companies. Similarly East German companies increased their exports to the EU by a mean value of 23 percentage points, compared to 5 percentage points for the Hungarian ones (significant at the 10 per cent level).

- *Variables capturing a company's know-how requirements, new production methods and forms of work organisation introduced* (Hypothesis 4)

To assess the extent to which a company has a 'knowledge gap' I asked managers to assess the extent to which their new products required more, equal or less: 1) technological know-how; 2) modern production technology and technological know-how; 3) organisational knowledge; 4) qualified and trained personnel. The experiences of the companies in the two country samples seem to have been very similar in terms of the additional know-how required after 1990, giving the know-how variable a mean of 3.3 in Hungary and of 3.4 in Germany. At no time was it claimed in any company that less know-how was required in any area. It is noticeable that in Germany there were generally less complaints about shortages in organisational and managerial skills, but in both countries the overriding concerns were with technological know-how and the training new technologies required.

I also enquired about the new production methods required by a company's upgraded product range. Interview partners were asked whether they had newly introduced or significantly upgraded their computing facilities in the commercial area, in production planing, in production coordination, in R&D, in the management of their stocks as well as their CAD systems, industrial robots etc. I found that the East German companies tended to introduce significantly (at the 1 per cent level) fewer new production methods.[30]

Lastly interview partners were required to state whether they had introduced quality control groups, job rotation, job enrichment, flexible working hours, project groups and other new forms of work organisation. I find that 77 per cent of the East German companies did so, but only 54 per cent of the Hungarian ones.

Both in Hungary and East Germany the introduction of new working methods tended to meet with a mixed response. Whereas flexible working hours were usually accepted as a necessity, project groups tended to attract negative comments: 'Our investor decided to introduce project groups. We were given leaflets explaining "our values" and how these project groups would improve both productivity and quality. The investor thought that this was all new to us. It wasn't. Previously such groups were called socialist brigades and our mission statements weren't on leaflets but on banners. The investor did not understand the general apathy which greeted his initiative, nor why these groups were no success.'[31]

- *Investment related variables: total investment, investment as a fraction of sales and a variable capturing the extent to which a company benefits from up-to-date machinery* (Hypothesis 5)

For the East German and Hungarian companies accumulative investment between 1990 and 1996 tended to be of the same size as, respectively, 30 per cent and 44 per cent of sales in 1996. The companies' machinery tends to be characterised by an overall comparable degree of obsolescence. In both countries the mean value of this variable suggests that by 1996(7) the typical company's machines still have between 47 per cent and 41 per cent of their technical lifetime left.

From the interviews it was quite clear that if a company was unable to obtain money from an institutional investor, domestic or foreign, or to float on the stock exchange, it needed a direct investor to ease its liquidity constraints. The former options were typically open to only a few large Hungarian companies. In the East German case the Treuhand generally did not encourage any alternative methods of privatisation. In this sense investors do seem to play an important role in easing liquidity constraints, but in Hungary this is mostly a function of the underdeveloped domestic banking and stock markets rather than of the subsidiary's wish to obtain foreign involvement and know-how. Several Hungarian interview partners also made the claim that, given the finances, Hungarian managers will always want to buy the best and most up-to-date technology they can possibly afford, while foreign direct investors tend to give them second-hand machinery from Western subsidiaries.

'Usually we get machines which have been replaced in Western factories. We are expected to be happy with outdated machines and generally there is very little investment by foreigners which is of a high quality.'[32]

***

> 'It is easy for Western factories to have a higher productivity: even the greenfield site which has been recently build does not operate with the latest technology which most similar Western factories would be employing. We have the latest technology in some areas, but has also received second hand machines from the investor.'[33]
>
> ***
>
> 'We continuously upgrade our production methods and were on par with our Western competitors already in the early 1990s. We always buy into the best technology we can conceivably afford when making new capital investments.'[34]

- *Variables capturing the extent to which a company relies on domestic suppliers and on suppliers pre-dating 1990* (Hypothesis 6)

It is a reflection of the overall greater stability in the supply networks of the Hungarian companies that 50 per cent of their suppliers tend to pre-date 1990, while this variable obtains a mean of only 28 per cent in East Germany (significant at the 1 per cent level). Hungarian companies also tend to rely to a greater extent on domestic suppliers, a trend which is especially pronounced if one only compares manufacturing companies with each other, allowing for the relatively large number of construction companies in the East German data.

4 Confronting the Hypotheses

This section presents the statistical evidence obtained with respect to Hypotheses 1–6 in my data set. Tables 5.4a and 5.4b in Appendix E summarise the associations found for the variables introduced.

HYPOTHESIS 1:

- *a positive association between profitability/ export performance to Western European markets (as proxies for successful restructuring) and functional integration with the investor/companies in which the investor is the main force in managerial training (as proxies for knowledge transfer).*
  Summary: both in the East German and Hungarian data investors have introduced a relatively high number of changes to their subsidiaries' product range. Only in East Germany, however, are these restructuring measures associated with improved profitability and export performance. In the Hungarian context the quality improvements achieved through new

Table 5.1 Summary of the main statistical findings

Hypothesis	East Germany	Hungary
1	YES – foreign investors introduce an above average number of changes to the subsidiaries' product range. These changes are associated with improved profitability and export performance	NO – there is no evidence that companies with FDI outperform those without – the quality improvements achieved through new production methods seems to be a key factor influencing performance, rather than the introduction of new products
2 and 3	NO – all associations with FDI are insignificant in this respect – closures are indicative of a managed winding down of a companies' operations rather than of strategic restructuring	NO
4 and 5	YES – high investment levels are associated with good performance and there is evidence that FDI eases liquidity constraints	Generally NO, with the exception that companies with FDI introduce a relatively large number of changes the subsidiaries' work organisation
6	YES	NO

production methods rather than new products seem to be key features influencing a company's relative performance. There is no evidence that in the Hungarian data companies with FDI outperform those without.

The East German data clearly supports the contention that companies which have restructured their product range and production methods effectively tend to achieve higher relative exports.[35] For example companies which have experienced more changes in their general product range (0.54, 10 per cent)[36] benefit from an improved export performance. My data also indicates that companies which have introduced an above average number of new production methods have not only achieved high rates of export growth (0.58, 10 per cent) but also have above average total exports in 1996 (0.50, 10 per cent).

The next question is whether East German companies which have restructured effectively have done so because of their investor's contributions. In the east German data functional integration with the investor is associated with an investor who is also the main force in the restructuring of the subsidiary's product range and production methods (0.78, 1 per cent in both cases). Furthermore investors who are active in the restructuring of the production methods also tend to be the main force in managerial training (0.73, 5 per cent).[37] The clearest indication of the value of the know-how provided by investors is the fact that by 1997 companies in which the investor is active in the training of local managers are more likely to be profitable (0.60, 10 per cent) and have also introduced more new products than others (0.52, 10 per cent). Companies in which the investor was the main force in the restructuring of the product range also benefit from high export growth (0.72, 5 per cent) and total exports (0.71, 5 per cent).[38]

In the Hungarian data I find that there is no clear relationship between restructuring measures affecting a company's product range and better performance both in terms of exports or profitability.[39] I do find, however, that companies introducing a large number of new production methods have benefited from above average export growth (0.68, 5 per cent). In addition increases in exports tended to go to the EU (0.56, 5 per cent) and a good export performance to the EU tends to be associated with a high probability of being profitable (0.56, 5 per cent).

The policies of investors are similar in the East German and Hungarian companies: As in the East German data set I find that companies with FDI have tended to be more active in the restructuring of their product range. They have introduced more overall changes (0.59, 5 per cent),[40] closed more horizontal product groups[41] and also introduced more new ones (0.46, 10 per cent).[42] In contrast to the East German data there is little evidence, however, that they have introduced an above average number of new production methods.

My data suggests that in Hungary investors do not seem to be achieving the desired results with their restructuring measures. All the investor related variables are entirely insignificant with respect to a company's export performance and have negative but statistically insignificant associations with profitability. In stark contrast to the East German data the contribution of investors seems to have been neutral at best in the Hungarian context.

HYPOTHESIS 2:

- *a positive association between the introduction of new products and the closure of old ones in companies with FDI only.*

HYPOTHESIS 3:

- *a positive association between FDI and the introduction of new products.*

In the East German data there is no evidence whatsoever that the companies experiencing a large number of closures are also the ones introducing new product lines. Nor is there any evidence that companies with FDI behave any differently in terms of the number of closures and new products introduced. The mere fact that a company is closing down horizontal product lines is more likely to indicate a managed winding down of its operations than the presence of strategic restructuring.

In the Hungarian data I again find no overall relationship between the closure of old product lines and the introduction of new ones. As argued in the context of Hypotheses 1a and b companies with FDI are, however, more likely than average to be highly active in both areas, without achieving noticeable improvements in their relative performance.

HYPOTHESIS 4:

- *a positive association between FDI and the introduction of new production methods and forms of work organisation.*

HYPOTHESIS 5:

- *a positive association between FDI and relative investment levels.* *Summary: both in the German and Hungarian data high relative investment levels are significantly related to a company's performance, suggesting a virtuous investment circle. The East German data supports the role of foreign direct investors in easing liquidity constraints. It also indicates their contribution to the introduction of new production and work methods, especially by helping to close the subsidiary's knowledge gap. My findings also stress, however, the importance of a company's pre-existing knowledge base in determining its ability to engage in strategic restructuring.*

In the Hungarian data there is little evidence that FDI has played a unique role in easing liquidity constraints, since some companies had access to the stock market or institutional investors. I do find, however, that Hungarian companies with FDI engage in a disproportionate number of changes to their work organisation. In contrast to the East German data there is no evidence suggesting that investors contribute to closing a Hungarian company's knowledge gap or that the organisational innovations they introduce enhance the subsidiary's performance.

In the East German data I find a clear support for Hypothesis 4. Companies with FDI tend to introduce an above average number of new production methods (0.60, 5 per cent). Changes in a company's production methods are conducive to both higher total exports in 1996 (0.50, 10 per cent) and greater overall export growth (0.58, 10 per cent). Similarly companies in which the investor is the main force in managerial training are also likely to introduce more changes to their work organisation (0.60, 5 per cent). These changes increase a company's probability of being profitable, both in 1995 (0.48, 10 per cent) and especially by 1997 (1, 1 per cent).

A precondition for the introduction of new production and work methods is the availability of the necessary funds. Consistently my East German data suggests that companies which tended to introduce a large number of changes to their work organisation also had high relative investment levels (0.50, 10 per cent). These high investment levels clearly resulted in more up-to-date machinery in these companies, since changes to the organisation of work are also associated with a lower degree of technical obsolescence (-0.67, 5 per cent).

The role of investors in easing liquidity constraints is supported by the finding that companies in which the investor was the main force in restructuring the product range experienced both higher relative (0.57, 10 per cent) and total (0.48, 10 per cent) investment levels.

As would be expected, higher relative investment levels are associated with a greater probability of being profitable (0.50, 10 per cent). In this context it needs to be stated that the flow of causation is ambiguous: Companies might be profitable because they have higher investment levels enabling them to introduce more new products etc., or their higher profitability might give them the retained earnings needed to finance investment. In either case profitable companies are likely to be in a virtuous investment circle.

In the Hungarian data there is little evidence that changes in a company's production methods are in any way associated with FDI. Rather the determining factors seem to be the relative investment levels a company has experienced (0.71, 1 per cent). Since in the Hungarian data there are companies without FDI which were able to raise significant funds by either floating on the stock market or having an institutional investor FDI was not necessarily a high precondition for high investment levels. High relative investment levels are significantly related to a company's performance: they are associated with higher total exports in 1997 (0.61, 5 per cent), higher export growth (0.75, 1 per cent) and a higher probability of being profitable (0.48, 10 per cent).[43] Since interview partners usually indicated that retained earnings are a major source of investment funds it is likely that there is a two-way causation.

The Hungarian data supports the notion that the investors who are active in the restructuring of the product range (0.60, 5 per cent) and in managerial training (0.69, 1 per cent) are also strongly predisposed towards introducing changes in the subsidiary's work organisation. In contrast to the East German data, however, in 1996 these changes in the organisation of work do not yet seem to achieve their desired results be it in terms of improving the Hungarian subsidiary's relative export performance or profitability.

HYPOTHESIS 6:

- *a negative association between FDI and companies using local suppliers Summary: only the East German data supports Hypothesis 6. In both countries a continued reliance on pre-existing suppliers, whether local or foreign, tends to be associated with a general lack of investment and of changes to the company's product range and production methods. A restructuring of a company's supply arrangements seems to be a concomitant of strategic restructuring.*

The East German data strongly supports this hypothesis, both with respect to investors in general (-0.83, 1 per cent) and investors who are the main force in the restructuring of the product range (-0.53, 10 per cent). The data also suggests that a continued reliance on East German suppliers is associated with few general changes to the company's product range (-0.61, 5 per cent) and production methods (-0.48, 10 per cent) as well as with lower than average total (-0.58, 10 per cent) and relative (-0.57, 10 per cent) investment levels. The finding that companies relying on East German suppliers have also experienced below average export growth (-0.67, 5 per cent) and total exports (-0.69, 5 per cent) is partly due to the fact that in this data set it is mainly construction companies who still rely on local suppliers and customers.

In the Hungarian data there is no indication that companies with FDI rely less on local suppliers. What the data does, however, support is the notion that a continued reliance on pre-existing Hungarian (and foreign) suppliers[44] is indicative of a general lack of strategic restructuring. Companies which have introduced a large number of new products (-0.42, 10 per cent), production methods (-0.47, 10 per cent) and have experienced above average relative investment (-0.42, 10 per cent) are all less likely to continue using their pre-existing suppliers. I also find that companies which heavily rely on their old supplies tend to have lower additional know-how requirements (-0.44, 10 per cent). This is consistent with the previous finding that strategic restructuring not only tends to entail the need to restructure a company's supply arrangements but also to increase its know-how requirements.

5 Conclusions and Interpretations[45]

A hypothesis emerges which has not been clearly formulated in the surveyed literature: the pre-existing social, cultural and economic structures will have a large bearing on how effective a blanket approach to enterprise restructuring will be.

The problems associated with a blanket approach to restructuring are illustrated by my main general finding that both in the East German and Hungarian companies investors have tended to introduce more overall changes to their subsidiaries' product range, but only in the East German case do these strategic restructuring measures seem to have achieved the desired effect in terms of exports and profitability.

The East German data supports the performance enhancing effect of the knowledge transferred by the investor. Functional integration with the investor is associated with investors taking an active interest in training the local management and the restructuring of the subsidiary's product range and production methods. All these policies are in turn associated with an improved export performance and profitability in the subsidiary. Clearly the restructuring measures and training endorsed by active investors and the knowledge directly transferred through functional integration provide the subsidiary with valuable inputs and a viable strategy.[46]

It is in rather strong contrast that the investors who are the main force in the restructuring of the Hungarian subsidiaries' product range and production methods and are involved in the training of the local management[47] pursue similar policies as in the East German context without having a noticeably positive result. In the Hungarian context the performance enhancing effect of improvements in a company's production methods seems to outweigh benefits obtained from introducing entirely new products. Although investors have a disproportionate tendency to close old product lines and introduce new ones, they seem to focus more on the introduction of new forms of work organisation rather than on providing the Hungarian subsidiary with the most up-to-date production methods and high relative investment levels.[48] In contrast to East Germany, in the Hungarian context investors also have no appreciable effect on their subsidiary's knowledge gap and the organisational innovations they introduce do not seem to be performance enhancing.

The question to arise from these conclusions is why a) the same restructuring measures are being endorsed by investors both in East Germany and Hungary and b) why they are proving successful in the East German context but not the Hungarian one. In this context my case studies provide anecdotal evidence that the value of the knowledge (frequently West German) investors transfer to their East German subsidiaries is very high. Due to the shared language, cultural background, competitors, rules and regulations functional as well as restructuring skills developed in West Germany are easily transferable to the East German context. This hypothesis is supported by the fact that the companies which reported problems with their investor in this respect tended to have genuinely 'foreign' investors.

In Hungary anecdotal evidence suggests that investors were frequently unaware of the demand and cultural idiosyncrasies they were facing, making the potential input of local managers all the more important. Even if local managers frequently lack functional skills, their knowledge of the context in which new strategies need to be developed and implemented in meant that they have important restructuring skills. Investors who did not tap into this source of relevant knowledge and skills frequently ended up endorsing restructuring measures which made little sense in the Hungarian context. Since, for example, Hungarian consumers frequently have a strong loyalty to local brands it makes more sense to improve the quality of these products by introducing new production methods and engaging in process innovation rather than to simply replace them by Western brands. In East Germany on the other hand such demand patterns were relatively rare, making the total replacement of old products a much more attractive strategy.

The simple answer to the first part of the question is, therefore, that investors pursued the same restructuring measures in both East Germany and Hungary because they were frequently unaware of local idiosyncrasies. The strategies endorsed proved to be appropriate in the East German context, but not in the Hungarian one for one main reason: the East German context is sufficiently 'similar' to the Western and especially West German one for managerial approaches which have been developed elsewhere to work well.

For an investment to be successful in a highly idiosyncratic context, however, a mutual learning process has to take place; a simple one-way diffusion process from the investor to the local management is not enough. A mutual learning process involving several feedback loops makes it unlikely that a company will find it desirable to implement a 'revolutionary' process of change affecting all aspects of its operation simultaneously. The reason is that revolutionary processes of change are likely to be exclusively based on the investors 'vision', not to say his preconceived ideas, while a more sequential process of change allows for learning, sequential adaptation and the temporary preservation of options which might become valuable in the future.[49]

Time is, however, a precondition for a sequential learning process and the exploration of future options. The East German companies suffered much stronger competitive pressures following reunification which entailed the loss of all forms of protection. Consequently one could argue that in East Germany there was not only less need to adapt restructuring approaches developed elsewhere to local conditions but that there was also less time to do so. In Hungary we might be observing not so much the failure of strategies endorsed by investors, but rather stages in a two-way learning process.

The last issue which needs to be considered is the extent to which any knowledge diffusion processes are taking place not only from the investor to the subsidiary but also within the wider economy. In this context I find that in both Hungary and East Germany companies which have strategically restructured[50] also have tended to seek out new suppliers. In the Hungarian context all companies seem to continue to extensively use local suppliers, whether these pre-date 1990 or not. Only in East Germany is there a noticeable tendency for companies with FDI to disproportionately rely on 'foreign' suppliers. This might well indicate that in East Germany investors are building 'cathedrals in the desert'. It is, however, difficult to say whether in East Germany the general industrial devastation[51] left investors with no other choice than to 'import' inputs, or whether investors have in part caused this deindustrialisation by excessively relying on their pre-existing Western supply networks and never giving East German suppliers a chance. Due to the reliance on 'foreign' suppliers there is little evidence that the valuable knowledge transferred to East German subsidiaries is being diffused down a local supply chain, while in the Hungarian context it is not clear how valuable the knowledge being diffused really is.

Notes

1 The '*horizontal product range*' will only refer to physical products which do not use other internally produced physical products as inputs and are not themselves inputs to physical products which are further up the value added chain. Whether we are concerned with changes in horizontal product range rather than vertical integration depends on which section of the value-added chain the affected product range is on. If a company closes down the manufacturing of a product which it uses as an input or which uses internally produced inputs, then it is reducing its vertical integration. If, on the other hand, it closes

down a final product which is not used as an input into another product made by the company, then it has reduced its horizontal product range.

2 See, for example, Grosfeld and Roland, 1995, p. 10, Carlin, Van Reenen and Wolfe, 1995, pp. 448 ff., Carlin and Landesmann, 1997, p. 77 and Meyerand Moller, 1998, p. 412.

3 See, for example, Grabher, 1996, pp. 181 ff.

4 Grabher and Stark (1996, p. 18ff.) discuss the advantages of such 'loose coupling' from an evolutionary perspective, arguing that it increases a company's learning interface and helps to avoid possible cognitive lock-ins.

5 The procurement manager in H2 stated, for example: 'When we give tenders, we find that Hungarian companies have a lower amount of experience and economic knowledge than foreign ones. An exception to this previous statement are Hungarian companies with FDI, which are even more confused than those without an investor because their investors are constantly introducing new systems and procedures.' Baden-Fuller and Volberda (1997) claim as well that too much change will lead to chaos, loss of cultural glue, fatigue and organisational breakdown. They argue that the scope of change should be contained either through spatial or temporal separation.

6 The case study evidence not only serves as a basis for the statistical variables used in Section 4, but will also help to interpret the statistical results obtained.

7 Table 5.1 lists and explains all the variables used. Table 5.2 summarises the extent and type of functional integration companies have with their investor. Tables 5.3a and b summarise the variables and their respective means. Tables 5.4a and b show the correlation matrices obtained. All tables can be found in Appendix E.

In order to examine whether differences between the means of two country specific variables are significant a small-sample t-test was used for continuous variables and a chi-square test of independence for dummies. Such a procedure effectively tests whether it can be assumed that the Hungarian and East German data has been generated by the same underlying processes, that is we are testing for homogeneity between the two countries. Unless it is otherwise stated the null cannot be rejected for the variables used in my case studies. If the null hypothesis of homogeneity cannot be rejected, then the two country specific variables can be pooled. Correlation matrices were obtained for the pooled data but did generally not contradict previous findings or add something new.

8 Notes on a round table discussion with the personnel, procurement and technical managers in D7.

9 This list reflects the findings made by Estrin et al. (1995).

10 D4, D5, D6, H1, H2, H4, H5, H7, H9, H11.

11 D6, D7, H1, H3, H4, H5, H6, H7, H8.

12 H1, H4, H5, H7, H8, H10, H11.

13 H2, H7, H9, H10, H11, D1, D4.

14 D5, D6, D7, D9, H10.

15 H10, H11, D9.

16 Although there is a relatively large difference between these percentages, the assumption of homogeneity cannot be rejected.

17 D2, D8, D9, H2, H3, H7, H9, H10.

18 The investor of D2 explicitly had such a policy.

19 Interview with the general manager of H2's Budapest factory.

20 Interview with the manager in charge of change management in company D8.

21 H4, H7, H9.

22 H4.
23 H4.
24 D4, D5, D8, D9.
25 H2, H3, H7, D7.
26 H7 was very unusual in the fact that ever since 1957 it (rather than a central government agency) was in charge of its own export activities and had a very high proportion of its output being exported into Western countries.
27 All quotes from an interview with H7's trade union representative.
28 H3, D8.
29 Personnel manager in H2.
30 This finding is not due to the possibility that the East German companies had a better pre-existing stock of capital. If anything, the Hungarian companies had a more up-to-date starting point after the investment drive in the 1980s in many 'key' sectors.
31 Interview with the manager in charge of change management in company D8.
32 Production manager in H2.
33 Managing director in H3.
34 Deputy CEO of H5. Similar comments were made in H8 and H11.
35 In order to assess why for 1995 the data suggests that there is a negative relationship between a company's export performance and its profitability (at the 5 per cent level) one would have to examine the companies' competitive situation in their export markets. One possibility is that companies initially achieved relatively high exports by having a loss leadership strategy. Alternatively newly exporting companies might have encountered very hostile competitors in their target markets.
36 The numbers in parentheses indicate the association found and its statistical significance. Statements along the lines of 'companies which have introduced a higher than average number of new production methods have experienced higher than average increases in their export performance' are meant to indicate that in the case studies there is, for example, a significant positive association between the number of new production methods introduced and the export variable.
37 Similarly companies which are highly functionally integrated with their investors tend to have investors who are active in managerial training (0.53, 10 per cent).
38 In addition FDI in general is associated with higher export growth (0.52, 10 per cent).
39 The association which appear to be significant in this context are entirely due to H7, who is an outlier both in terms of its export performance and the number of its overall restructuring measures, especially in terms of the closure of horizontal product ranges. The footnotes to Table 4b provide scattergrams to illustrate this point. Scattergrams were obtained for all the major associations. They are only reported when their visual inspection revealed that a seemingly significant association is entirely due to one or two outliers.
40 This association also holds for companies in which the investor was the main force in the restructuring of the product range (0.62, 5 per cent), for companies who are highly integrated with their investor (0.58, 5 per cent) and for companies in which the investor is the main force in managerial training (0.64, 5 per cent).
41 This association is especially strong for companies which are highly integrated with the investor (0.61, 5 per cent).
42 This association also holds for companies in which the investor was the main force in the restructuring of the production methods (0.43, 10 per cent) and who are tightly integrated with their investor (0.57, 5 per cent).

43 With the exception of export growth similar relationships hold for total investment as well.

44 Pre-existing suppliers tended to be mainly Hungarian ones (0.44, 10 per cent), but not exclusively so.

45 This section is best started by a caveat: All my conclusions relate only to my 20 case studies. Although I am hence unable to make statements about trends pertaining to Hungarian and East German companies in general, my case studies nevertheless are well suited to show the degree of support found for the hypotheses studied.

46 My East German data also supports the important role foreign investors have played in easing liquidity constraints, while in Hungary some companies had access to institutional investors and the stock market. My Hungarian data provides examples of companies who were able to obtain these investment funds without FDI and are using them to implement a successful strategy they have independently developed. Whether they have a direct investor or not in both countries profitable firms seem to be in a virtuous investment cycle, with their retained earnings financing investment into new products and production methods which in turn enhance their future performance.

47 It should be noted again that in several Hungarian subsidiaries 'being active in the training of the local management' frequently really meant 'keeping them on a very close lead and making sure that they faithfully implement the investor's policies'.

48 In both countries closures of products lines tend to be indicative of a managed winding down of the subsidiary's operations rather than of strategic restructuring. The closure of uncompetitive products is a necessary step in re-focusing the company's activities, but not a substitute for actual restructuring. Strategic restructuring clearly involves not just the introduction of new products, but also the use of new production methods.

49 An example of a 'revolutionary' approach would be the almost immediate closure of several old product lines and their replacement by entirely new ones. The closure of the worst old products and the introduction of new production methods to improve the quality of the most promising old product lines would be an example of a more sequential approach.

50 (That is have high investment levels and have engaged in an extensive restructuring of their product range and production methods.)

51 See Carlin (1994) for an account of the extent of deindustrialisation in East Germany following reunification.

References

Baden-Fuller, C. and Volberda, W. (1997), 'Strategic renewal: How large complex organisation prepare for the future', *International Studies of Management and Organisation, Summer.*

Carlin, W. (1994), 'Privatisation and deindustrialisation in East Germany', in Estrin, S. (ed.), *Privatisation in Central and Eastern Europe*, Longman.

Carlin, W. and Aghion, P. (1996), 'Restructuring outcomes and the evolution of ownership patterns in Central and Eastern Europe', *Economics of Transition*, Vol. 4 (2).

Carlin, W. and Landesmann, M. (1997), 'From theory into practice? Restructuring and dynamism in transition economies', *Oxford Review of Economic Policy*, Vol. 13 (2).

Carlin, W., Van Reenen, J. and Wolfe, T. (1995), 'Enterprise restructuring in early transition : the case study evidence from Central and eastern Europe', *Economics of Transition*, Vol. 3 (4).

Dyck, A. (1997), 'Privatisation in Eastern Germany: Management selection and economic transition', *American Economic Review*, September.

Ericson, R. (1998), 'Restructuring in transition: Conception and measurement', *Comparative Economic Studies*, Summer.

Estrin, S., Brada, J., Gelb, A. and Singh, I. (1995), *Restructuring and privatisation in Central and Eastern Europe: Case studies of firms in transition*, Sharpe.

Grabher, G. (1996), 'Adaptation at the cost of adaptability? Restructuring the East German regional economy', in Grabher, G. and Stark, D. (eds), *Restructuring networks in postsocialism*, Oxford University Press.

Grabher, G. and Stark, D. (1996), 'Organising diversity: Evolutionary theory, network analysis and postsocialist transformations', in Grabher, G. and Stark, D. (eds), *Restructuring networks in postsocialism*, Oxford University Press.

Grosfeld, I. and Roland, G. (1995), 'Defensive and strategic restructuring in Central European enterprises', *CEPR, Discussion Chapter No. 1135.*

Grossman, S. and Hart, O. (1986), 'The costs and benefits of ownership: a theory of vertical and lateral integration', *Journal of Political Economy*, Vol. 94 (4).

Meyer, K. and Moller, I. (1998), 'Managing deep restructuring: Danish experiences in Eastern Germany', *European Management Journal*, Vol. 16 (4).

6 Changing Markets: The Economic Geography of Transition and the Companies' Competitive Situation after Trade Liberalisation

This chapter examines the changes which have occurred in the companies' forward and backward linkages. Transition induced trade liberalisation is found to have had a profound effect on the companies' supply arrangements, export orientation and competitive situation. Supplier and customer relationships have shown a much greater stability in the Hungarian data. The East German companies have generally deserted their domestic suppliers in favour of pre-existing West German and EU suppliers who are not suffering from the challenges posed by transition. At the same time in their output markets the East German companies themselves have been largely deserted by their customers, be it due to the availability of more attractive substitutes from the West or due to a collapse in East German industrial demand. Both data sets show that a pre-existing exporting capability is a deciding factor in whether a company can meet the supply side challenges posed by transition. Since the rigidities of the previous economic system meant that especially in East Germany few companies had direct experience with foreign markets, extensive and sudden trade liberalisation early on in the transition process is argued to have lead to the destruction of an excessive proportion of East German industry. Hungary arguably provides an example of how gradual but fully credible trade liberalisation provides restructuring incentives without decimating the domestic manufacturing base.

Introduction

Companies do not operate in isolation. Hence no study on enterprise restructuring would be complete without considering changes in a company's backward and forward linkages. Transition induced trade liberalisation is likely to affect a company's supply arrangements as well as its export performance and domestic competitive situation profoundly. Using the literature on economic geography as an interpretative framework this chapter examines how in the 20 companies studied between 1990 and 1996:

- the geographical distribution of supply arrangements changed (section 2);
- the geographical distribution of sales changed. In particular I examine whether have there been any noticeable changes in the companies' export orientation (section 3).

Acknowledging that trade liberalisation not only gives domestic companies better access to foreign markets, but also foreign companies to domestic ones, the chapter proceeds to examine:

- how the companies' competitive situation and domestic market have changed (section 4);
- the main dimensions of competition and the importance of different regional characteristics for the companies' competitive success (section 5).

Section 1 provides a survey of the literature which serves as an interpretative framework for the empirical evidence presented in sections 2–5. Section 6 concludes by highlighting the main results.

1 Literature Survey: Trade Liberalisation and Economic Geography

As a consequence of their history of central planning and COMECON orientated trade East Germany and Hungary started the transition process in 1990 sharing many a priori similarities in their likely comparative advantage and underlying production structures. Kornai (1992, pp. 341ff.) and van Brabant (1994, p. 165) especially emphasise that trade decisions were bureaucratically controlled and not based on real economic scarcity indicators, world prices or genuine comparative advantage. Trade within the COMECON also followed the logic of bureaucratic coordination (Kornai, 1992, p. 356).

The underlying idea of international specialisation lead to severe distortions in locational decisions, giving rise to industries in some countries which probably would not have developed there on the basis of comparative advantage considerations.[1] Prices as well were distorted in COMECON trade, with, for example, Central European countries exporting overpriced manufacturing goods and importing underpriced energy in their trade with the Soviets (Marer, 1991, p. 329). As part of the policy goal of limiting dependence on the West, many Eastern European countries also sought to restrict international trade with market economies (Hamilton and Winters, 1992, p. 353). Even when official policy was one of export encouragement, however, producers were frequently unenthusiastic about selling to a buyers' market abroad when they enjoyed a sellers' market domestically (Kornai, 1992, p. 349).[2]

All these factors contributed to a domestic economy which was both distorted and inflexible in its underlying supply structures as well as sheltered from internal and external competition. In such a context a strong case can be made for trade liberalisation, which can be expected to lead to improved allocative and productive efficiency by, for example, providing competition in previously monopolised domestic markets, exposing domestic production to world prices and allowing firms to obtain better economies of scale and scope due to their increased exports.

Van Brabant (1994, p. 167) points out, however, that rapid trade liberalisation can only be expected to lead to such benefits once domestic markets function sufficiently well to allow for flexible adjustments to new demand and supply patterns. He warns that extensive trade liberalisation, if introduced too early in the transition period, 'might eliminate an inordinate share of domestic production'. On the other hand the question arises whether delayed liberalisation just forestalls the collapse of negative-value added firms[3] and sacrifices the positive restructuring incentives trade liberalisation offers to viable companies in the form of improved price formation and increased competition.

Not only the desirable speed of trade liberalisation is disputed, but also the likely comparative advantage Central European transition economies enjoy. In particular the notion that similarly to Southern Europe, Central Europe's comparative advantage might lie in unsophisticated, low-tech and labour-intensive goods (Neven, 1994) has been challenged. Amsden et al. (1994, p. 8), for example, claim that lowering real wages in order to specialise according to factor-price comparative advantage 'makes no sense at all in a semi-developed country, defined as already having a broad base of industries, especially mid-tech, and a stock of accumulated human skills'. Hamilton and Winters (1992) argue that on the basis of its very high stock of human capital, especially Hungary should become an exporter of sophisticated goods with a high R&D content. Indeed Carlin and Landesman (1997, pp. 78, 92 ff.) conclude that by 1995 the representation of R&D and skill intensive exports in Hungary's exports to the EU was similar to that of overall exports from the rest of the world to the EU.

East Germany experienced very sudden total trade liberalisation with West Germany through reunification. In addition as East Germany and Hungary become increasingly integrated into the EU as well we can generally expect shifts in the spatial agglomeration patterns of economic activity, including the location and export decisions of companies. For example this chapter will show how by 1996 the companies in the Hungarian data set maintained a stronger focus on their domestic sales, while the East German companies have more strongly re-orientated themselves to EU and especially West German markets. In contrast to the 'New Economic Geography' literature[4] considerations based on comparative advantage do not help to explain why two countries which had similar starting points in terms of their comparative advantage might end up on different development paths subsequently. In this context an important difference is that East Germany integrated very suddenly with West Germany, while Hungary has still maintained its own currency and some tariff and non-tariff trade barriers with the EU.[5]

In deciding on whether to agglomerate their activities or to disperse more evenly over a region companies face countervailing centrifugal and centripetal forces (see, for example, Krugman and Venables, 1990, 1995; Martin, 1999; Venables, 1998). Centripetal forces essentially consist of Marshallian localisation externalities arising from labour market pooling, technological spillovers and intermediate supply and demand linkages (Martin, 1999, p. 68).

Assuming increasing returns to scale, market size effects play an especially large role in generating pecuniary externalities between agglomerating firms. This gives companies an incentive to locate in or at least re-orientate their activities towards areas already enjoying good access to large markets.[6] Newly arriving companies generate higher expenditure on the intermediate products produced by already existing firms and agglomeration also leads to transaction cost savings as more inputs can be procured in spatial proximity (Krugman and Venables, 1995). In addition integration might increase labour mobility across a region, in which case the purchases of the employees of newly arriving firms add to the demand linkages and market size effects between agglomerating companies (Krugman, 1991). Empirical evidence surveyed by Brülhart

(1998, p. 792 ff.) and Amiti (1998) supports the importance of scale economies, intermediate-good intensity as well as market size effects in encouraging the geographical concentration of production.[7]

This discussion of the factors favouring a process of agglomeration indicates an underlying logic of cumulative causation (Venables, 1998, p. 4) or path dependence (Martin, 1999, p. 69): Firms want to locate in a given region because there are already other firms there. It is through the backward and forward linkages with pre-existing companies that positive externalities are transmitted. This also suggests that regions might have to reach a critical mass of industry before agglomeration and learning processes take off (Ottaviano and Puga, 1998, p. 722; Porter, 1998). Allowing such a critical mass to develop might provide a basis for infant industry arguments (Lall, 1998, p. 67; Porter, 1998).

Agglomerating companies are, however, also subject to centrifugal forces putting a stop on unlimited clustering. Centrifugal forces derive from product and factor market competition as well as from pure external diseconomies such as congestion. All these factors intensify with the number of companies locating in proximity to each other. Local product market competition can be circumvented by exporting to markets which are further away, but this incurs trade and transportation costs. Immobile factors and land rents lead to intensifying factor market competition between clustering companies and are likely to be only partially mitigated through the migration of workers from the surrounding regions.

A general result from new trade theory models is that if the trading costs between two regions are gradually reduced the relative balance between centripetal and centrifugal forces shifts over time (Ottaviano and Puga, 1998, p. 722; Krugman and Venables, 1995). With high trading costs firms concentrate on supplying their local markets and manufacturing will be evenly divided between the two regions.

As trading costs fall, this increasingly allows for a separation of production and consumption (Venables, 1998, p. 3), easing the centrifugal tendencies caused by product market competition. Consequently at intermediate levels of trade barriers we will observe a predominance of the centripetal forces. There will be a tendency for industry to cluster in a core region, deserting what is becoming the periphery. For example Krugman and Venables' (1990) model of trade integration between a large core country and a small peripheral region has the implication that for finite trading costs and increasing returns the core country becomes a net exporter of manufactures, effectively leading to the deindustrialisation of the periphery. In this context Martin (1998, p.

760) expresses the concern that European integration might lead to a situation where increasing returns to scale industries are concentrated in the core of Europe, while the periphery might end up specialising in constant returns to scale industries such as agriculture and low technology industries.

As the number of firms in the core increases, centrifugal forces based on the increased competition for immobile factors will raise their head. Prices for these immobile inputs, for example labour, are bid up in the core, creating a wage differential to the periphery region. As trade costs become small enough, firms will relocate to the periphery region to take advantage of lower factor prices there. Consequently with low trade costs, we should expect a more even distribution of industry across the region to develop, resulting in factor price equalisation in the long run (Krugman and Venables, 1995). As integration progresses further the presence of immobile factors is crucial in reversing the agglomeration tendencies which characterised intermediate levels of trade costs.

The predictions from these chapters are that as trade costs decrease between two regions, they are likely to start off with a relatively even distribution of industry, progress to a core-periphery structure and eventually end up again with a more even distribution at very low levels of trade costs. A question which still needs to be asked is where clusters are likely to form in the agglomeration phase. Since market size and access considerations are important in determining the scale economies and transportation cost savings a company can obtain, we can expect locations in the centre of a region to be more likely to experience clustering (Krugman, 1993).

Other regional characteristics are also likely to be important: for example a region characterised by a bad infrastructure will suffer from bad market access and is hence more likely to become a peripheral region. Consequently a well-developed infrastructure is considered to be an important tool in regional convergence (Martin, 1998, p. 758) and has been found to be an important determinant of foreign direct investment flows (Markusen, 1998, p. 736[8]). Similarly in order to allow companies to benefit from the labour pooling externalities and the knowledge spillovers involved in clustering a core region will also have to offer a pool of highly trained employees (ibid.; Porter, 1998). A region which has a rich supply of third-party research institutions such as universities will also be able to provide knowledge inputs to relocating firms, increasing its attractiveness (Audretsch, 1998, p. 21).[9]

2 The Implications of the Literature on Trade Liberalisation and Economic Geography for Companies in Hungary and East Germany

In 1990 East Germany and Hungary shared many underlying production structures, but arguably the Hungarian economy was less distorted, more decentralised and open as a consequence of the gradualist reform process which started after 1956 and accelerated in the 1980s. This makes it likely that many Hungarian companies who had accumulated some experience in, for example, directly dealing with Western customers were in an a priori better position to provide flexible responses to the supply-side challenges posed by transition. The greater rigidity in the East German economy and the extreme form of trade liberalisation it experienced with reunification lead to a situation where 'before we were even able to spell market economy we were already being competed to death.[10]' This echoes van Brabant's (1994, p. 167) warning that extensive trade liberalisation too early in the transition process can devastate domestic industry.

The literature on economic geography points in a similar direction. East Germany rapidly integrated with a region (West Germany) which already had pre-existing areas with strong industrial agglomeration, such as the Ruhr valley, where companies were enjoying increasing returns to scale as well as localisation externalities. The relative proximity of East Germany to these clusters meant that companies were unlikely to gain access to previously unobtainable markets by relocating to East Germany. After the collapse of the COMECON trading system the most important new market was East Germany itself, which could easily be served from West German production sites. Market access and market size considerations provided few reasons for maintaining production in East Germany. These arguments suggest two conclusions: West German companies had few reasons to relocate to East Germany and, following the logic of cumulative causation, East German companies had every reason to re-orientate their economic activity to West Germany. As would be predicted by Krugman and Venables' (1990) model, East Germany became West Germany's periphery, generating a trend towards deindustrialisation in East Germany. This deindustrialisation[11] entailed a process of dis-agglomeration in East Germany, opening up the possibility that East Germany might loose its 'critical mass' of domestic industry. A likely exception is the construction sector, which due to high transportation costs has an incentive to maintain its East German operations.

As trade costs decrease further one would expect a renewed strengthening of centrifugal forces away from West German clusters, favouring production in East Germany. For such centrifugal forces to set in, however, it is crucial that factor market competition intensifies between companies, increasing the wage differential between the core and periphery. At sufficiently high productivity levels such a wage differential would give East German companies a comparative advantage in terms of factor prices. Unfortunately East German workers are highly mobile between East and West Germany and trade union pressure has meant that after reunification wage levels have rapidly equalised.

This means that companies in West German clusters are unlikely to be 'pushed' eastwards due to labour shortages nor are they likely to be 'pulled' by low labour costs.[12] The implication is that the crucial forces evening out spatial disparities in regions with very low trade costs are unlikely to kick in and reverse the core-periphery pattern which has evolved after reunification, leaving the prospects for a reindustrialisation of East Germany rather bleak.

Hungarian industry, on the other hand, has not only benefited from the protection implied by higher trade costs. Hungary as a location has also exerted a 'pull' as a consequence of its low labour costs and extremely highly trained workforce. Consequently Hungarian companies not only had good reasons to stay put in Hungary, but also foreign companies had good reasons to invest there.[13] On the basis of the literature surveyed we would hence expect a much more stable industrial base in Hungary than in East Germany.[14] Due to its favourable location in the centre of Europe and anticipated EU membership, one can expect Hungary to increasingly serve as an exporting base both east- and westwards, especially in sectors such as food processing where capacity is relatively large compared to domestic market size.[15]

This chapter will proceed by examining statistically *questions which arise from the literature surveyed.*[16] With respect to each question I also ask whether there are any significant differences between the East German and Hungarian data. The first question examines changes in the companies' backward linkages, that is in their supply arrangements. Trade liberalisation and economic integration both give companies a wider spectrum of suppliers to choose from. The choice criteria companies use in this context and the relative attractiveness of domestic suppliers are of particular interest.

1 How and why has the geographical distribution of supply arrangements changed between 1990 and 1996?

The next two questions arise from the consideration that trade liberalisation both enables companies to export more easily abroad as well as gives foreign companies better access to domestic markets.

2 How has the geographical distribution of sales changed between 1990 and 1996? In particular, have there been any noticeable changes in the companies' export orientation?
3 How has the company's competitive situation and domestic market changed between 1990 and 1996?

In trying to interpret the overall trends found, I will ask:

4 what are the main dimensions of competition? Are companies specialising in low-tech cheap products? How important are different regional characteristics for the companies' competitive success? For example, how important is the availability of a cheap workforce?

Section 2 provides a description of the geographical shifts which have taken place and section 2.2 provides qualitative evidence which is of help in interpreting the observed trends.

2.1 Description of the Changes in the Geographical Structure of Supply Relationships

In my *1990* data[17] there were few differences between the Hungarian and East German manufacturing companies' procurement policies.[18] They tended to rely predominantly on domestic suppliers and Eastern European ones. The fact that Hungarian companies seem to have had a overall stronger reliance on EU and worldwide suppliers is notable but not statistically significant.

For 1990 I find that in the complete (manufacturing) East German data set the 'average' company[19] procured 79 per cent (66 per cent)[20] of its input in East Germany, 8.7 per cent (16 per cent) in West Germany, 11 per cent (16 per cent) in Eastern Europe, 1 per cent (2 per cent) in the EU and no company procured inputs on a worldwide scale. All companies depended to 70 per cent or more on input supplies from the GDR. The only exception is the pharmaceuticals company which procured inputs for medications worldwide through state organisations as there was no significant pharmaceuticals input synthesis in the former GDR.

The 'average' company in my Hungarian data set procured 54.5 per cent of its inputs in Hungary, 23.6 in the EU (including West Germany) and 10.9 per cent each in Eastern Europe and worldwide.

By *1996* significant shifts and differences emerge. Now the 'average' company in my East German data procures only 38.3 per cent of its inputs

Table 6.1 Summary of the main statistical findings

<table>
<tr><th>Question</th><th>East Germany</th><th>Hungary</th></tr>
<tr><td>1 How and why has the geographical distribution of supply arrangements changed between 1990 and 1996?</td><td colspan="2">The mean values of the variables indicating the geographical distribution of supply arrangements suggest that from similar starting points by 1996 strongly diverging developments have taken place in the East German and Hungarian data set. Most importantly, the Hungarian companies continue to show a much stronger reliance on their local suppliers. At the same time the fact that East German companies have been predominantly switching to suppliers from West Germany and other countries in the EU, while Hungarian companies have been experiencing a much smaller increase in their reliance on these markets.</td></tr>
<tr><td>2 How has the geographical distribution of sales changed between 1990 and 1996? In particular, have there been any noticeable changes in the companies' export orientation?</td><td colspan="2">The diverging geographical shifts which have taken place in terms of input markets are mirrored in the companies' output markets. Although Hungarian companies had higher exports worldwide and to the EU in 1990, I find that by 1996 the East German companies have experienced far larger increases in their exports, especially to West Germany, and decreases in their domestic sales.</td></tr>
<tr><td>3 How has the company's competitive situation and domestic market changed between 1990 and 1996?</td><td colspan="2">From similar starting points, between 1990 and 1996 the average Hungarian manufacturing company has only experienced a 3 percentage point fall in its market share, while the fall experienced by East German companies tended to be closer to 74 percentage points (significant at the 1 per cent level), resulting in the typical East German company having a significantly (at the 1 per cent level) lower overall market share in 1996.</td></tr>
<tr><td>4. What are the main dimensions of competition? Are companies specialising in low-tech cheap products? How important are different regional characteristics for the companies' competitive success?</td><td colspan="2">With respect to the role of regional characteristics and of different dimensions of competition the case studies confirm the important role played by net labour cost advantages in maintaining the attractiveness of Central Europe as a manufacturing location. In this context the rapid wage assimilation between West and East Germany posed a particular problem to East German companies. Since it is net labour costs which count in this context, it is not enough for a workforce to be cheap, but it also has to be well-trained and sufficiently productive to constitute a competitive advantage. It is this combination which allows both East German and Hungarian companies to strive for niches in which they provide products of Western quality at lower prices.</td></tr>
</table>

locally. If we consider the five manufacturing companies only, then this average is as little as 13.5 per cent. West Germany directly accounts for 34.7 per cent (39 per cent) of inputs, but we have to bear in mind that the true role of West German companies is much larger because East German suppliers usually tend to be subsidiaries of West German companies. Input procurement from Eastern Europe has generally all but collapsed. The average company procures 13 per cent (24 per cent) of its inputs in the EU and 3.5 per cent (6 per cent) worldwide. Overall[21] between 1990 and 1996 the 'average' East German company in my data set has reduced input procurement from companies located in East Germany by 41 percentage points (52) and from those located in Eastern Europe by 10 percentage points (14), while increasing its procurement from West Germany by 26 percentage points (23), from the EU by 12 percentage points (22) and from companies worldwide by 3.5 percentage points (6).

In stark contrast between 1990 and *1996* the pattern of input procurement as changed surprisingly little in the Hungarian data. In my data on average input procurement from Hungary has decreased by 4.3 percentage points to 50.2 per cent. The mean value for input procurement from the EU remains unchanged, procurement from Eastern Europe increased by 4 percentage points to an average of 15 per cent and input procurement on a worldwide scale has essentially remained unchanged at 10.6 per cent.[22]

The mean values of the variables indicating the geographical distribution of supply arrangements suggest that from similar starting points by 1996 strongly diverging developments have taken place in the East German and Hungarian data set. Most importantly, the Hungarian companies continue to show a much stronger reliance on their local suppliers.[23] At the same time the fact that East German companies have been predominantly switching to suppliers from West Germany and other countries in the EU, while Hungarian companies have been experiencing a much smaller increase in their reliance on these markets. This results in Hungarian companies procuring significantly fewer (at the 5 per cent level) inputs from the EU and West Germany in 1996.[24]

There are few differences between the Hungarian and German companies in the extent of their reliance on worldwide and Eastern European markets in 1996. The general trend has been for companies to reduce their reliance on Eastern European suppliers, but both in the East German and Hungarian data set we have one company each which has strongly increased its reliance on suppliers from this region, leading to very small overall average changes. The East German manufacturing companies have almost all been increasing their reliance on worldwide markets, while in Hungary we observe, from a higher starting point, a more mixed trend which averages out to very little

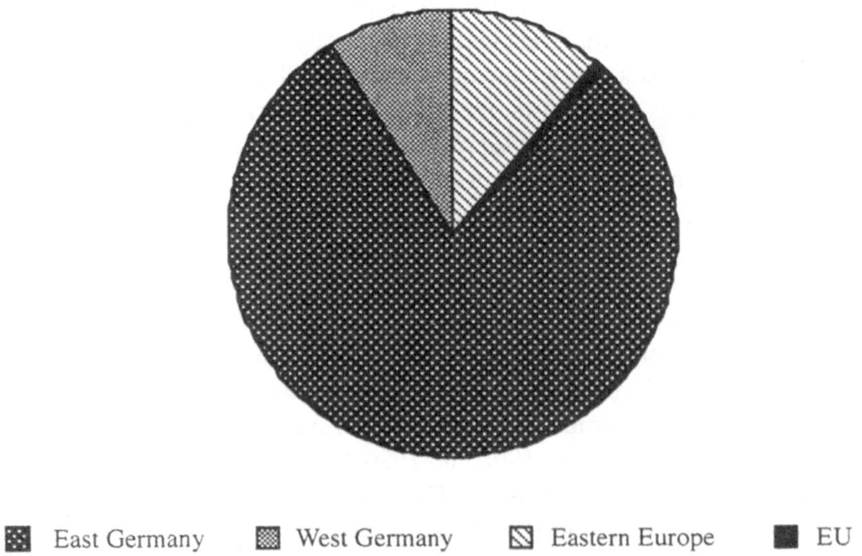

Diagram 6.1 Geographical distribution of input procurement in 1990, mean values for the complete East German data

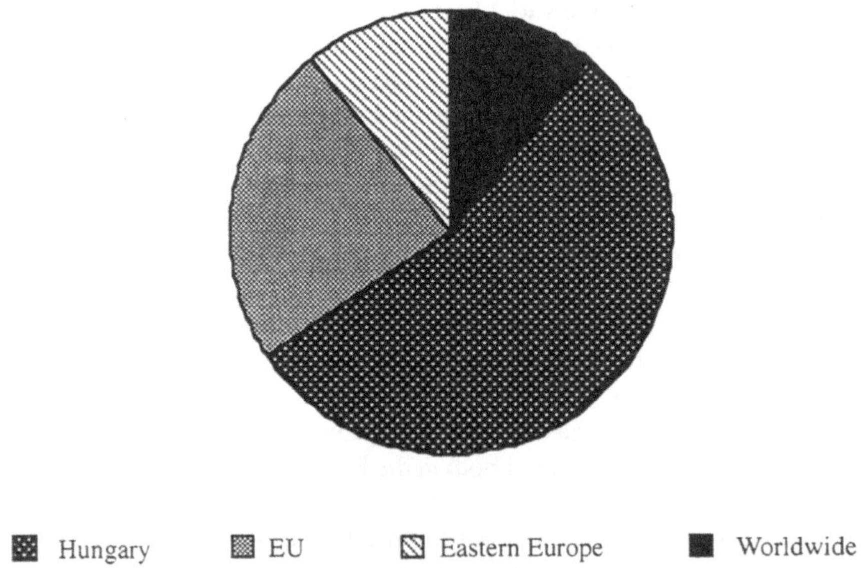

Diagram 6.2 Geographical distribution of input procurement in 1990, mean values for the Hungarian data

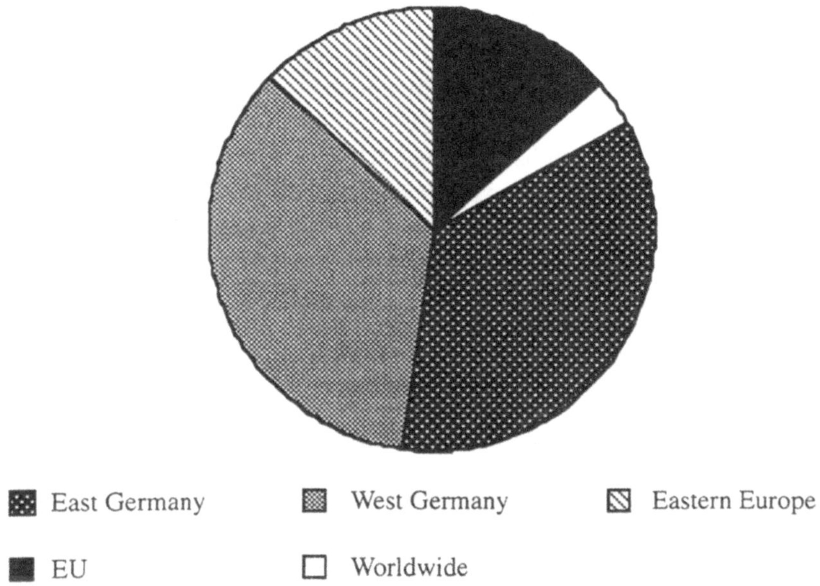

Diagram 6.3 Geographical distribution of input procurement in 1996, complete East German data[25]

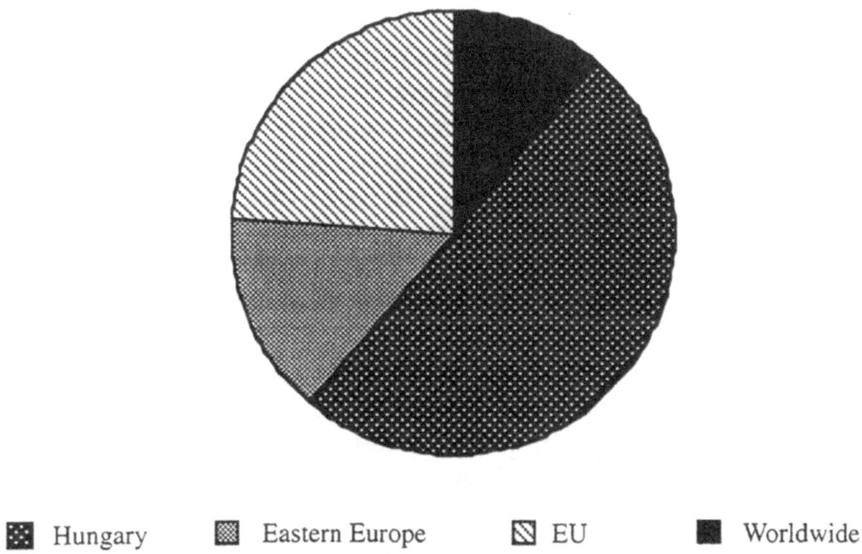

Diagram 6.4 Geographical distribution of input procurement in 1996, Hungarian data set

average change in this area. Consequently in 1996 we have a situation were the average East Germany manufacturing company shows the same reliance on worldwide suppliers as its Hungarian counterpart, even though the East German company's reliance on these markets has increased at a noticeably higher rate.

Considering the relatively large changes the East German companies have been making in their supply arrangements it should not come as a surprise that only 28 per cent of their suppliers predate 1990. In Hungary this number is significantly (at the 1 per cent level) higher at 64 per cent. Interview partners tended to indicate that in East Germany 'old' suppliers are predominantly pre-existing West-German and EU suppliers, while in Hungary they tend to be domestic suppliers.[26]

2.2 *Searching for the Driving Forces behind these Geographical Shifts in Supply Arrangements*

To examine the driving forces behind the diverging geographical shifts in greater detail I obtained qualitative data on a) why companies stopped dealing with (domestic) 'old' suppliers, b) whether they think that there are any significant differences between domestic suppliers and those in the EU/West Germany and c) on which future developments they anticipate in their supply arrangements. All the answers are summarised in Tables 6.3a and b.

The East German interview partners indicated that the main reason for abandoning pre-existing East German supply relationships, other than that the supplier goes out of business,[27] is that supplies were not up to scratch as far as quality requirements[28] and, less frequently, price competitiveness[29] go. The response to such problems has generally been to discontinue pre-existing supply arrangements and to turn to suppliers from the EU and West Germany. The companies continuing to rely on East German suppliers are predominantly construction companies. In this case it is clearly transportation cost consideration which maintain the East German suppliers' competitiveness.

Both Hungarian and East German companies turning to EU suppliers indicated that they are highly concerned about the quality of their inputs and hence willing to forgo the transportation cost savings offered by domestic supplier, confirming that quality is an area where many domestic suppliers still have problems. Interview partners also suggested that worldwide suppliers are mainly sought out on the basis of price. However, the companies searching out worldwide customers do not tend to procure homogenous goods, which could be obtained in greater proximity at a transportation cost saving but rather it is customers buying idiosyncratic products who are searching for a good price from worldwide suppliers.[30]

When I asked Hungarian interview partners for the main reasons behind abandoning 'old' Hungarian suppliers, insufficient product quality is mentioned by seven companies[31] and unreliability and lack of punctuality is mentioned by six companies.[32] On the other hand, uncompetitive prices and bankruptcy are only pointed out by two companies.[33]

Next I asked interview partners whether in their opinion there are significant differences between West and surviving East German/ Hungarian suppliers. As Table 6.3a indicates the general answer was that the surviving East German suppliers are not significantly different. However some companies perceive differences which favour East German suppliers: Interview partners in D5 refer a sense of solidarity, while the need to build a good reputation induces the East German suppliers of D6 and D8 to be more cooperative and flexible than West German ones. D9 claims that East German suppliers are better than West German ones because they have more modern machinery and production methods.

On the other hand when I asked Hungarian interview partners whether there remain any generic differences between domestic and foreign suppliers in 1997, companies tended to give an affirmative answer. Most frequently interview partners claim that some of the quality problems experienced in the initial phases of transition still persist. At the same time, however, the general tenor is that Hungarian suppliers are reaching Western standards fast and that, given that they are financially stable and have up-to-date technology, they offer relatively price competitive and, due to their proximity, also flexible and accommodating business partners.

To conclude this section I enquired how supply relationships were expected to change in the medium-run.[34] East German interview partners generally indicated that the structure of supply relationships is not expected to change significantly in the near future. If anything companies tend to aim at consolidating their relationship with a set of core suppliers (D5, D7, D8, D9). Thus the structure of the new supply arrangements, which are based on the West German and EU supply networks to which especially the East German companies receiving FDI have gained access to, is expected to consolidate itself without any major structural shifts. Consequently we cannot expect a greater reliance on East German inputs to develop in the near future.

When I asked Hungarian interview partners how they expected the supply arrangements in their company to develop in the next five years, the most frequently cited aim was to develop a set of core (frequently Hungarian) suppliers with which the company was hoping to develop long-term relationships offering the additional non-price benefits of greater cooperation.[35]

3 How has the Geographical Distribution of Sales Changed between 1990 and 1996? In Particular, Have there been any Noticeable Changes in the Companies' Export Orientation?

I find that in *1990* the 'average'[36] *East German* company was heavily focused on its domestic market, selling 85 per cent of its output locally and generally exporting, if at all, to Eastern Europe.[37] West Germany and the European Union accounted for as little as 1.8 and 0.7 per cent of sales on average.

By *1996* the geographical distribution of sales has shifted quite dramatically. The average company now sells only 61.6 per cent of its total output in East Germany and exports 38.3 per cent. This constitutes an average net increase[38] in exports of 23.3 percentage points between 1990 and 1996. The most important export markets are now West Germany,[39] accounting for 24.6 per cent of sales, followed by the European Union (8.3 per cent), Eastern Europe (5.3 per cent) and the rest of the world (1.1 per cent).[40] Interview partners indicated that breaking into the West German market was a matter of survival for all companies who did not have a fairly captive pre-existing export market due to a fairly inelastic demand (as is the case in pharmaceuticals) or who are localised in their operations due to high transportation costs (as is the case in the construction business).

These overall figures hide even greater changes in the manufacturing, rather than construction, sector. The average of output sold in east Germany is only 25 per cent for the manufacturing companies in 1996, down from 80 per cent in 1990. This constitutes an increase of 55 percentage points in net exports for the average manufacturing company in my German data set.[41] The average manufacturing company now exports 43 per cent of its total output to West Germany (an increase of about 40 percentage points since 1990), 15 per cent to the European Union (up from 0.7 per cent) and 9 per cent to Eastern Europe (down from 14 per cent). The proportion of output being sold worldwide is essentially unchanged at 2 per cent.

Associations found in Table 6.6a suggest pre-existing sales to West Germany and the EU were central in enabling companies to expand their sales in Western markets.[42] Eastern European markets have played no statistically discernible role in absorbing sales which were redirected from the East German market after 1990. If anything there has been a trend for a retrenchment for the Eastern European market: companies which had high exports to Eastern Europe are likely to have reduced these by 1996 (-0.62, 5 per cent) and companies without previous experience in the region have not entered Eastern European markets between 1990 and 1996 (0.95, 1 per cent).

When examining changes in the *Hungarian* companies' product markets find that already in *1990* the average company exported 35 per cent of its total output. Even the civil engineering company, H10, exported 13 per cent of its output by winning infrastructure projects in the Soviet Union and Libya.[43] Eastern Europe was the most important export market with on average 19 per cent of total sales, with the Soviet Union typically accounting for the lion's share in this category. The European Union and the worldwide market took similar shares with 8 per cent and 9 per cent of total sales respectively. A comparison of these 'averages' with those found in the East German data suggests that by 1990 Hungary's greater tradition of openness and gradualist reform resulted in Hungarian companies noticeably less output domestically and exporting significantly more to the EU (significant at the 5 per cent level for the complete data set and at the 10 per cent level for the manufacturing companies[44]) and worldwide (significant at 10 per cent level).

Table 6.6b indicates companies with exports to the European Union are also likely to have exported worldwide (0.72, 1 per cent) in 1990. This suggests that my data contains a group of companies which specialised in exporting to the European Union and worldwide (especially H5 and H7), rather than to COMECON countries (as H1, H6, H9, H10).[45]

By *1996* there have been significant changes in the two countries' relative comparative export orientation resulting in the observation that the average Hungarian manufacturing company realises a much larger proportion of total sales domestically (60 per cent as compared to 25 per cent, significant at the 10 per cent level). These comparatively high domestic sales for the Hungarian companies are reflected in their significantly lower exports in general and exports to the EU (including West Germany: 12 per cent in the Hungarian data and 58 per cent in the East German one, significant at the 10 per cent level).[46]

To the extent that the Hungarian companies have been increasing their exports this has been done by redirecting sales from Hungary to the European Union.[47] Consequently domestic sales fall on average 5 percentage points to 60 per cent of total output. In contrast to East German interview partners none of the Hungarian companies complains about a sustained fall in the overall volume of domestic demand, although the food industry tends to find fault with smaller than anticipated demand growth.[48] Overall average total exports increased by 5 percentage points to 40 per cent of output.[49] Exports

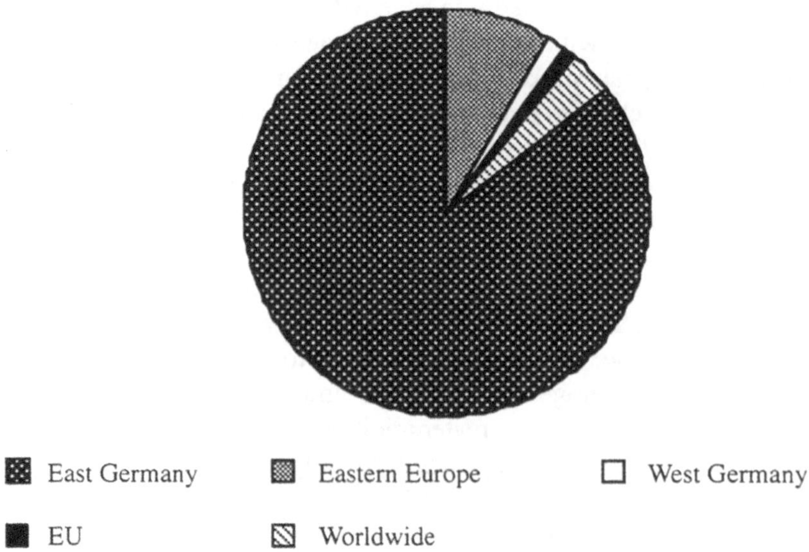

Diagram 6.5 Geographical distribution of the average East German company's sales in 1990

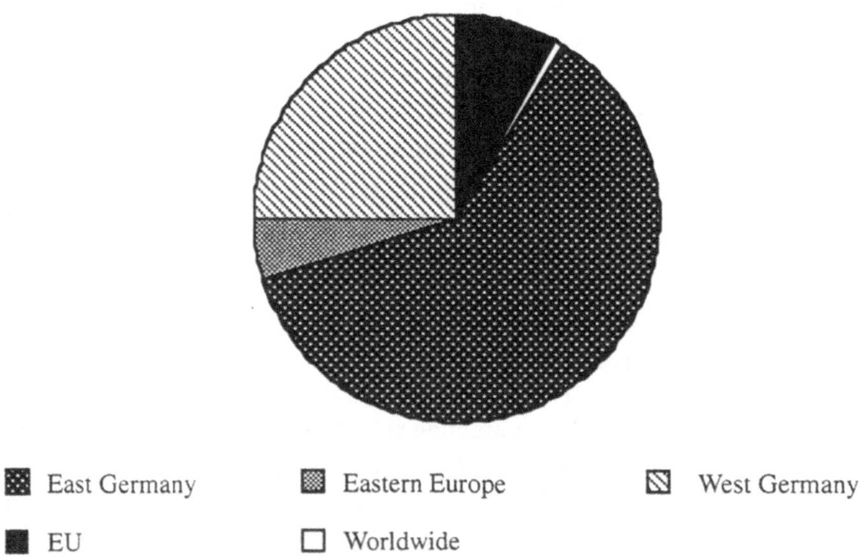

Diagram 6.6 Geographical distribution of the average East German company's sales in 1996, complete data set

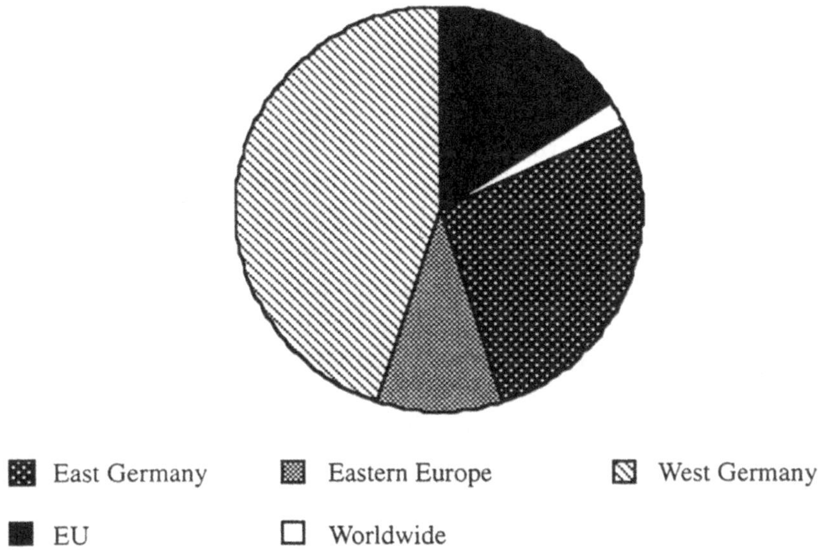

Diagram 6.7 Geographical distribution of the average East German manufacturing company's sales in 1996

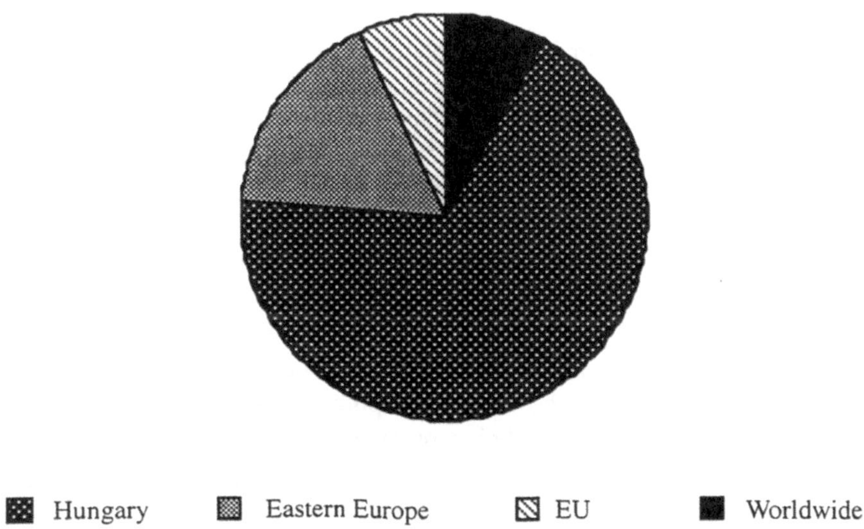

Diagram 6.8 The geographical distribution of the average Hungarian company's sales in 1990

to the EU increased by an average of 4 percentage points to 12 per cent of total output, while worldwide sales have been overall stable.

Sales to Eastern Europe increased by an average of 2 percentage points to 21 per cent of total output. In this case it is important to distinguish between sales going to the former Soviet Union and those going to Central Europe. Sales to the former Soviet Union have generally fallen dramatically, usually both in relative or absolute terms, mainly due to the inability of these customers to pay (H6, H7 and H10 all illustrate this problem). My data suggests that the worldwide markets have been playing an important role in absorbing sales displaced from the Eastern European market (-0.71, 1 per cent).

On the other hand some companies have been experiencing dramatic increase in sales to other transition economies in Central Europe. This is especially true of companies in the food and the related packaging industry (H1, H3, H8). Their previous competitive disadvantage has turned into a competitive advantage as income levels rise in Central Europe for a significant proportion of the population. People are now willing to pay a higher price for better quality products, but many are not willing to pay the extra it takes to purchase, for example, sweets made by Western, rather than the relatively cheaper, Hungarian companies. The interviews indicate that many managers are increasingly thinking in regional terms which typically include the Czech Republic, Poland, Slovenia, Austria and Switzerland rather than in historic categories.

Associations found in Table 6.6b support the impression of a general persistence of historical trends: companies which were relatively strongly focused on the Hungarian market in 1990 remain so in 1996,[50] while a high export orientation in 1990 is associated with high exports in 1996 (0.93, 1 per cent); companies which have a high export orientation to Eastern Europe in 1996 have historically sold a high proportion of their output in this market (0.88, 1 per cent); companies which have high exports to the EU in 1996 also did so in 1990 (0.96, 1 per cent); companies which had a high worldwide export orientation in 1996 had both higher than average worldwide exports (0.68, 5 per cent) and exports to the EU (0.72, 1 per cent) in 1990.

A remaining question is how the geographical distribution of a companies' sales affects its probability of being profitable. Table 6.6a suggests that in 1995 a high focus on the East German market[51] was associated with higher profitability (0.64, 5 per cent), a trend which is insignificant by 1997. Similarly the trend that high exports (-0.64, 5 per cent) are associated with lower profitability becomes insignificant by 1997. The negative results achieved by export orientated companies in 1995 are mainly due to a strong negative

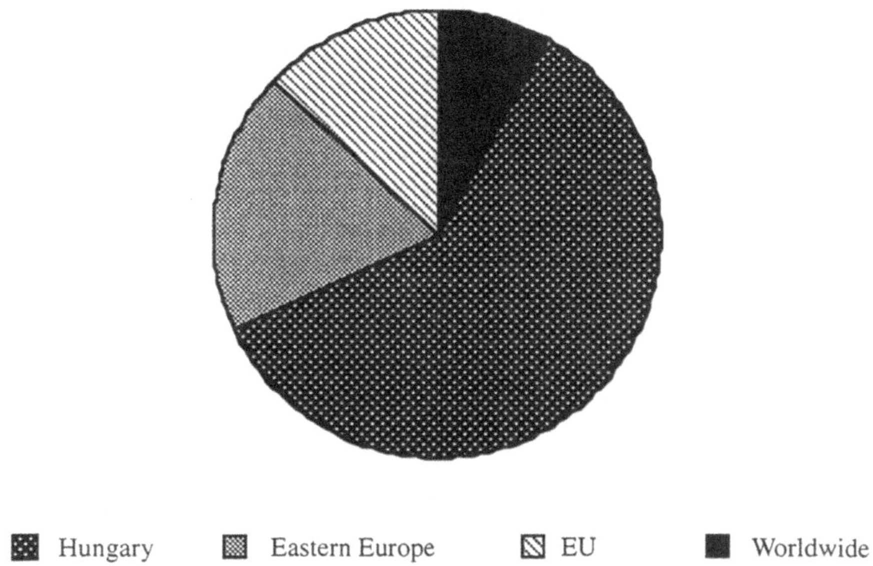

Diagram 6.9 The geographical distribution of the average Hungarian company's sales in 1996

association between profitability and exports to West Germany (-0.66, 5 per cent) on the one hand and to the European Union (-0.56,10 per cent) on the other. A possible explanation of these trends is that in 1995 we still have a situation where:

1 a residual inelasticity in demand due to 'patriotism' or historic factors can cushion some East German companies (especially D5, D8 and D4) in the short-run before entrants can fully affect their market share and profitability while;
2 other companies are experiencing the medium-run costs of trying to break into fairly saturated and sometimes collusive West German and European Union markets. The frequently strong demand decline in the traditional East German and East European markets usually occurred much faster than companies were able to break into new markets. Consequently many interviewees indicated that they spent the first few years of transition trying to break into unwelcoming Western markets while having lost much their traditional sales outlets.

It seems that by 1997 the companies which have strongly refocused their sales westwards have managed to sufficiently overcome these entry costs and to increase their sales in these markets to be no less profitable on average than the companies which have experienced smaller demand declines and hence have restructured the geographical orientation of their sales less.[52]

The Hungarian data supports the importance of a pre-existing exporting capability. I find that companies which already sold a high proportion of their output in the EU (0.57,5 per cent) or worldwide (0.55, 5 per cent) in 1990 are more likely to be profitable than average in 1996. High sales in the EU in 1996 are also positively associated with profits (0.56, 5 per cent). A good export performance to EU markets not only indicates that the company is producing internationally competitive products but also suggests that these companies have been better equipped to meet the challenges posed by transition.

4 How has the Company's Competitive Situation and Domestic Market Changed between 1990 and 1996?[53]

This section examines the extent to which increased market access by western competitors affected East German and Hungarian companies. Table 6.5a indicates that in *1990* almost all of the *East German* companies, with the exception of the pharmaceuticals company, were local monopolists. On average their products covered 89 per cent of the local market. By 1996 each company's market share has dramatically dropped by 74 per cent on average to only 15 per cent. High market shares in 1990 are associated with a greater decrease by 1996 (-0.75, 1 per cent). This suggests that the more monopolised a sector was, the more competition and entry (in the form of 'imports') it has attracted upon reunification.

Companies which had a strong export orientation (to Eastern Europe) before and after 1990 have tended to experience the smallest decreases by *1996* (0.65, 5 per cent), mainly because they had smaller domestic market shares to start off with (-0.64, 5 per cent). These trends especially hold for manufacturing companies. One possible reason is that (West German) entrants might well have faced smaller entry costs into the construction sector,[54] which has seen an almost immediate transfer of the West German market structure to the East German market. Any East German companies which survive in the construction sector do so as the subsidiaries of a Western firm, that is because in this instance entry was via acquisition, rather than by driving the local competitor out of the market.[55] Furthermore, when giving construction contacts a company's solvency and hence ability to finish the project is an important consideration, a factor which will have operated against East German companies without financial backing from the West.

The smallest drops in market share were suffered by the pharmaceuticals company D5 (who had a small market share to start off with and is somewhat protected by a low demand elasticity for its products) and the turbine manufacturer D8 who has found a niche in servicing old turbines which have it has built in the past. D9 has seen its entire market collapse together with the East German car industry and D1, D2, D7 are left with very small residual markets after a large number of financially solvent West German competitors have entered the East German construction sector. D6, who also suffered a fall in market share of over 90 percentage points, is plagued not only by a large number of financially strong competitors as the other construction companies as well, but in addition by the fact that these competitors are operating a tacit cartel in a saturated market.

Given these considerations it is not surprising that almost all companies claim to face a large number of competitors. The exception is D9 whose parent is part of a West German duopoly. All companies claim that their main competitors are larger and solvent companies. In addition four out of nine companies also face important small competitors.

The geographical location of the companies' main competitors reflects their sales orientation. Eight out of nine companies claim that important competitors are located in West Germany. The only exception is D3, who is a member of a West German cartel and is hence only concerned about non-German competitors. The five companies which claim that they also face important East German competitors are usually quick to add that these East German companies are subsidiaries of West German parents. Three companies face important competitors who are located in Eastern (or rather Central) Europe and only one company (D6) is touched by competition originating from the rest of the world.

Table 6.6a suggests that companies which in 1996 are more likely than others to be concerned about East German competitors sell a high proportion of their output in East Germany (0.60, 5 per cent) and a smaller than average proportion in West Germany (-0.75, 1 per cent). All the companies which are concerned about East European competition have experienced above average falls in the sales they realised in Eastern Europe (-0.76, 1 per cent). This indicates that overall the East German companies in the data set are not very successfully defending their traditional export markets in Eastern Europe.

Table 6.5a indicates that in *1990* the average company in the *Hungarian* data set had a 60 per cent market share.[56] By *1996* the average market share has fallen to 56 per cent, that is by 4 percentage points only. Several companies (H3, H7, H8) have even experienced increases in their market share.[57] Transportation or physical input cost[58] considerations play an important import deterring role in almost all these cases. In addition interview partners in all the Hungarian companies indicated that they enjoy a net labour cost advantage, even after differences in their relative productivity have been taken account of. These differential cost conditions faced by domestic firms and importers means that in many sectors entry using a strategy of cost leadership is not a feasible strategy. The alternative is for a potential importer to offer a higher quality product at a price differential which covers his higher production and transportation costs. The Hungarian companies which have increased their market share have all drastically improved the quality of their products, making this second entry strategy unattractive as well.[59]

The largest fall in market share was suffered by H4 who, like all its Hungarian competitors, has been suffering from the effects of entry by multinationals into the pharmaceuticals market. The fall in H10's and in H11's market share are also a direct consequence of entry form abroad. Only H2 claims that newly established (smaller) Hungarian entrants into the 'small sweets' (that is candies, small chocolate bars etc.) market have been affecting its sales.

Even though companies have generally maintained their market shares (0.89, 1 per cent) this by no means entails an absence of competitive pressure with 58 per cent of the companies interviewed claiming that they face small competitors as well as large ones and only one company, H1, claiming that it does not face any large competitors at all.[60] Although companies with a high market share in 1996 tend to have fewer than average number of competitors (-0.53, 5 per cent)[61] and are less likely to face domestic competitors (-0.59, 5 per cent), they are also concerned about the price (-0.42, 10 per cent) and quality (-0.43, 10 per cent) of their products. In conjunction with the good export performance of these companies,[62] this suggests that in a small and reasonably open economy a high domestic market share does not entail a lack of international competition.

Since the Hungarian companies have been increasing their exports to the EU and most foreign entrants into the Hungarian markets tend to originate from the EU as well it is not surprising that we find in Table 6.5b that nine out of the 11 companies interviewed state that they have important competitors who originate from the EU. The second most frequently cited geographical origin of competitors is Hungary (cited six times). Especially companies from the food processing industry tend to claim that their main competitors are Hungarian subsidiaries of Western companies (0.56, 5 per cent). Four out of 11 companies indicate that they face important competitors originating from outside Europe and only H8 locates important competitors in Eastern Europe.

The observation that Hungarian companies with a high market share in 1990/6 are more likely to be profitable is only weakly significant (0.49/0.48, 10 per cent). That this association is not stronger is likely to be due to fact that it is the companies which are large domestically which are also tend to have a good export performance. Consequently they frequently face competition in their foreign markets, even if they have some monopoly power domestically. Consistently with this interpretation I find that in general companies which face a large number of competitors are less likely to be profitable (-0.56, 5 per cent). Similarly in 1997 an East German companies' profitability is adversely affected by Eastern European (-0.76, 5 per cent), EU (-0.76, 5 per cent) and worldwide competitors (-0.66, 10 per cent).

The next section is going to explore the finer details of the East German and Hungarian companies' competitive situation. By examining the main dimensions of competition and importance of different regional factors I am trying to find indicators of the companies' implicit comparative advantage.

5 What are the Main Dimensions of Competition? Are Companies Specialising in Low-tech Cheap Products? How Important are Different Regional Characteristics for the Companies' Competitive Success? For Example, How Important is the Availability of a Cheap Workforce?

Interviews in which East German managers were asked to describe their company's main competitive advantages and challenges generally suggested that the companies focus on providing high (but not usually cutting edge) quality at lower prices than their main competitors.[63] Consistently they are very concerned about achieving further product and service quality improvements[64] and cost reductions.[65] Price wars and the acceptance or lack of it by West German cartels are also recurring themes.[66] In stark contrast the Hungarian case studies many East German interview partners also complained about the negative image of East German products and a lack of brand loyalty in domestic consumers.[67]

Table 6.6a supports the importance of price factors in the East German companies' competitive success by indicating that obtaining lower wage costs are especially important to companies which ascribe a high importance to price competition (0.50, 10 per cent) and in 1996 export a high proportion of their output to the EU (0.63, 5 per cent) and worldwide (0.50, 10 per cent).

Companies which had a high export orientation in 1990 are less worried about quality, punctuality and design (all significant at a 10 per cent level), suggesting that a high export orientation forced these companies to approach international standards with respect to these dimensions of competition. Nevertheless, companies which export a high proportion of their output in 1996 are very quality conscious (-0.55, 10 per cent). A focus on product quality tends to be associated with a focus on punctuality, which reflects the quality of the services provided by the company (0.67, 5 per cent).

Companies which have been increasing their exports generally (0.72, 5 per cent) and especially their sales in the European Union (0.72, 5 per cent) and worldwide (0.86, 1 per cent) tend to view high design standards as less important determinants of their success. This suggests the possibility that companies have been finding it easiest to increase their exports if they are producing products which are of a homogenous design internationally, which means that once the international standard (in processed steel, turbines or gears) is reached, the company does not has to compete along this dimension.

Common themes also emerged form interviews in which Hungarian interviewees were asked to describe their company's main competitive advantage and challenges: again successful Hungarian companies tend to focus on providing Western level quality and service at lower prices than multinational companies.[68] Further cost reductions[69] and quality improvements[70] are the main internal changes with which the companies are hoping to improve their competitiveness.[71]

The main message is that the Hungarian companies tend to mention Western standard quality at lower prices as the main determinant of their success, rather than any of these factors individually. Three companies (H5, H8, H10) even rank quality above prices, something only the duopolist D9 did in the German data. Punctuality again figures a lot lower than either price or quality. Nevertheless when exporting to the EU (-0.54, 5 per cent) and worldwide (-0.50, 10 per cent) Hungarian companies are primarily competing on price, without experiencing too many problems in their product quality.[72]

Punctuality is considered less important by companies with high export growth to Eastern Europe (0.68, 5 per cent), while companies increasing their exports worldwide rank punctuality highly (-0.57, 5 per cent). Assuming that punctuality is of the same importance to customers all over the world this indicates that Hungarian companies can still 'get away with' being less punctual in Eastern Europe. Nevertheless companies increasing their sales in Eastern Europe have been generally aiming to provide good product quality (0.45, 10 per cent).

The interviews showed that all the Hungarian companies (H9, H10, H5, H8) which assign a relatively low importance to price competition tend to have a degree of monopoly power, either by dominating the domestic market (H5, H8), being a member in a cartel (H10) or by operating in a small niche with few direct competitors (H9). The effect of a company facing small as well as large competitors is that it ranks price competition more highly than average (-0.83, 1 per cent), indicating that in these industries the small entrants serve to drive prices down. Additional competition from small companies also enhances a company's incentives for punctual delivery (0.83, 1 per cent).

I also enquired about the importance of various regional characteristics for the economic success of the company interviewed.[73] The means of the relevant variables (Tables 6.5a and b) indicate that for East German interview partners the availability of a highly qualified workforce is a very important factor for all companies, while the availability of a cheap workforce is attributed a medium importance by three companies only. Similarly in the Hungarian data the difference between the mean of the variable capturing the importance of a highly trained workforce and the mean score for a cheap workforce is significant at the 1 per cent level,[74] indicating that there too the availability of a cheap workforce is clearly a secondary factor when compared with the importance of well trained employees. This result provides a counterargument to the popular claim that cheap labour is what is making Eastern Europe attractive to investors.[75] What makes Eastern Europe and especially Hungary attractive to investors is not cheap labour, but rather the combination of a cheaper and very highly trained workforce. It is of essential importance for the future economic success and recovery of the region to maintain its currently high levels of human capital, that is the good provision of technical and nontechnical training and of general schooling.

Confirming market access considerations the East German companies also emphasise the importance of having a well developed infrastructure in the region.[76] Similarly in the Hungarian data the considerations which closely follow a well-trained workforce all relate to the proximity of the companies' markets and the state of the infrastructure the companies have to rely upon in order to obtain access to different geographical markets. The Hungarian companies place, however, a much higher valuation on being close to their most important customers and input providers (both significant at the 1 per cent level). East German companies would probably not be indifferent about having more customers and suppliers in close proximity, enabling them to have, for example, transportation cost savings. Whether East German manufacturing companies would like to have customers and suppliers in close proximity is not, however, really the relevant question. More to the point, they cannot have them because they usually do not exist. On the other hand the Hungarian companies predominantly have domestic customers and suppliers who, all the better, tend to be in close proximity.[77] Since services are usually not tradable, it is no contradiction to find that the East German companies value proximity to their service providers just as highly as the Hungarian ones.[78]

Although the Hungarian and German companies do not significantly differ in their assessment of the absolute importance of the three public goods the Hungarian companies' give a very low relative ranking two public goods, namely the proximity to research institutions and a competent local government.[79] At times (especially in the case of H1) proximity of research institutions is judged to be unimportant because the company has its own internal R&D department, while in the East German data there is a general lack of R&D. The Hungarian data provides some evidence that companies purchasing R&D from surrounding institutions have an above average export performance to the EU (0.52, 10 per cent) and worldwide (0.51, 10 per cent), especially in terms of export growth between 1990 and 1996 (0.71, 1 per cent and 0.45, 10 per cent respectively). Even though these companies are exporting products with a high R&D content, price competition remains their dominant consideration (-0.64, 5 per cent).

Tables 6.5a and b also make some interesting suggesting concerning a companies' relative probability of being profitable. For example with respect to different regional characteristics I find that companies which assign a high importance to the importance of a competent local government are more likely to be profitable both in 1995 (0.65, 10 per cent) and 1997 (0.68, 5 per cent). The interviews showed that companies which assign a high importance to a competent local government do so because they feel that their local government is of great value to the company in dealing with the social dimensions of its restructuring process or, in the construction sector, in securing contracts for the company.

In 1995 there was a strong negative association between East German companies which ascribe a high importance to a well-developed regional infrastructure (-0.91, 1 per cent) and those which are profitable. Since East Germany suffered from some backwardness (relative to West Germany) in, for example, its telecommunications and road networks it should not come as a surprise that companies which have an above average dependency on this relatively backwards infrastructure suffered a competitive disadvantage. By 1997 this association is insignificant which suggests that the large investments into infrastructure projects which took place in East Germany since 1990 seem to be succeeding in alleviating the infrastructure related problems especially manufacturing companies tended to face.[80]

6 Conclusions

My qualitative and quantitative data suggests that both East German and Hungarian suppliers experienced similar initial problems, especially with the quality of their products. They also suffered from a generally weak financial position and from transition specific problems such as a lack of punctuality and reliability. The response of East German and Hungarian customers to the problems faced by their domestic suppliers has been very different. Faced with very low trade costs East German customers generally abandoned their domestic suppliers because they had easy access to pre-existing supply networks in the West. Hungarian suppliers on the other hand benefited from the protection offered to them by Hungary's own currency and generally higher transportation costs to Hungary. These factors, however, merely gave them some breathing space. The threat of competition from the EU remains very real, especially in sectors in which quality is very important. There is evidence that Hungarian suppliers are responding by rapidly increasing their product quality and by being highly accommodating to their customers.

The diverging geographical shifts which have taken place in terms of input markets are mirrored in the companies' output markets. Although Hungarian companies had higher exports worldwide and to the EU in 1990, I find that by 1996 the East German companies have experienced far larger increases in their exports, especially to West Germany, and decreases in their domestic sales. The overall shifts are in accordance with the literature surveyed: Trade liberalisation has resulted in increased exports to the EU from companies in both countries. The increase in exports has been especially large in the case where trade barriers have been entirely abolished, namely from East German companies to West Germany. The interviews indicated that market size consideration were instrumental in re-focusing East German companies to the West German market: not only did the West German market present many new opportunities, but many East German customers vanished. Domestic companies interviewees supplied with inputs ceased, greatly changed or reduced their operations. In some sectors, such as steel, tyres, gears and turbines interview partners indicated that the East German market of industrial customers had all but ceased to exist, suggesting a process of disaglomeration. In addition East German final consumers showed a strong lack of brand loyalty, while Hungarian consumers were more prone to be sceptical about Western brands. Consistently with market access and transportation cost considerations interviews with Hungarian companies provided some evidence for an increasingly regional focus on Central Europe defined as a 1000 km radius both east- and westwards.

The persistence of historical trends in both data sets suggests that a pre-existing exporting capability is a precondition for being able to provide a flexible supply response to the opportunities presented by trade liberalisation. Since few East German companies had a pre-existing exporting capability and even fewer any direct experiences with Western customers the hypothesis presents itself that the extremely rapid trade liberalisation which took place not only enabled the survivors to re-orientated themselves westwards, but also forced them to do so by 'eliminating an inordinate share of domestic production' (van Brabant, 1994, p. 167) and hence demand.

The devastation suffered by East German industry is also reflected in the companies' market shares. From similar starting points, between 1990 and 1996 the average Hungarian manufacturing company has only experienced a 3 percentage point fall in its market share, while the fall experienced by East German companies tended to be closer to 74 percentage points (significant at the 1 per cent level), resulting in the typical East German company having a significantly (at the 1 per cent level) lower overall market share in 1996. The combination of the vanishing industrial and frequently also consumer demand for traditional East German products and of the unfettered market access enjoyed by Western companies has resulted in a situation where locally East German companies are not only frequently facing a smaller pie but are also obtaining a much smaller slice of what is left. This is a recipe for eliminating companies rather than for restructuring them.

The protection afforded to the Hungarian companies in the form of higher transportation costs to Hungary and their labour cost advantage are crucial in giving them a chance in competing with western multinationals. Reductions in market share which occurred nevertheless have generally been the result of entry by multinationals, rather than the consequence of indigenously grown new Hungarian competitors.

I find no evidence that in manufacturing the rapid expansion of the small and medium-sized firm sector has occurred which was hoped to 'ensure output growth, generate new employment, provide a tax base and generally augment the flexibility and dynamism of these economies' (Svejnar, 1991, p. 133). This observation makes the successful restructuring of the existing manufacturing base all the more imperative.

It is clear from the interviews that their continuing cost advantages are not, however, making the Hungarian companies complacent. They respond to the threat of competition by improving the quality of their products while maintaining relatively low prices. Since Hungary is a small economy, it is also important to bear in mind that being large in terms of domestic market share by no means entails being inappropriately big from the point of view of international scale economies and competitiveness. I find that it is exactly the companies which have a large domestic market share which are also strong exporters. A policy of domestic demonopolisation might well have adversely affected this exporting capability without providing incentives for restructuring which are not obtainable from continuing and gradual trade liberalisation with the aim of eventual EU membership.

With respect to the role of regional characteristics and of different dimensions of competition the case studies confirm the important role played by net labour cost advantages in maintaining the attractiveness of Central Europe as a manufacturing location. In this context the rapid wage assimilation between West and East Germany posed a particular problem to East German companies. Since it is net labour costs which count in this context, it is not enough for a workforce to be cheap, but it also has to be well-trained and sufficiently productive to constitute a competitive advantage. It is this combination which allows both East German and Hungarian companies to strive for niches in which they provide products of Western quality at lower prices.

There is some evidence, however, that the (indigenous) R&D content of the East German products is lower, making East German companies mainly successful in exporting product of a relatively homogenous design to western markets. Hungarian companies not only have a greater wage cost advantages, but have also maintained a greater R&D capacity. Although in their case as well price remains the primary competitive focus, there is some evidence that this greater R&D content allows for high export growth to EU and worldwide markets.

The very high importance ascribed in both data sets to a well-developed infrastructure underlines the role played by market access and transportation costs in influencing the companies' ability to compete internationally. In this context it is notable, however, that Hungarian companies have a significantly (at the 1 per cent level) higher valuation of being in proximity to their most important customers and input providers. This suggests that local agglomeration forces and the logic of cumulative causation are working in favour of manufacturing in Hungary.

The question arises whether the extensive destruction of the East German manufacturing base has resulted in dis-agglomeration, that is a situation where in most industrial sectors (with the clear exception of construction) the critical mass of domestic industry has been lost. In conjunction with the rapid wage assimilation between East and West Germany this results in a situation where the general lack of centrifugal and centripetal forces favouring East Germany as a production site makes East German re-industrialisation an unlikely prospect even in the longer term. Hungary on the other hand provides an example of how gradual but fully credible trade liberalisation with the aim of future integration with the EU provide restructuring incentives without destroying a country's manufacturing base.

Notes

1 Arguably one example is the presence of a relatively large oil refining industry in Hungary.
2 Hungary's investment drive in the 1980s nevertheless succeeded in raising hard currency exports from $4.4 bn in 1980 to $7 bn in 1990 (Amsden et al., 1994, pp. 104 ff.).
3 Using data from four transition countries and shadow profit rates Hughes and Hare (1994) provide estimates of which sectors might have a negative value-added at world prices.
4 See Ottaviano and Puga (1998), Martin (1999) and Krugman (1998) for recent surveys.
5 For an exposition of the 1994 Europe Agreements between the EU and Poland, Hungary the Czech and Slovak Republics see, for example, Reynolds (1994).
6 Leamer (1997, pp. 515 ff.) argues that Central Europe enjoys excellent market access which on the basis of 'distance to GDP' consideration should enable it to reach per capita income levels comparable to those of, for example, Austria. He argues that Western European trade barriers act like a 500-mile increase in distance between East and West.
7 Audretsch (1998) and Morgan (1997) emphasise the importance of information exchange and technological spillovers made possible by proximity, providing hence an incentive for clustering. Porter (1998) similarly argues that geographical concentration occurs because spatial, cultural and institutional proximity serves to amplify many of the productivity and innovation benefits of clustering.
8 He also emphasises a minimum threshold of per capita income (consistent with market size considerations) as an important determinant of FDI flows. The fact that FDI is attracted by high growth and robust demand means that it reinforces, rather than corrects, initial differences in regional trends (Kozul-Wright and Rowthorn, 1998, p. 76).
9 One of Martin's (1999, pp. 70 ff.) main criticisms against the 'New Economic Geography' is that the relevant characteristics determining a region's relative attractiveness are by no way exhausted by the list provided in the preceding paragraphs. On his account economists show a general neglect of the social, cultural and institutional factors involved in spatial

economic development. The argument is that since economic activity is embedded in these wider factors, the possibilities and constraints on spatial development are also determined by the networks of trust, cooperation, competition and governance that characterise regions and the clusters they contain (ibid., p. 79). See, for example, Granovetter (1995) for an exploration of the 'social' element in interfirm relations and Nelson (1995, p. 78) on the importance of a firm's institutional environment.

10 Interview with the production manager in D4.

11 See Carlin (1994) for an account of the extent of deindustrialisation in East Germany following reunification.

12 Nuti (1994, p. 452) similarly argues that due to the assimilation of wage levels East Germany still faces 'a risk of protracted underdevelopment as German and foreign investors are attracted by central-eastern European countries with much lower wages and similar economic structures'.

13 One only has to look at Hungary's ability to attract FDI since 1990.

14 For example both with respect to the forward and backward linkages of the 10 Hungarian companies they examine Whitely et al. (1996, pp. 404 ff.) find a relatively limited extent of change.

15 Interview partners from the food sector not only complained about relatively large overacapacity due to investors' overoptimistic initial demand expectations but also about a fragmentation of production processes due to the different investors' desire to be present in numerous market segments. This fragmentation destroyed the previously existing division of labour in the Hungarian food processing industry and makes obtaining scale economies through exports all the more imperative.

16 The literature on economic geography does not easily lend itself to narrowly defined hypotheses/predictions which are empirically tractable. This might be a contributing factor to the relative scarcity of empirical work in this area (see, for example, Krugman, 1998, p. 15).

17 All the procurement and sales figures have been obtained from interviews. Although based on memory, the 1990 figures are reasonably reliable, since in the previous economic order there was not much change in these areas. The variables used are defined in Table 6.1 in Appendix F.

18 The larger number of construction companies in the East German data is significant at the 10 per cent level, as is the high number of food companies in the Hungarian data. These differences in the composition of the two data sets could introduce biases when making comparisons, should I find that either construction companies or food companies systematically differ from manufacturing ones. My data suggests that in their procurement policies food companies on aggregate tend to diverge little from other manufacturing companies. Furthermore there are such large differences within this group itself, that their inclusion is unlikely to lead to systematic biases. Including construction companies can, however, lead to systematic biases, since they face high transportation costs and are hence strongly localised in their operations. These biases will be referred to explicitly throughout this discussion. Tables 6.2a and b contain more information on this issue.

19 The 'averages' refer to the means of the variables listed in Tables 6.2a and b.

20 Values in parentheses indicate the mean values obtained for the manufacturing companies only.

21 All these statements refer to changes in the percentage of total inputs procured from a given geographical area. See Table 1 for the descriptions of the relevant variables.

22 The relative stability of overall procurement is clearly supported by the fact that when I obtained the associations for the percentage of input procured in 1990 and 1996 from a given geographical area, I found associations which were significant at the 1 per cent level in each case between the percentage of inputs procured from Hungary, Eastern Europe, the EU and worldwide respectively in 1990 and the relevant percentages for each geographical area in 1997. Reporting on ten Hungarian case studies, Whitley et al. (1996, pp. 409 ff.) also report a surprising stability in supply arrangements.

23 Although insignificant for the complete data set, for the manufacturing companies only the extent to which East German companies use fewer local suppliers in 1996 is significant at the 5 per cent level (Table 6.2a).

24 The differences in the magnitude of the switch away from domestic suppliers and in favour of EU suppliers are both significant at the 1 per cent level, suggesting that in 1996 Hungarian companies not only rely more heavily on domestic suppliers in total but have also tended to maintain the overall level of their orders by not switching away from the Hungarian market.

25 Taking the averages for the complete data set introduces two biases: the extent to which companies still rely on Eastern European suppliers is overstated by the inclusion of the strong outlier D3, whose owner, a Slovak steel mill, is also its main supplier. The second bias is that including construction companies biases downwards the extent to which companies have switched away from East German suppliers in comparison with the Hungarian data.

26 When I obtained associations for the percentage of old suppliers a company has in 1996 and its supply arrangements in 1990 I found that East German companies which have a large number of old suppliers already procured a relatively high proportion of their inputs from the EU in 1990 (significant at the 5 per cent level). For the Hungarian data I found that companies with a large number of old suppliers showed a greater than average total reliance (significant at the 10 per cent level) and increase in their reliance on Hungarian suppliers (significant at the 10 per cent level).

27 This factor is explicitly mentioned by D3, D6, D8, D9.

28 This is mentioned by D1, D2, D3, D4, D5, D6, D8.

29 This is mentioned by D7, D8.

30 This point was made, for example, by the procurement managers in both the pharmaceutical companies D5 and H4.

31 H1, H2, H3, H5, H6 H7, H10.

32 H2, H3, H5, H6, H8, H11.

33 H2, H10 and H3, H11 respectively. Far more common are stories about problems which can be termed transition specific: Bankruptcy (H3, H4, H11), an inability to agree on payment methods (H3), opportunism (H4, H11), financial instability on the side of the supplier or customer (H6, H7) and an inability to adjust to the customer's new demands and product range (H7, H9, H10) all feature.

34 Tables 6.3a and b summarise the answers.

35 H2, H3, H4, H6, H11. In this context it was frequently claimed the current level of economic uncertainty and instability forces the company to make contracts of a suboptimal length (that is they are shorter than would be desirable given a more stable environment) which entail large renegotiation costs.

36 Throughout the 'averages' refer to the means of the variables listed in Tables 6.5a and b.

37 Table 6.6a confirms this: in 1990 there is a negative association (-0.77, 1 per cent level) between the proportion of sales a company realises in East Germany and those it exports to Eastern Europe. Furthermore exports to Eastern Europe are associated at the 1 per cent level (-0.77) with total exports, while the associations between total exports and all other geographical areas are insignificant.

38 All these statements refer to changes in the percentage of total sales realised in a given geographical area. See Table 6.4 for the descriptions of the relevant variables.

39 Although after reunification sales to West Germany do not cross country borders, I will still refer to them as exports in order to be able to compare the geographical distribution of sales in 1990 with that in 1996 using the same categories.

40 The new relative importance of different export markets is reflected in Table 6.6a. Companies which in 1996 sell a small proportion of their output in East Germany are strongly focused on West Germany instead (-0.91, 1 per cent), secondarily on the European Union (-0.63, 5 per cent) and thirdly on the worldwide market (-0.56, 10 per cent). Increases in exports are associated with increased sales in these three markets, especially the West German one (significant at the 1 per cent and 5 per cent level respectively).

41 Any statistical trends which are specific to the manufacturing sector are captured by the manufacturing dummy in Table 6.6a which confirms that manufacturing companies have experienced above average reductions in the proportion of sales realised in East Germany (-0.74, 5 per cent), strong increases in the proportion of sales going to West Germany (0.68, 5 per cent), reductions in the proportion of sales realised in Eastern Europe (-0.55, 10 per cent) and increases in the proportion of sales going to the European Union (0.57, 5 per cent).

42 Companies which exported to West Germany in 1990 already have found it easier to reduce their overall dependence on the East Germany market by 1996 (-0.57, 10 per cent). The Furthermore, the higher the proportion of sales a company realised in West Germany in 1990, the higher the total sales it realises there in 1996 as well (0.71, 5 per cent) and the higher the increase in the company's West German sales (0.65, 5 per cent level). In addition it appears that experiences gained in the European Union were conducive to breaking into the West German market by 1996, both in terms of the total percentage of sales going to this market (0.59, 5 per cent) and of higher than average increases in these sales (0.58, 5 per cent).

43 Some of the lowest exporters can be found in the sweets' industry. H2 and H3's main problems seemed to have been that in 1990 they were producing goods which were generally of an inferior quality to that acceptable on Western markets but which were of a superior quality and crucially higher price than sweets produced by local companies in potential Eastern European export markets. H8 (packaging materials) faced similar problems.

44 These significance levels relate to t-tests on the means of pairs of country-specific variables.

45 Only H4 exported in even proportions to Eastern Europe on the one hand and the EU and worldwide markets on the other.

46 No statistically significant differences emerge in the manufacturing companies' exports to Eastern Europe and worldwide. The East German companies have experienced significantly greater increases in their total exports and reductions in the proportion of output sold domestically (both significant at the 1 per cent level). The relatively larger increases in exports are mainly due to the East German companies' strong reorientation to the West German market (significant at the 5 per cent level).

47 In 1996 high sales to the European Union are associated with high worldwide exports (0.81, 1 per cent), high falls in domestic sales (-0.87, 1 per cent) and also with high growth in exports in general (0.54, 5 per cent) and to the EU in particular (0.66, 5 per cent). It is worth noting that not only was a company's export orientation statistically insignificant in determining whether a company received FDI after 1990, but also whether a company had FDI or not seems to have been entirely immaterial in determining subsequent changes in the geographical distribution of its sales.

48 The extent to which companies face increased competition and hence smaller residual domestic demand curves is going to be discussed later on.

49 The companies to experience the largest increases in their total exports are H3, whose chocolate bars in particular are increasingly popular in Central Europe, and H7 who has expanded its already impressive exporting base to 90 per cent of its total output.

50 The percentage of output sold in Hungary in 1996 is positively correlated with the percentage of output sold domestically in 1996 (0.93, 1 per cent) and negatively associated with the 1990 levels of exports to Eastern Europe (-0.64, 5 per cent), to the European Union (-0.46, 10 per cent), exports worldwide (-0.73, 1 per cent) and exports in general (-0.93, 1 per cent).

51 When I obtained the relevant associations I found that the geographical distribution of input procurement tends to be generally insignificant with respect to a companies' relative performance.

52 By 1997 only two companies are not profitable, namely D6 and D3. Their problems are industry specific and the associations found in the Dpr97 column reflect the average (usually of one very high and one very low value) of the entries for D6 and D3 rather than trends they share in the geographical distribution of their sales.

53 In the East German data I again consider East Germany, rather than re-unified Germany, to be 'domestic' in order to be able to compare data for 1990 with that for 1996. All the companies interviewed clearly distinguished between West- and East German sales and market shares.

54 If we assume that many West German manufacturing companies had excess capacity in 1990, then they could simply transport their finished products to the East German market, so that the capital costs of entry are not necessarily higher in manufacturing, although manufacturing is more capital intensive. However to realise sales in the construction sector one merely has to win contracts and one does not require a network of, for example, local sales outlets and distributors. In the construction sector one also has to convince only one customer (usually the local or state government) rather than the general public to buy one's end-product. Entry into the manufacturing sector consequently tends to necessitate advertising outlays, which add to the net costs of entry.

55 I encountered abundant anecdotal evidence of the latter strategy. Interview partners also repeatedly claimed that some of the former East German companies had been merely acquired to be ruined, i.e. that acquisition is frequently just another version of a strategy to drive out the local competitor.

56 This is not significantly different from the 'average' market share prevalent in the East German data for 1990.

57 H3 now focuses on chocolate bars which are smaller (and cheaper) than Western ones. Like this people can still treat themselves and their children without having to spend much money, a fact which makes these bars especially popular with lower income groups and with children spending their pocket money. H8 has increased the quality and range of its products to an extent which makes importing more packaging materials unattractive.

58 These factors are especially important for H5, H11 and H1.

59 Table 6.6b suggests that companies which have a high domestic market share in 1996 rank the importance of the quality of their products very highly (-0.43, 10 per cent). In addition companies which have been increasing their domestic sales have been emphasising quality (-0.48, 10 per cent) rather than price (-0.56, 10 per cent). These observations are consistent with the assumption that increasing product and service quality is an important way of inhibiting entry from abroad in sectors where entry with a strategy of cost leadership is not feasible.

60 Only three companies (H1, H5, H7) claim that they face few or no competitors. In all three cases this constitutes a continuation of a pre-existing monopoly situation in a market where the capital requirements for domestic entrants are prohibitive and where foreign entrants are deterred for the reasons discussed above.

61 Table 6.6b suggests that companies which in 1996 claim to be facing a large number of competitors tended to be strongly focused on the Hungarian market (0.52, 10 per cent), to be exporting less to the European Union (-0.60, 5 per cent) and worldwide (-0.45, 10 per cent).

62 Table 6.6b also suggests that both in 1990 and 1996 companies which had a large market share in 1990 tend to sell a below average proportion of their overall output in Hungary (-0.49, 10 per cent) and have high export levels (0.49, 10 per cent). Due to the fact that Hungary is a small market being big in terms of output frequently entailed not just a large domestic market share but also a significant export orientation.

63 Explicitly mentioned by interview partners in D1, D2, D3, D6, D7, D8. There is almost universal agreement that punctuality is secondary and design relatively unimportant. See also Table 4a. The variables capturing the importance of different dimensions of competition yield means which are not significantly different for the two country data sets.

64 D3, D4, D5.

65 D7, D8, D9.

66 These comments are especially prevalent in the building (D1, D2, D6, D7) and steel processing sectors (D3).

67 One East German interview partner expressed this sentiment by stating that 'In the beginning you could not even sell milk from East German cows to East German consumers' (interview with the personnel manager in D4). On the other hand especially interview partners in the Hungarian food processing industry regularly recounted stories in which investors were forced to reintroduce domestic brands after hastily discontinuing them in favour of their own Western ones. Strong brand loyalty and an intimate knowledge of an idiosyncratic market were explicit mentioned as a competitive advantage in H1, H2, H4.

68 This strategy is explicitly referred to by H1, H3, H4, H5, H8, H11.

69 H3, H5, H6, H10, H11.

70 H7, H9.

71 Some companies (H1, H4) wish to expand their product range and to improve their marketing approach (H2). The companies tend to suffer from transition specific external problems: The lack of stability in the economy and society are a recurring theme, with companies complaining about legal uncertainty, uncertainty in Hungary's economic policies regarding taxation, exchange and interest rates. Worries about future political stability and GDP growth are also common. Only two companies complain about industry specific external problems: Cartels (H10) and lack of payment discipline (H8).

72 Two types of companies tended to assign a high importance to competition in terms of quality: those who excel in this dimension and those which still face problems in this area.

73 The interviewees were asked to ascribe strengths to their preferences and to order factors according to their importance. The first two questions relate to characteristics of the workforce, the next three to proximity of relevant input and output markets and the last three deal with public good provision, for example the quality of the local infrastructure.

74 I obtain a test statistic of 3.57, while the critical value for 1 per cent significance is 2.52 for a t-distribution with 20 degrees of freedom. In comparison to the East German companies the Hungarian companies ascribe a significantly (at the 5 per cent level) higher overall importance to the fact that their workforce is relatively cheap. This is not a reflection of the fact that the East German companies would not like to have a relatively cheap workforce, rather they have few labour cost advantages over West German and EU companies because of the fast rise in East German wages to levels which are very close to West German ones.

75 In the Hungarian data companies with FDI especially value the availability of a highly trained workforce (0.62, 5 per cent) rather than a cheap one. In addition companies which ascribe a high importance to having a cheap workforce also tend to appreciate high standards of training (0.54, 5 per cent).

76 East German companies which value having a good infrastructure tend to sell a relatively small proportion of their output in East Germany (-0.64, 5 per cent) and a high proportion in West Germany (0.61, 5 per cent) and the EU (0.53, 10 per cent) in 1996. Due to their high export levels westwards they also assign a high importance to both price (-0.65, 5 per cent) and quality (-0.62, 5 per cent) competition.

77 East German companies which value proximity to their customers as well as input providers (0.65, 10 per cent) tend to be construction companies (-0.82, 1 per cent) who are strongly localised in their operations (0.83, 1 per cent). Competition in product quality and punctuality is relatively unimportant to these companies (0.72, 5 per cent and 0.78, 1 per cent for example in the cost of companies valuing proximity to their suppliers) probably because once a contract has been won predominantly based on price considerations, the customer experiences significant transaction specific sunk costs for any given building project. There is no evidence for any such trends in the Hungarian data, were proximity to their input and output markets is more uniformly considered to be important.

78 Since proximity to service providers greatly enhances a companies' flexibility it should come as no surprise that in both data sets companies which value proximity to their service providers are export orientated, experiencing especially rapid export growth westwards between 1990 and 1996 (in the East German data: 0.53, 10 per cent for export growth to the EU, 0.48, 10 per cent for export growth worldwide; in the Hungarian data: 0.61, 5 per cent for total export growth, 0.53, 5 per cent for export growth to the EU. These Hungarian companies also ascribe a very high importance to price competition: -0.81, 1 per cent).

79 Hungarian companies which assign a high importance to one of these factors tend to also do so for the other (0.81, 1 per cent), suggestion that these are companies who are generally more tightly integrated into the institutional structures surrounding them. Similarly East German companies ascribing a high importance to their local government are more localised than average in their operations and have low exports to the EU (-0.54, 10 per cent). East German companies tend to praise their local government while in Hungary

the tenor tends to be, especially when foreign managers are being interviewed: 'If a competent local government was of any importance to us, we would not be here' (interview with the MD of Douwe-Egberts).

80 The Hungarian data merely indicates that in 1996 companies which value proximity to their customers are more likely to be profitable than average (0.56, 5 per cent), while those valuing proximity to their input suppliers are less likely to be profitable (-0.48, 10 per cent).

References

Amsden, A., Kochanowicz, J. and Taylor, L. (1994), *The market meets its match*, Harvard University Press.

Amiti, M. (1998), 'New trade theories and industrial location in the EU: A survey of evidence', *Oxford Review of Economic Policy*, Vol. 14.

Audretsch, D. (1998), 'Agglomeration and the location of innovative activity', *Oxford Review of Economic Policy*, Vol. 14.

Brabant, van J. (1994), 'Trade, integration and transformation in Eastern Europe', *Journal of International Affairs*, Summer.

Brülhart, M. (1998), 'Economic geography, industry location and trade: the evidence', *World Economy*, August.

Carlin, W. (1994), 'Privatisation and deindustrialisation in East Germany', in Estrin, S. (ed.), *Privatisation in Central and Eastern Europe*, Longman.

Carlin, W. and Landesmann, M. (1997), 'From theory into practice? Restructuring and dynamism in transition economies', *Oxford Review of Economic Policy*, Vol. 13 (2).

Granovetter, M. (1995), 'Coase revisited: Business groups in the modern economy', *Industrial and Corporate Change*, Vol. 4 (1).

Hamilton, C. and Winters, L. (1992), 'Trade with Eastern Europe', *Economic Policy*, April, reprinted in Hare, P. and Davis, J. (eds) (1997), *Transition to the market economy, Volume III*, Routledge.

Hughes, G. and Hare, P. (1994), 'The international competitiveness of industries in Bulgaria, Czechoslovakia, Hungary and Poland', *Oxford Economic Chapters*, reprinted in Hare, P. and Davis, J. (eds) (1997), *Transition to the market economy, Volume III*, Routledge.

Kornai, J. (1992), *The political economy of communism*, Clarendon Press.

Kozul-Wright, R. and Rowthorn, R. (1998), 'Spoilt for choice? Multinational corporations and the geography of international production', *Oxford Review of Economic Policy*, Vol. 14 (2).

Krugman, P. (1998), 'What's new about the new economic geography?', *Oxford Review of Economic Policy*, Vol. 14 (2).

Krugman, P. (1993), 'First nature, second nature and metropolitan location', *Journal of Regional Science*, Vol. 33.

Krugman, P. (1991), 'Increasing returns and economic geography', *Journal of Political Economy*, Vol. 99.

Krugman, P. and Venables, A. (1990), 'Integration and the competitiveness of peripheral industry', in Bliss, C. and Braga de Macedo, J. (eds), *Unity with diversity in the European Community*, Cambridge University Press.

Krugman, P. and Venables, A. (1995), 'Globalisation and the Inequality of nations', *CEPR Discussion Chapter No.1015 and Quarterly Journal of Economics*, Vol. 110.

Lall, S. (1998), 'Exports of manufactures by developing counties: Emerging patterns of trade and location', *Oxford Review of Economic Policy*, Vol. 14 (2).

Leamer, E. (1997), 'Access to Western markets and Eastern effort levels', in Zecchini, S. (ed.), *Lessons from the economic transition*, Kluwer.

Marer, P. (1991), 'Foreign economic liberalisation in Hungary and Poland', *AEA Chapters and Proceedings*, May.

Markusen, J. (1998), 'Multinational firms, location and trade', *World Economy*, August.

Martin, P. (1998), 'Can regional policies affect growth and geography in Europe?', *World Economy*, August.

Martin, R. (1999), 'The new "geographical turn" in economics: some critical reflections', *Cambridge Journal of Economics*, Vol. 23.

Morgan, K. (1997), 'The learning region: Institutions, innovation and regional renewal', *Regional Studies*, July.

Nelson, R. (1995), 'Recent evolutionary theoretising about economic change', *Journal of Economic Literature*, March.

Neven, D. (1994), 'Trade liberalisation with eastern nations, how sensitive?', *Economic Policy Research, July 1994*, reprinted in Hare, P. and Davis, J. (1997), *Transition to the market economy, Volume III*, Routledge.

Nuti, D. (1994), 'The impact of systemic transition on the European Community', *CIS, Middle Europe Centre Discussion Chapter Series, No. 10*, May, reprinted in Hare, P. and Davis, J. (1997), *Transition to the market economy, Volume III*, Routledge.

Ottaviano, G. and Puga, D. (1998), 'Agglomeration in the global economy: A survey of the "New Economic Geography"', *World Economy*, August.

Porter, M. (1998), 'The Adam Smith address: Location, clusters and the "new" microeconomics of competition', *Business Economics*, January.

Reynolds, M. (1994), 'Central and Eastern Europe moving closer to the EU', *International Financial Law Review*, September.

Svejnar, J. (1991), 'Microeconomic issues in the transition to a market economy', *Journal of Economic Perspectives*, Fall.

Venables, A. (1998), 'The assessment: Trade and location', *Oxford Review of Economic Policy*, Vol. 14 (2).

Whitley, R., Henderson, J., Czaban, L. and Lengyel, G. (1996), 'Trust and contractual relations in an emerging capitalist economy: The changing trading relationships of ten large Hungarian enterprises', *Organisation Studies*, Vol. 17 (3).

7 Conclusions

A noticeable pattern is that the academic literature and investors frequently endorsed restructuring measures which turned out to be 'right' for the East German companies and 'wrong' for the Hungarian ones. The second startling feature of my case studies is the evidence of total industrial devastation in East Germany. In this conclusion I argue that these observations are related to three recurring themes: local idiosyncrasies matter, the past matters and the future should not be rushed.

That *local idiosyncrasies matter* might seem banal, but it is not. My case studies show that academics, as well as foreign direct investors, frequently endorse catch-all restructuring measures. In doing so they implicitly assume that the wider social, legal, economic and cultural transition environment is already sufficiently similar to that of a developed and stable market economy for policies developed elsewhere to work well. Especially policy prescriptions assuming in any way that markets work well and information is abundant are not suited to address situations in which creating markets under a high degree of uncertainty is the problem to be addressed in the first place. The surprise many western managers expressed, for example, about unexpected responses by Hungarian consumers, suppliers, employees etc. shows not only a general lack of awareness of the fact that restructuring measures a constrained by and interact with their wider environment, but also of the critical dimensions of difference.

To illustrate the problems associated with a blanket approach to restructuring imagine that there are two successful football managers from northern Italy, who both speak no English. One of them is asked to take over an ailing second division team in southern Italy and the other an English team. They arrive at their respective new jobs in the firm belief that their experiences gained and methods used in northern Italy will soon catapult their new teams into the first division. Whom would you expect to have a greater a priori change of succeeding?

A comparison between enterprise restructuring in East Germany and Hungary is especially well-suited to examine these issues. Not only does East Germany share strong language and cultural ties with West Germany, but through reunification East Germany adopted West German laws, financial and political institutions and became part of the West German industry structure. Over night all the 'right' institutions and incentives were in place. In Hungary, however, local idiosyncrasies persist, which cannot simply be put down to widespread illegality and chaos. Unlike less fortunate transition economies, Hungary does not provide an illustration of how agents behave when the legal system is entirely ineffective, ethnic tension is high, corruption is rife and/or the Mafia is the main rule-enforcement agency. Hungary is reasonably stable in all these main dimensions underpinning the transformation process and nevertheless it still yields different restructuring outcomes from those in East Germany.

A clear illustration is provided in chapter 3. The observation that under central planning companies were far more vertically integrated than is customary in market economies has resulted in the general assumption that vertical disintegration is going to be performance enhancing. In my case studies Western managers, for example, showed a strong tendency to 'slim' their companies down by closing non-core units. On the other hand Hungarian managers, keen to reduce the unemployment impact of restructuring, tended to favour a policy of separating out non-core units, with the parent company frequently maintaining an ownership share in these newly founded subsidiaries. In the academic literature this 'Hungarian-style' restructuring of the boundaries of the firm has been generally interpreted as 'ambiguous' at best, with more sympathetic authors pointing to the risk spreading properties of cross-ownership and more critical ones suspecting that these measures merely create a cloud of confusion behind which non-restructuring or even criminal activities can take place.

Contrary to what might be expected my case studies clearly show that, in contrast to East Germany, vertical disintegration is not performance enhancing in the Hungarian companies examined. In retrospect the main reason seems rather obvious: For subcontracting to be viable a well-functioning supply market is necessary. Without the developed, competitive and stable West German background industry East German companies had direct access to, Hungarian companies benefit from remaining integrated or creating their own suppliers through 'ambiguous' restructuring measures.

Chapter 4 makes a similar point, only this time with respect to the internal provision of social services. In most market economies the provision of social services such as crèches and doctor's surgeries is not generally seen as the role of the enterprise sector. Consequently the suggestion is frequently made that the extent to which a company in a transition economy has shed the internal provision of such nonproductive activities is one indicator of the extent of restructuring in that company. My East German data does indeed suggest that the internal provision of social services was almost without exception the first thing to go. In Hungary, however, the situation is different. Even companies with FDI show a strong persistence in social service provision. What is more, companies showing such persistence outperform others in terms of their profits, domestic market share and exports.

Maintaining the internal provision of social services has different efficiency implications in Hungary and East Germany. Employees in East German companies became integrated into the West German social security system and experienced rapid wage assimilation. For this reason abolishing the internal provision of social services caused little friction and enabled the companies' to increase their per capita productivity. On the other hand, many Hungarian employees not only feel that social service provision is an intrinsic part of their company's traditions, one of the few tangible benefits of decades of building socialism, but they also fear that there would be few alternative providers they could afford. A general tenor is 'if you want to close these services pay us Western-level wages first'. Even though happy employees are not necessarily productive ones, disgruntled employees can certainly cause a lot of conflict which hinders the restructuring process overall. My case studies show that foreign investors' first instinct tended to be try and extensively cut these services back in Hungarian subsidiaries as well, but they soon relented when such measures invariably caused severe friction with their workforce. On the other hand culturally sensitive and 'humane' managers were generally rewarded by a cooperative workforce willing to do its bit for the company's long-term survival.

Chapter 5 most clearly illustrates the notion that local idiosyncrasies matter. The widespread assumption that companies with FDI will outperform their rivals because of knowledge transfer from their investor and his role in introducing new products and production methods is borne out in the East German data only. My Hungarian case studies provide many examples in which investors endorsed inappropriate restructuring measures by not realising, for example, the popularity of local brands or the analogy between socialist brigades and project groups. In this context successful companies give competent local managers a say in the restructuring process. They might need to be trained in areas such as marketing and finance, but at the same time they process valuable historical and cultural knowledge. Transition is a two-way learning process: since enterprises have to restructure in a way which is appropriate to their local environment, investors frequently find that what works well in their head offices and domestic markets does not work well in their subsidiary. What might be optimal in one context is not necessarily so in another. Competent local managers can help investors understand why.

The idea that local idiosyncrasies matter closely relates to a second underlying theme, namely that *history matters,* not only in the sense that it frequently gives rise to and explains local idiosyncrasies. Chapter 6 illustrates how historical factors also influence a company's underlying restructuring capability. Flexible supply side responses to the challenges posed by transition are much more likely in companies which have a pre-existing export experience, that is they are used to producing internationally competitive products and have experience in international markets. There is no clean slate in enterprise restructuring, frequently the past provides the building blocks for the future.

The last recurring theme is also most clearly illustrated by chapter 6: *the future should not be rushed.* There is an underlying tension between experiencing too little pressure for change, resulting in insufficient restructuring, and too much pressure for change, resulting in destruction rather than restructuring. In other words, is evolution preferable to revolution? My case studies show that if the transition process overall is sufficiently credible, a lot can be said for a slower pace of change.

For example, trade liberalisation is a fully credible policy goal in both Hungary and East Germany. Crucially, however, in the case of East Germany trade liberalisation occurred almost over night with reunification, while Hungary is more gradually preparing for EU membership. In addition Hungarian wage levels are approaching Western-levels much more slowly than East German ones.

The result of early and radical trade liberalisation in East Germany has been the devastation of its manufacturing base. With the exception of the construction sector, East German companies have deserted their domestic suppliers in favour of stable West German and EU suppliers. At the same time in their domestic output markets the East German companies examined have experienced radical falls in their overall demand and market share as a consequence of the availability of attractive substitutes from the West and a near-total collapse in industrial demand. Breaking into a frequently hostile West German market became a matter of survival. The prospects for East German re-industrialisation in the foreseeable future are bleak: market access, agglomeration and wage cost considerations do not clearly favour East German production sites over West German ones, especially when many West German industrial sectors are characterised by overcapacity.

On the other hand cost advantages and demand idiosyncrasies have partially protected many Hungarian industrial sectors from unfettered competition by multinationals. This has enabled capable companies to genuinely restructure. Restructuring is a complex learning process which takes time to implement. The immediate and intense competition suffered by the East German companies left them with no time to learn. Excessively speedy trade liberalisation became a recipe for enterprise destruction rather than restructuring.

The notion that there is only that much simultaneous change an organisation or individual can cope with was also all-pervasive in the personal accounts given to me by interviewees. For example Hungarian subsidiaries of foreign companies were in one instance judged to be the worst possible suppliers because the multitude of their investors' change initiatives left them in even more chaos than usual. Many trade union representatives gave illustrations of the apathy and feeling of powerlessness which yet another initiative to encourage 'self-determination', 'responsibility', 'efficient work practices' etc. brought about in employees.

In a transition environment the pressures for change crush down on a company from all sides: customers are making new demands, suppliers are overburdened, new competitors and new opportunities arise, the rules of the game change. In this situation it is tempting to try and address all problems at once. There is a Hungarian saying, however, that people who grab much end up holding little. Sometimes there is no time for evolution. If there is, however, a company can benefit from carefully working out its most profound problem, which usually relates to its products and product markets, and then introduce change in that area. Afterwards it will become clear how the organisation as a whole is affected by this initiative and which follow-on changes are necessary. To maintain an organisation's efficiency, change has to be genuine and targeted during radical restructuring processes.

APPENDICES

Appendix A

English Translation of the Questionnaire used: East German Version[1]

Interviews were conducted in East Germany between August and December 1996, in Hungary between March and August 1997, follow-up phone calls were made in 1998.

A The Situation in 1996, 1997

Interview partner
Name, Date, Company, Position in the company, Responsibilities
Name of the company
Address
Industrial sector
Name of the investor

Number of employees in 1996, expectation for 2001 (2Pt = 1Ft)
Part-time
Full-time
Blue-collar
White-collar
Sales volume after tax in million DM
Are you profitable? Yes/No

B The Situation before 1990

Interview partner
Name, Date, Company, Position in the company, Responsibilities

1 To which conglomerate (*Kombinat*) did your company last belong?
2 Where was the head office of this conglomerate?

PRODUCT

3 Which were the most important products of your company before 1990?
4 Number of employees in 1990
Part-time
Full-time
Blue-collar
White-collar

KNOW-HOW

5 Did the company with this address have a particular responsibility in the conglomerate for
– certain commercial activities
– certain activities on the value added chain
– certain product groups
– certain markets

MARKETS

6 Which percentage of your final output did you sell before 1990?
– within the *Bezirk* (corresponded to an administrative unit of about the size of a county) in which you are located
– within the former GDR
– within countries of the former Eastern Block
– within West Germany
– to other companies in your conglomerate
– other

INTEGRATION

7 Which functions were catered for (1) directly in this company [separate internal division], (2) in other companies belonging to the same Conglomerate (3) bought from external sources?
– *Bilanzierung* (basically seeing whether production is following the plan given from above)
– investment planning
– personnel
– product development

– process development
– input procurement
– maintenance
– distribution
– transportation

8 Which social functions (e.g. summer camps, kindergartens ...) were integrated into your company?

C Changes since the Acquisition by the Investor

Interview partner
Name, Date, Company, Position in the company, Responsibilities

1 When were you acquired? (All the companies in the sample have a 100% ownership by the investor.)

2 How high is the size of the employment guarantees and the investment guarantees given by the innovator to the Treuhand (guarantees given, until 1996 fulfilled, expected up to 2001)?

3 Which sanctions were agreed upon in the acquisition deal?

PRODUCTION

4 Which are your most important products (since when in production, proportion of total sales before FDI, expectation until 2001)?

5 For the products which you have kept on producing after FDI, to what extent has their value added changed?

6 For your new products: would you say that they require, in comparison to your old products more, equal or less
– technological know-how
– modern production technology
– organisational knowledge
– qualified personnel

7 From where did the main impulses for the changes in your products come?
- investor
- Treuhand
- management consultancies
- important customers
- industrial associations
- exhibitions, fairs
- the 'old' managers
- R&D
- other

8 Who controls how frequently and using which criteria whether the goals you are aiming for through these changes in your products are achieved?

INTEGRATION

9 Which activities are at the moment being a) internally supplied, b) supplied by the investor or are being c) bought from external sources?
- R&D
- design
- computing facilities
- supply procurement
- quality control
- maintenance
- transportation
- sales
- marketing
- customer services
- personnel

10 What are in your opinion the main advantages and disadvantages of this division of labour?

11 How would you like to see this division of labour develop up to the year 2001?

12 According to which criteria have you changed your position on the value-added-chain?
- costs
- capacity
- know-how
- flexibility

MARKET

13 Which percentage of your total output do you sell in
- the Land in which you are located?
- the new Länder
- the old Länder
- the EU
- directly to your investor
- other

14 How has your market shares changed? (1990, 1996, expected 2001)
- East Germany
- West Germany
- Eastern Europe
- EU
- overseas

15 How would you characterise the competition which you face? (before FDI, after FDI)
- mainly small companies
- mainly large companies
- a large number of competitors
- a small number of competitors

16 Where were your main competitors located before 1990?

17 (agree/do not agree 1 to 6) The main dimension of competition is nowadays ...
- price
- quality
- punctuality in delivery

- design
- other

18 What is in your judgement the main reason why your business partners turn to you rather than your competitors?

19 Which changes would improve upon your competitive situation?
- internal (e.g. service, quality, organisation ...)
- external (improvements in the infrastructure, policy changes ...)

PRODUCTION METHODS

20 To what extent has the composition of overall production methods changed (before FDI, 1996, 2001)?
- production runs comprising individual units
- small series
- large series
- mass production

21 Since the FDI, which were the three largest investments into the production process?

22 Judging by sales volume, which were the three largest closures in production?

23 Which of the following technologies/processes do you use in your company (before FDI, since FDI, expectation)?
- computers in the commercial area
- computers in production planning
- computers in production coordination
- computers in R&D
- computers in the management of your stocks
- CAD
- NC
- CNC
- industrial robots

24 How old are (on average) the machines which are most important for your production?

25 How long is the average technical lifetime of your machines?

26 From where did the main impulses for the changes in production come?
External:
- investor
- Treuhand
- management consultancies
- important customers
- trade associations
- trade fairs
- other
Internal:
- 'old' management
- R&D
- other

27 Who controls using which criteria the attainment of the goals envisaged by the changes in production?

D The Relationship to your Investor

Interview partner
Name, Date, Company, Position in the company, Responsibilities

1.1 Where there is vertical integration between you and your investor: how high is the procentual proportion of your total output that you sell directly to your investor?

1.2 How high is the proportion of total output that you sell to your other main customer, who is not your investor?

2.1 How would you describe the price of 'in-house-sales'?
- prices with profit margins which are typical of those obtained in this company
- prices with profit margins which are typical of our industrial sector
- prices with a narrow profit margin
- just or hardly cost covering prices

2.2 How would you describe the prices which you obtain for 'out-of house' sales?
- prices with profit margins which are typical of those obtained in this company
- prices with profit margins which are typical of our industrial sector
- prices with a narrow profit margin
- just or hardly cost covering prices

3 For the proportion of your output that you sell out of house, how is the pricing decision made?

4 How binding are quality control requirements demanded a) by your investor b) by your other main customer?
- absolutely binding?
- relatively binding?
- have the proposal nature?

5 What happens if the quality control procedures which have been suggested by a) your investor and b) by your other main customer are not implemented?
- the requested procedures are implemented
- nothing
- the dissolution of the business contact might be threatened
- we have to expect the loss of the contract
- other

6 How frequently are there control inspections by a) your investor and b) your other main customer?

7 To the extent that there have been in the past disagreements over issues such as the interpretation of a contract or quality control issues, how have these been resolved in your judgement?
- a fair compromise was found
- the supplier had to make the main concessions
- the customer had to make the main compromise

8 Are there any tasks that you solve together with a) your investor b) your other main customer?
- R&D

- common investment into tools/machines
- common management of the stocks
- other

9 Should serious problems develop in your supply relationship with a) your investor b) your other main customer, how are these resolved?
- there is close co-operation and common problem solving
- the parties are allocated separate problem areas but there is co-operation
- there is rather sporadic communication concerning the most important matters
- everybody solves there problems, to the extent that this is possible separately

10 How strongly does a) your investor b) your other main customer take into consideration (not at all:1 → very strongly 6)
10.1 principles of fairness
10.2 ideas of far-reaching cooperation
10.3 your wishes and ideas

E Changes in human resource management (twice, one interview with the personnel manager and one with the trade union representative)

Interview partner
Name, Date, Company, Position in the company, Responsibilities

1 Number of employees in 1990, 1996, expectation for 2001 (2Pt = 1Ft)
Part-time
Full-time
Blue-collar
White-collar

2 Which percentage of your employees is unionised? (Not applicable in German companies.)

3 To which union do your employees belong?

4 Which are the main challenges which your company faces in its personnel policies?

5 How were the dismissals which became necessary in the context of restructuring handled?

6 In your opinion, do the new production methods which have been introduced since FDI (or, were applicable after 1990) higher equally or less qualified personnel?

7.1 Which further training became necessary as a consequence of the changes in production?
7.2 Who has provided and financed this training?
7.3 Which importance does your company ascribe to further training?
- unimportant
- secondary, but not unimportant
- very important but time constraints ( ) or financial consideration ( ) hardly make it possible for us to provide our workforce with additional training
- very important, and even though we face the above problems, we make it possible for employees to occasionally visit courses etc.
- very important, and we make sure that each employee receives further training

7.4 How company specific are the skills acquired through this further training?

8.1 Have you introduced new forms of work organisation?
- quality control groups
- job rotation
- job enrichment
- flexible working hours
- project groups
- other

8.2 Why have you introduced the changes in 8.1
8.3 Are there any forms of work organisation which you have abandoned?
8.4 Why did you stop the forms in 8.3?
8.5 How has labour productivity developed?

9.1 Are there any (*übertarifliche Sozialleistungen*) social services which are provided by your company over and above those incorporated into the *Tarifvertrag*?
9.2 If yes, which are these?

9.3 Which social services have been stopped since FDI?

10.1 Are there demands on the side of the employees concerning:
- company social services
- personnel policies
- involvement in the introduction of new technologies/production methods
- work load
- work organisation
- other

10.2 In case there are demands, do you think that they are justified? (1 very justified → 6 unjustified)

10.3 If you think that the demands in 10.1 are rather unjustified, what do you think they are due to (1 entirely, 2 partly)
- the interests of individual employees
- the policies of the trade union representative
- dissatisfaction with the work
- bad company climate
- good company climate
- political interests
- illusions
- other

11 Please try to characterise your company (1 agree → 6 do not agree)

Our company

1.1 uses conservative and traditional management principles

1.2 uses modern organisational approaches

2 interprets itself as the social community of the workforce

3 sees employees mainly from the perspective of economically rational human capital usage

4.1 attempts to enhance the independence of employees

4.2 limits the independence of the employees in the interest of clearly defined areas of responsibility

In our company

5.1 conflicts are seen as avoidable

5.2 conflicts are seen as necessary for finding and implementing real solutions to problems

6.1 we view the *Betriebrat* as a legal requirement but a disturbance

6.2 we view the trade union representative as an important Partner in decisions concerning our company

F The Regional Effects of FDI: Structural Changes

1 How important are the following regional characteristics for the success of your company? (large, small, insignificant)
- availability of a highly qualified workforce
- availability of a cheap workforce
- proximity to the most important customers
- proximity to the most important input suppliers
- proximity to the suppliers of services needed by the company
- proximity to research institutions
- a competent local government
- a relatively well developed infrastructure in the region
- other

2 How important were the following regional characteristics for the investment decision of your investor? (large, small, insignificant)
- availability of a highly qualified workforce
- availability of a cheap workforce
- proximity to the most important customers
- proximity to the most important input suppliers
- proximity to the suppliers of services needed by the company
- proximity to research institutions
- a competent local government
- a relatively well developed infrastructure in the region
- other

3 How has the geographical distribution of your input suppliers changed? (Please give approximate percentages, 1990, 1996, 2001)
- Berlin/Brandenburg area
- East Germany
- West Germany
- Eastern Europe
- EU
- other

4 How high is the proportion of standardised merchandise (catalogue listed products) in your entire input demanded?

5 From where do you primarily procure such standardised products? (primary source/ secondary source)
- Berlin/ Brandenburg area
- East Germany
- West Germany
- Eastern Europe
- EU
- other

6 According to which criteria have you changed (indicate nature of the change) your position of the vertical chain? (primarily, secondarily, unimportant)
- costs
- capacity utilisation
- know-how
- flexibility

7.1 How high is the proportion of 'old' suppliers (those which whom you were in contact before your investor approached you) in relation to the total number of suppliers?
- standard products_____%
- customised products________%

7.2 How high is the proportion of suppliers which also belong to your investor?
- standard products_____%
- customised products________%

8 Which were the main reasons to maintain your contact with the 'old' suppliers? (primarily, secondarily, unimportant)
- price
- quality
- proximity
- good experiences in the past
- willingness to cater for special requests

9 According to which criteria do you choose your new suppliers? (primarily, secondarily, unimportant)
- price
- quality
- existence of quality control processes
- punctuality
- belonging to the same conglomerate
- other

10 What were the main reasons why you have stopped using certain old suppliers?

11 Do you think that there is a difference between suppliers located in East Germany and those located in West Germany?

12 How do you think your supply arrangements will develop in the next 3 to 5 years?

G The Relationship to your Suppliers

1.1 How frequently do you evaluate your suppliers according to a set routine?
1.2 Which factors do you consider in your evaluation?
- punctuality
- proportion of faulty supplies
- quality standard of the products supplied
- quality control procedures
- other

2.1 What kind of agreements do you have with your suppliers concerning quality purchased?
- a fixed number of units
- binding quantity agreements
- minimum number of units/ quantity
- other

2.2 (1 agree → 6 disagree) We take into consideration the need of our suppliers for stable and continuous orders.

3 How long are your contracts with suppliers normally?

4 What are the main reasons for this time-frame?

5 Are there any tasks which you solve together with your suppliers? (frequently, seldom, never)
- R&D
- common investment into tools/ machinery
- common stock management
- other

6 With which arguments do you try to get your suppliers to make maximal concessions?
- buying at the competitors
- stopping the supply relationship
- situation in the final market
- other

7 To the extent that there have been disagreements between you and a supplier concerning the interpretation of, for example, the supply contract or the implementation of quality control processes, how would you describe the resolution of these differences? (1 applies → 6 does not apply)
- we have found a fair compromise
- the supplier had to make the largest concessions
- the customer (we) had to make the main concessions

8 Should serious problems develop in your supply relationship with one of your suppliers, how are these resolved?
- there is close co-operation and common problem solving
- the parties are allocated separate problem areas but there is co-operation
- there is rather sporadic communication concerning the most important matters
- everybody solves there problems, to the extent that this is possible separately

9 How strongly do your suppliers take into consideration (1 very strongly → 6 not at all)

9.1 principles of fairness
9.2 ideas of fair-reaching co-operation
9.3 your wishes and ideas

9.4 I trust my suppliers not to take advantage of my company should the opportunity arise. (1 very strongly → not at all)

9.5 Our suppliers trust my company not to take advantage of them should the possibility arise (1 very strongly → 6 not at all)

10 We keep to agreements with our suppliers because (1 agree → 6 do not at all agree)

10.1 We are contractually bound

10.2 We would like to maintain the business relationship with our suppliers in the future

10.3 We are concerned about our reputation with other companies

10.4 This is the common practice in our industrial sector

10.5 Personal friendship with the suppliers leads me to keep to agreements

10.6 Personal honour (I always keep my promises) motivates me to keep to agreements

11 Why do you think your suppliers keep to agreements with you? (1 agree → 6 do not at all agree)

11.1 They are contractually bound

11.2 They would like to maintain the business relationship with us in the future

11.3 They are concerned about their reputation with other companies

11.4 This is the common practice in their industrial sector

11.5 Personal friendship with us leads them to keep to agreements

11.6 Personal honour (I always keep my promises) motivates them to keep to agreements

12 What characterises in your judgement a successful relationship with a supplier?

13 What determines the success of a business relationship with a supplier? (1 agree → 6 do not at all agree)

- our willingness to cater for extra-contractual requests of our suppliers is important
- our supplier's willingness to cater for our extra-contractual requests is important
- mutual co-operation is important
- mutual trust is important

- personal contact is important
- a prompt payment of the inputs bought by us is important
- mutual information concerning technological developments is important
- it is very important that our supplier informs us about reductions in his raw material costs

Note

1 In designing this questionnaire I am deeply indebted to Professor Gernot Grabher and Professor Bruce Lyons.

Appendix B

The Statistical Questions Involved[1]

Throughout I examine whether the variables collected in the case studies yield any statistically significant associations, that is whether I can detect ant statistical regularities in may data. I am fully aware that I have a rather small number of observations for such an enterprise. The first thing to stress is that throughout I do not generalise to entire populations. I do not, for example, claim that *all* Hungarian companies behave in a certain way. Rather on the basis of the statistical regularities which hold for met data set only I generalise to theoretical propositions. Nevertheless even the use of small-sample significance tests cannot fully eliminate the problems posed by the small number of observations. Consequently especially associations of a 10 per cent significance levels should be treated with some care and they should not serve as the basis for any strong conclusions. Rather they indicate fruitful avenues for future research benefiting from a larger data set.

What I am interested in my study is a) the existence of an association, b) its direction and c) its statistical significance, but *not* in assigning a precise numerical value to the association in order to give it an economic interpretation. All the correlations reported in the relevant tables were obtained using Excel.[2]

1 For testing the significance of an association between two dummy variables a chi-square test of independence using contingency tables is used.[3] Chi-square tests are non-parametric and require no assumption about the exact shape of the population distribution. The null hypothesis is that the two variables are independent, which is another way of saying that there is no association between them. The null hypothesis can be rejected if X^2 (obtained/corrected) > X^2 (critical) and in this case the association between the two dummies is unlikely to have been generated by chance alone.

In the cases where the data set is large enough to generate expected frequencies of more than 5 in each cell in the relevant contingency table the following formula is used:

$$X^2 \text{ (obtained)} = \Sigma (f_o - f_e)^2 / f_e$$

The degrees of freedom of this X^2 test statistic is given by the formula:

$$df = (r - 1) \bullet (c-1),$$

where (r-1) is the number of rows in the contingency table minus one and (c-1) is the number of columns minus one. For two-times-two tables where the expected frequency in at least one cell is less than five, the above formula is modified by applying Yate's correction for continuity:

$$X^2 \text{ (corrected)} = \Sigma (|f_o - f_e| - 0.5)^2 / f_e .$$

A two-times-two table always has one degree of freedom regardless of the number of cases in the sample.

2 When testing the significance of the correlation between a dummy and a continuous variable a t-test is used which tests whether the differences in the means of the two data subgroups (of the continuous variable) generated by the dummy are significant or not. This test is appropriate for small sample sizes, especially when the population standard deviation is unknown. However, when using t-tests in general, one has to assume that one is dealing with independent random samples, the level of measurement is the interval ratio, the two samples have equal population variances and the sampling distribution is normal.[4] The null hypothesis is that the means of the two sub-samples are identical, that is $\mu_1 - \mu_2 = 0$. If one can reject the null because t (obtained) > t (critical) we can conclude that the differences between the means of the two (continuous variable) subgroups generated by the dummy are significant and that therefore the correlation between the dummy and the continuous variables is significant. The relevant test statistic for differences in means of small samples is:

$$t = \mu_1 - \mu_2 - \delta / \sqrt{} [\{(n_1 - 1) s_1{}^2 + (n_2 - 1) s_2{}^2 / n_1 + n_2 - 2\} \bullet (1/n_1 + 1/n_2)].$$ [5]

This statistic has $n_1 + n_2 - 2$ degrees of freedom.

3 When testing for the significance of the correlation between two continuous variables we again use a small sample t-test.[6] As before, this assumes random sampling, that the level of measurement is the interval ratio and that both variables are normally distributed. In addition, this t-test also assumes that the relationship between the two variables is roughly linear in form and fulfils the assumption of homoscedasticity, that is that the errors, u_i in a given bivariate regression (this is what correlations effectively are) have a common variance. Differently formulated, homoscedasticity requires that the variance of the scores for variable *Y* are uniform for all values of *X*. For our purposes the visual inspection of a scattergram should usually be sufficient to appraise the extent to which the relationship at hand conforms to the assumption of homoscedasticity. The null hypothesis tested is that $\rho = 0$. If we can reject the null [*t* (obtained) > *t* (critical)], this indicates that the correlation between the two variables at hand is significant.

The formula for the relevant t-statistic is:

$$t = [r \bullet \sqrt{(n-2)}] / \sqrt{(1-r^2)},$$

where r is the correlation coefficient for the two variables at hand and n is the number of (pairs of) observations. This t-statistic has n-2 degrees of freedom.

Notes

1 I would like to thank Dr Dennis Leach for his help in statistical matters. This section is based on *Statistics* by Joseph F. Healy, 4th edition, Wadsworth Publishing Company, 1996, *Modern Elementary Statistics* by John E. Freund, 7th edition, Prentice-Hall, 1988 and *Statistics for Business and Economics* by Paul Newbold, 3rd edition, Prentice-Hall, 1991.

2 The correlation coefficients are all based on Pearson's *r*, which is essentially a measure of a linear association between two interval-ratio variables. However, my data also contains associations involving dummies (qualitative variables which are measured at the nominal level). I find that firstly, nominal based measures of association such as LAMBDA and PHI yield similar numerical values as those obtained from Excel. Secondly, even if I used nominal rather than the interval ratio based measures of association, the numerical values obtained could not be given a precise economic interpretation in my study. For the purposes of hypothesis testing I treat the discrete variables in my data set as continuous ones.

3 The same approach was used for testing the hypothesis that the observations for two country-specific dummies can be pooled, that is when examining whether there are significant country-specific differences in the data set.

4 It is worth noting that in this case these assumptions apply to the sample means which are the objects of our tests, not the series of dummies which have generated the means in the first place.

5 The most general formulation of the null hypothesis is that $\mu_1 - \mu_2 = \delta$. If we are, as in my case, testing the null that $\mu_1 - \mu_å = 0$, then $\delta = 0$ in the above formula. n_1 and n_2 are the

number of observations in sub-sample one and two respectively. This test (rather than the appropriate *z* test) is used when, as in my case, $n_1 < 30$ or $n_2 < 30$. s_1^2 and s_2^2 are the sample variance of sub-sample one and two respectively. They are in each case calculated using the formula: $s_i^2 = \Sigma (x - \mu_i)^2 / (n_i - 1)$, where x is an individual observation in sample i, μ_i is its mean and n_i is the number of observations in i.

6 This test was also used when I explored whether there are significant differences between the means of two country-specific continuous variables.

Appendix C

Data and Tables for Chapter 3

Table 3.1a Vertical integration in the East German companies before 1990[1]

Co.	*Bilanzierung*[2]	Investment	Personnel planning[2]	Product development	Process development	Input procurement	Maintenance	Distribution	Transportation
D1	I, K	I, K	I	I (very small scale)	I (very small scale)	I	I, K	N.A, was incorporated into the plan	I
D2	I	I	I	I	I	I	I	N.A	I
D3	I, K	I, K	I	I	I	I	I	I	I
D4	I	I	I	I	I	I	I	I	I
D5	I	I	I	I	I	I	I	I	I
D6	I	I	I	I	I	I	I	I	I
D7	I	I	I	I	I	I	I	I	I
D8[3]	K	I, K	I, K	I, K	I, K	I	I, K	I, K	I
D9	I	I	I	I	I	I	I	I	I

Notes

1 Which function were catered for (I) directly in this company (in a separate internal division), (K) in other companies belonging to the same *Kombinat* or (E) bought from external sources?

2 *Bilanzierung* refers to checking whether production in the company is running according to the plan given from the ministry. *Bilanzierung* and Investment planning were specific to the previous economic system and thus do not have a narrowly corresponding activity in Table 2a.

3 K in the case of company D8 effectively stands for conmpany D6, since company D6 was the *Stammbetrieb* of the *Kombinat* to which company D8 belonged as well.

Table 3.1b Vertical integration in the Hungarian companies before 1990*

Co.	*Bilanzierung*	Investment	Personnel planning	Product develop-ment	Process develop-ment	Input procure-ment	Mainten-ance	Distribution	Transport-ation
H1	I	I	I	I	I	I	I	I	I
H2	I, K	I	I	I	I	I	I	I	E
H3	K	I,K	I,K	K	I,K	I,K	I	I,K	K
H4	I	I	I	I	I	I	I	I	I
H5	I	I	I	I	I	I	I	I	I
H6	I	I	I	I	I	I	I	I	I
H7	I	I	I	I	I	I	I	I	I
H8	I	I	I	I	I	I	I	I	I
H9	K	I, K	I	I	I	I	I	I, K	I
H10	I	I	I	I	I	I	I	I	I
H11	I, (plus central plans)	I, (plus central plans)	I	I	I	I	I	I	I

Note

* See footnotes to Table 3.1a

Table 3.2a Vertical integration in the East German companies in 1996[1]

Co.	Personnel	Design[2]	Quality control	R&D	Procurement	Maintenance	Sales[3]	Transportation	Marketing[4]	Customer services	Computing facilities
D1	I	INV	I	None	I	E (sub)	I	E (sub)	I	quality guarantees	I
D2	I	None	I	None	I	E	None	I (logistics),E	word of mouth	quality guarantees	I
D3	I	None	I	None	I	I,E	I	I (logistics),E	I	no separate department	I
D4	I	INV	I	INV	INV	I	I	E	I	I	I, INV
D5	I	I, INV	I	I, INV	I	I	I	I (logistics),E	I	I	I
D6[5]	I	I	I	I, E	I	N.A	I	N.A	I	quality guarantees	I
D7	I	E	I	E	I	E (sub), I	I	E (sub)	I,E	none	I,E
D8	I	I, INV	I	I, INV	I	E (sub)	I	E (sub)	I	I	INV, E
D9	I	None	I	I, INV	I	I	I	I, E	I, E	I	I, INV

Notes

1 Which activities are at the moment being (I) internally supplied, (INV) supplied by the investor or are being (E) bought from external sources? E(sub) stands for independent external companies which are effectively subsidiaries of the company being interviewed, in the sense that these suppliers have been originally separated out from their customer and still maintain close ties with him, frequently including ownership ties.
2 Design, Quality control and R&D correspond to Product and Process developement in Table 3.1a.
3 Sales corresponds to Distribution in Table 3.1a.
4 Customers services, Marketing and highly developed Computing facilities can be all seen as 'new activities' with no equivalent entries in Table 3.1a.
5 This company does not currently have an investor.

Table 3.2b Vertical integration in the Hungarian companies in 1996/7*

Co.	Personnel	Design[2]	Quality control	R&D	Procurement	Maintenance	Sales[3]	Transportation	Marketing[4]	Customer services	Computing facilities
H1	I	I	I	I	I	I, E(sub)	I	I (raw materials), E (final products)	I	I	I, E
H2	INV	(I), E	I, INV	I, INV	(I), INV	I, E	INV	E	INV	INV	INV
H3	I	I, (INV)	I, (INV)	I, INV	I, INV	I, E (sub)	I., (INV)	E (sub)	I, (INV)	I	I
H4	I	I	I	I, INV	I, INV	I, E (sub)	I, INV (export)	E (sub)	I,) (INV	I	I, INV
H5	I	I	I	E (buy licenses)	I	(I), E (sub)	I	I, E (sub)	I	I	I
H6	I	I	I	I, E	I	I, E (sub)	I	E (sub)	I	I	I, E
H7	I	I, (INV)	I	I	I, INV	I	I	I, (INV)	I, INV	I	I
H8	I	I	I	I	I	I	I	E (sub)	I	I	I
H9	I	I, INV	I	I	I	I	I	I	I	I	I
H10	I	I	I, E	I, INV, E	I	I, INV, E	I	E	I	I	E
H11	I	I	I – subsidiary	I, E	I, universities	I – subsidiary	I	I	I	I – subsidiary	I

Note

* See footnotes to Table 3.1b

Table 3.3 List of variables summarising changes in physical and functional vertical integration

D π95	1 if the company is profitable in 1995, 0 otherwise
D π97	1 if the company is profitable in 1995 (97), 0 otherwise
H π96	1 if the company is profitable in 1995, 0 otherwise
D(H) size 90	Number of employees in 1990
D(H) size 96(7)	Number of employees in 1996/7, employees working for partially owned subsidiaries which have been separated out are not included
D (H) ancill	1 if the company has separated out ancillary services into new companies, 0 otherwise
D(H) standard	Percentage of total inputs which are standardised and obtainable, for example, from catalogues. This variable captures the extent to which the company in question procures a homogenous products with a low asset specificity
D(H) opport	Do you think that your suppliers would use an unforeseen eventuality to their advantage, that is are your suppliers opportunistic? (1, the supplier is not at all opportunistic → 6, the supplier is highly opportunistic)
H Pnew(vert)	Number of major vertical products which have been newly introduced[1]
D (H)Pclosed (vert)	Number of major product groups which have been closed down and where the closure constitutes a reduction in vertical integration
H Δ pvertint	H Pnew (vert) minus H Pclosed (vert): this variable captures the net effect on physical vertical integration of the closure of (vertical) product lines and the introduction of new ones[2]
D90 internal	Number of functions (out of a maximum of 9) which were catered for internally in 1990
D90 kombinat	Number of functions (out of a maximum of 9) which were catered for by other companies belonging to the same conglomerate (*Kombinat*) in 1990

H 90 external	Number of functions (out of a maximum of 9) which are subcontracted out to suppliers external to the conglomerate in 1990[3]
D (H)96(7) internal	Number of functions (out of a maximum of 11) which are catered for internally in 1996
D (H)96(7) investor	Number of functions (out of a maximum of 11) which are catered for by the investor (that is other companies in the acquiring conglomerate) in 1996
D (H) 96(7) subcontr	Number of functions (out of a maximum of 11) which are subcontracted out to suppliers which originally belonged to the company being interviewed and maintain close ties with it in 1996
D (H)96(7) external	The number of functions (out of a maximum of 11) which are subcontracted out to external suppliers in 1996 (7)
D (H)%90out	Percentage of functions (9=100%) which were catered for by outside units (that is other companies in the *Kombinat*)
D(H)%96(7) out	Percentage of functions (11=100%) which were catered for by outside units (that is by the investor, separated-out companies or external suppliers)
D(H)%Δ fvertint	D(H) %96(7)out minus D(H) %90out: this variable captures the net change in functional vertical integration (as a percentage of total functions which are catered for by external units) between 1990 and 1996 (7)
D (H)FDI	1 if the company has a foreign direct investor, 0 otherwise
D (H)IMPPR	1 if the investor was the most important force in determining changes in the product range 0.5 if the investor and the company's 'old' management had roughly the same influence 0 if the 'old' management was the main force in determining changes in the product range

Notes

1 In the German data set no new products have been introduced which constituted an increase in the vertical integration of the company. Consequently this variable is zero for all companies in the German data set and has not been included there.

2 Since no East German company has introduced any new vertical products the net change of physical vertical integration in East Germany is captured by D Pclosed (vert).

3 In East Germany in 1990 no functions were supplied by companies which did not at least belong to the same conglomerate (see Table 3.1a). Consequently this variable is zero for all companies in the German data set and has not been included there.

Table 3.4a Summary of the East German data on changes in physical and functional vertical integration

	D1	D2	D3	D4	D5	D6	D7	D8	D9	mean
Dπ95	1	1	0	0	1	0	1	0	0	0.44
Dπ97	1	1	0	1	1	0	1	1	1	0.77
Dsize90	2000	330	2021	9500	2700	6500	6800	4500	3000	4150
Dsize96	600	248	270	722	1033	320	800	500	700	577
D ancill	1	0	0	1	1	0	1	1	1	0.66
D standard	75	99	100	100	80	0	90	10	30	65
D oppor	2	1	3	2	3	6	2	6	3	3.11
D pclosed (vert)	0	0	0	1	1	0	1	0	0	0.33
D90 internal	6.5	8	8	9	9	9	9	5	9	8.5
D90 kombinat	1.5	0	1	0	0	0	0	4	0	0.72
D96 internal	6.5	5	7	6.5	9.5	8	5.5	7	8	7
D96 investor	1	0	0	3.5	1	0	0	1.5	1	0.88
D96 subcontr	2	0	0	0	0	0	1.5	2	0	0.38
D96 external	0	1.5	1	1	0.5	0.5	3	0.5	1	1.2
D% 90out	16	0	11	0	0	0	0	44	0	7.8
D% 96out	27.2	13.6	9	40.9	13.6	4.5	40.9	36	18.1	22.5
D% Δ fvertint	10.6	13.6	-3	40.9	13.6	4.5	40.9	-8	18.1	14.5
DFDI	1	1	1	1	1	0	0	1	1	0.77
DIMPPR	0	0	0	1	0.5	0	0	0.5	1	0.33

Table 3.4b Summary of the Hungarian data on changes in vertical integration and in the companies' horizontal product range

	H1	H2	H3	H4	H5	H6	H7	H8	H9	H10	H11	Mean
Hπ96	1	0	0	1	1	0	1	1	0	0	1	0.58
H size 90	2100	2400	2500	4500	5000	10500	14297	1000	450	650	40000	4430 excl.H11 7663incl.H11
H size 97	640	1396	800	2550	3500	3200	9952	580	100	250	14500	2270 excl.H11 3406incl.H11150
Hancill	1	0	1	1	1	1	1	1	0	0	1	0.75
H standard	100	90	100	90	100	65	10	100	80	100	100	85
H oppor	6	5	2	5	2	5	3	2	4	3	3	3.6
Hpclosed(vert)	0	0	0	0	0	0	0	0	0	1	0	0.08
Hpnew(vert)	0	0	0	0	1	0	1	0	0	1	0	0.25
HΔPvertint	0	0	0	0	1	0	1	0	0	0	0	0.16
H90internal	9	7.5	3.5	9	9	9	9	9	7	9	9	8.08
H90kombinat	0	0.5	5.5	0	0	0	0	0	2	0	0	0.75
H90External	0	1	0	0	0	0	0	0	0	0	0	0.16
H97Internal	9.5	2.5	6.5	7	9	8.5	9	10	10.5	6.66	10.5	8.18
H97 investor	0	6.5	3	2.5	0	0	2	0	0.5	0.66	0	1.26
H97subcontr	0.5	0	1.5	1.5	2	1.5	0	1	0	0	0	0.79
H97External	1	2	0	0	1	1	0	0	0	3.16	0.5	0.8
H%90out	0	5.5	61	0	0	0	0	0	22	0	0	8.35
H%97out	13.6	77.2	40.9	36.3	18.1	22.7	18.1	9.09	4.54	39.3	4.54	25.5
H%Δvertint	13.6	71.7	-20.5	36.3	18.1	22.7	18.1	9.09	-17.6	39.3	4.54	17.2
HIMPPR	0.5	1	0	0	0	0	1	0	1	1	0	0.45
HFDI	1	1	1	1	0	0	1	0	1	1	0	0.62

Table 3.5a Correlation matrix for the East German variables[1]

	Dπ95	Dπ97	D size90	D size96	D ancill	D stand	D oppor	Dp closed (vert)	D90 inter-nal	D90 komb-inat	D96 inter-nal	D96 inves-tor	D96 sub contr	D96 exter-nal	D% 90 out	D% 96 out	D% Δ fvertint	DFDI	D IMPPR
Dπ95	1.00	0.48	-0.39	0.33	0.16	**0.50 t**	**-0.60 t**	0.32	0.05	-0.24	-0.26	-0.32	0.27	0.27	-0.25	0.08	0.28	-0.06	-0.46
Dπ97		1.00	-0.02	0.60**t	**0.76**	0.21	-0.45	0.38	-0.18	0.09	-0.21	0.44	0.37	0.16	0.09	0.64**t	0.46	0.36	0.44
Dsize90			1.00	0.29	0.31	-0.13	0.24	**0.56 t**	0.30	-0.13	-0.01	**0.54 t**	0.02	0.24	-0.12	**0.55 t**	**0.57 t**	**-0.48 t**	0.36
Dsize96				1.00	0.84***t	0.14	-0.20	**0.77 t**	0.29	-0.20	0.43	0.41	0.11	0.11	-0.20	0.43	**0.54 t**	0.04	**0.50 t**
D ancill					1.00	-0.03	-0.09	**0.50 t**	-0.15	0.22	0.18	**0.59 t**	**0.49 t**	0.00	0.21	**0.73 t**	0.42	0.19	0.58
D standard						1.00	-0.87***t	0.48 t	0.27	-0.39	-0.43	0.08	-0.17	0.39	-0.39	0.18	**0.48 t**	0.28	-0.14
D oppor							1.00	-0.33	-0.33	**0.51 t**	**0.49 t**	-0.06	0.14	-0.41	**0.52 t**	-0.19	**-0.60 t**	-0.29	0.03

	D p closed (vert)	D90 internal	D90 kombinat	D96 internal	D96 investor	D96 subcontr	D96 external	D% 90out	D% 96out	D% D fvertint	DFDI	DIMPPR
D pclosed (vert)	1.00	**0.50 t**	-0.40	0.09	0.40	-0.09	0.43	-0.40	**0.49 t**	**0.76 t**	-0.19	0.29
D90 internal		1.00	**-0.95 t**	0.21	-0.07	**-0.74 t**	0.41	**-0.95 t**	-0.26	**0.61 t**	-0.38	0.17
D90 kombinat			1.00	-0.05	0.14	**0.70 t**	-0.37	**1.00 t**	0.31	**-0.62 t**	0.30	-0.04
D96 internal				1.00	0.10	-0.32	**-0.55 t**	-0.05	-0.43	-0.31	0.10	0.37
D96 investor					1.00	0.01	-0.28	0.14	**0.59 t**	0.36	0.44	**0.78 t**
D96 subcontr						1.00	0.00	**0.70 t**	**0.61 t**	-0.11	-0.08	-0.26
D96 external							1.00	-0.37	0.35	**0.62 t**	**-0.49 t**	-0.17
D% 90out								1.00	0.31	**-0.62 t**	0.30	-0.03
D% 96out									1.00	**0.56 t**	0.00	0.33
D% Δ fvertint										1.00	-0.27	0.31
DFDI											1.00	0.44
DIMPPR												1.00

Table 3.5b Correlation matrix for the Hungarian variables[2]

	Hπ96	H size 90	H size 97	Hancill	H standard	H oppor	HPclosed (vert)
Hπ96	1.00						
H size 90	0.35	1.00					
H size 97	0.47 *t	0.95	1.00				
Hancill	0.67 **nc	0.36	0.39	1.00			
H standard	-0.07	-0.15	-0.39	-0.12	1.00		
H oppor	-0.11	-0.12	-0.19	-0.16	-0.06	1.00	
HPclosed (vert)	-0.35	-0.20	-0.23	-0.52**t	0.18	-0.15	1.00

	Hπ96	H size 90	H size 97	Han cill	H stan dard	H oppor	HP (vert)	Hpnew closed (vert)	HΔ pvertint	H90 inter	H90 kombi	H90 exter	H97 inter	H97 inves	H97 subcon	H97 exter	H%90 out	H%97 out	H%Δ fvertint	H IMP PR	HFDI
Hpnew (vert)	0.15	-0.05	0.16	-0.08	-0.35	-0.43 *t	0.52 **t	1.00													
HΔ pvertint	0.43 *t	0.09 **t	0.35 ***t	0.29	-0.54	-0.39	-0.15	0.77	1.00												
H90 internal	0.55 **t	0.25	0.30	0.13	-0.17	0.25	0.16	0.31	0.24	1.00											
H90 komb	-0.49 *t	-0.23 ***t	-0.28	-0.04	0.16	-0.31	-0.14	-0.28	-0.21	-0.98	1.00										
H90 external	-0.35 **t	-0.15	-0.14	-0.52	0.06	0.32	-0.10	-0.19	-0.15	-0.13	-0.04	1.00									
H97 internal	0.49 *t	0.35 *t	0.33 ***t	0.43	-0.10	-0.22	-0.21	0.02	0.18	0.32	-0.18	-0.79	1.00								
H97 invest	-0.36 ***t	-0.22 ***t	-0.15	-0.37	-0.09	0.20	-0.12	-0.16	-0.09	-0.43	0.28	0.84	-0.89	1.00							
H97 subcon	0.15 **t	-0.25	-0.26	0.59	0.24	-0.19	-0.31	-0.05	0.17	-0.13	0.18	-0.31	0.03	-0.17	1.00						
H97 external	-0.42 *t	-0.18 **t	-0.24 ***t	-0.59 *t	0.27	0.17	0.77	0.38	-0.14	0.23	-0.31	0.39	-0.51	0.15	-0.29	1.00					
H%90 Out	-0.49 *t	-0.23 ***t	-0.28 ***t	-0.04	0.16	-0.31	-0.14	-0.28	-0.21	-0.98	1.00	-0.04	-0.18	0.28	0.18	-0.31	1.00				
H%97 Out	-0.49 *t	-0.35	-0.33	-0.43 *t	0.11	0.22	0.21	-0.02	-0.18	-0.32	0.18	0.79	-1.00 ***t	0.89 ***t	-0.03	0.51	0.18	1.00			
H%Δ fvertint	-0.05	-0.12	-0.07	-0.33	-0.03	0.41	0.28	0.18	0.01	0.45 *t	-0.58	0.69 ***t	-0.70 ***t	0.53 **t	-0.16	0.64 **t	-0.58 **t	0.70 ***t	1.00		
HIMPPR	-0.37	-0.27	-0.15	-0.77 **nc	-0.39	0.23	0.40	0.34	0.09	0.02	-0.09	0.40	-0.28	0.35	-0.78 ***t	0.42 *t	-0.09	0.28	0.30	1.00	
HFDI	-0.31	-0.45 *t	-0.35	-0.46	-0.18	0.35	0.24	0.04	-0.13	-0.38	0.34	0.24	-0.45 *t	0.54 **t	-0.40	0.13	0.34	0.45 *t	0.13	0.66 **nc	1.00

Notes to Tables 3.5a and b

1 In order to calculate the significance level of associations between two dummy variables contingency tables were used. A X^2 distribution with 1 degree of freedom has the following critical values: $X^2_{(critical\text{-}10\%)} = 2.7$, $X^2_{(critical\text{-}5\%)} = 3.84$, $X^2_{(critical\text{-}1\%)} = 6.63$. We find that the uncorrected X^2 statistic is significant at the 10% level for associations of 0.60 [$X^2 = 2.97$]. Consequently the association of 0.58 between DIMPPR and Dancill is insignificant (only significant at the 15% level). Associations of 0.71 are significant at the 5% level. Using uncorrected X^2 statistics ignores the fact due to the very small number of cases in my data set we will not fulfil the requirement of having at least five observations in each cell of the relevant contingency table. The association of 0.76 between Dancill and Dπ97 yields a corrected (4.17, merging 0.5 with 1 observations) and an uncorrected (9.07, for a X^2 distribution with two degrees of freedom) test statistic which are both significant at the 5% level. The significance levels reported in Table 3a refer to the uncorrected test statistics. Associations between a dummy and a continuous variable as well as those between two continuous variables are tested using small sample t-tests. The relevant t-statistics are: $t^7_{0.15} = 1.11$, $t^7_{0.10} = 1.41$, $t^7_{0.05} = 1.89$, $t^7_{0.01} = 2.99$. We find that in both cases all associations above 0.48 (t = 1.44) are significant at the 10% level, associations above 0.59 (t = 1.93) are significant at the 5% level and associations above 0.75 (t = 3.00) are significant at the 1% level.

2 In order to calculate the significance level of associations between two dummy variables contingency tables were used. A X^2 distribution with 1 degree of freedom has the following critical values: $X^2_{(critical\text{-}10\%)} = 2.7$, $X^2_{(critical\text{-}5\%)} = 3.84$, $X^2_{(critical\text{-}1\%)} = 6.63$. We find that the uncorrected X^2 statistic is insignificant for associations of -0.46 [$X^2 = 2.35$]. Associations of 0.66/67 are significant at the 5% level [$X^2 \approx 4.42$ uncorrected, insignificant corrected value]. Associations of -0.77 are significant at the 5% level [$X^2 = 5.19$, insignificant uncorrected value]. Using uncorrected X^2 statistics ignores the fact due to the very small number of cases in my data set we will not fulfil the requirement of having at least five observations in each cell of the relevant contingency table. Consequently any inferences drawn from uncorrected X^2 values should be interpreted with some care. Associations between a dummy and a continuous variable as well as those between two continuous variables are tested using small sample t-tests. The relevant t-statistics are: $t^9_{0.10} = 1.38$, $t^9_{0.05} = 1.83$, $t^9_{0.01} = 2.82$. We find that for both types of associations all correlation coefficients above 0.42 (t = 1.38) are significant at the 10% level, associations above 0.52 (t = 1.83) are significant at the 5% level and associations above 0.69 (t = 2.85) are significant at the 1% level.

Appendix D

Data and Tables for Chapter 4

Table 4.1 List of variables summarising the data on the internal provision of social services

D(H)FDI	1 if the company has a foreign direct investor, 0 otherwise
D(H)COOP	1 if the union co-operated in restructuring, 0 otherwise
D(H)SOCRES	1 if the company explicitly endorsed a socially responsible approach to labour shedding, 0 otherwise
D(H)LEAVING	percentage of employees leaving the company (1990 =100%)
D(H)UNEMP	percentage of employees (1990 = 100%) becoming unemployed
D(H)SOCIAL	1 if the level of social services in the company has stayed constant in real terms, 0 otherwise
DPROFIT95	1 if the company was profitable in 1995, 0 otherwise
DPROFIT97	1 if the company was profitable in 1997, 0 otherwise
HPROFIT96	1 if the company was profitable in 1996, 0 otherwise*
D(H)SIZE90	number of employees in 1990
D(H)SIZE96(97)	number of employees in 1996/7
D(H)BENNUM90	number of internally provided social services in 1990
D(H)BENNUM96(97)	number of internally provided social services in 1996/7
D(H)DELBEN	change in the number of benefits provided: D(H)BENNUM96/7 minus D(H)BENNUM90
HSOCIALINC	1 if in 1997 the level of social services has increased in real terms in the company, no East German company falls in this category

HSOCCONST	1 if in 1997 the level of social services has at least stayed constant in real terms in the company, no East German company falls in this category
HSOCREORG	1 if the delivery of the social services which the company continues to provide has been reorganised by 1997, no East German company falls in this category
D(H)MS90	market share of the East German (Hungarian) market in 1990
D(H)MS96(97)	market share of the East German (Hungarian) market in 1996/7
D(H)EXPORT96(97)	proportion of output exported worldwide or to the European Union in 1996/7

Note

* In 1997, when the Hungarian interviews were conducted, this was the latest available profit figure. The German profit figure for 1995 was obtained in the interviews conducted in 1996 and the one for 1997 was obtained in follow-up calls which were made in 1998 in order to update the East German data.

Table 4.2 List of the social services provided in 1990 and 1996/7

	Food		Childcare		Medical		Holiday		Commodity		Housing		Community	
	90	96/7	90	96/7	90	96/7	90	96/7	90	96/7	90	96/97[1]	90	96/7
D1	0	0	0	0	0	0	1	0	0	0	0	0	0	0
D2	0	0	0	0	0	0	0	0	0	0	0	0	0	0
D3	1	1	0	0	1	0	1	0	0	0	0	0	1	0
D4	1	1	1	0	1	0	1	0	0	0	0	0	1	0
D5	1	1	1	0	1	0	1	0	1	0	0	0	1	0
D6	0	0	1	0	1	0	1	1	1	1	0	0	1	1
D7	0	0	1	0	0	0	1	1	1	1	1	0	1	1
D8	1	0	1	0	1	0	1	0	1	0	0	0	0	0
D9	1	0	1	0	1	0	1	0	1	0	0	0	0	0
H1	1	1[2]	1	1[3]	1	1	1	1	1	1[4]	1	1	0	0
H2	1	1	1	1[5]	1	1	1	1	1	1	1	1[6]	1	1
H3	1	1	1	0	1	1	1	1	1	1	0	0	1	1
H4	1	1	1	1	1	1	1	1	1	1	1	1	1	1
H5	1	1	1	1	1	1	1	1	1	1	1	1	1	1
H6	1	1	1	1	1	1	1	1	1	1	1	1	1	1
H7	1	1	1	1	1	1	1	1	0	0	1	1	1	1
H8	0	1[7]	0	0	1	1	1	1	0	0	1	1	0	0
H9	1	0	0	0	0	0	1	1[8]	1	0	0	0	0	0
H10	1	0	0	0	0	0	1	1	1	1[9]	1	1	0	0
H11 [10]	1	1*	1	1*	1	1*	1	1	1	0	1	0	1	1
%D[11]	**55**	**33**	**66**	**0**	**66**	**0**	**88**	**22**	**55**	**22**	**11**	**0**	**55**	**22**
%H	**90**	**81**	**72**	**63**	**81**	**81**	**100**	**100**	**81**	**63**	**81**	**72**	**63**	**63**

Notes

1 Typically companies have closed their old dormitories and sold apartments they owned. What is not uncommon in 1997 is to give low interest loans to employees buying or building a house.
2 Employees of D1 had access to holiday facilities via their trade union.
3 The kindergarten has been given to the local government but maintains close links with H1 and is still fully operative.
4 H1 still gives Christmas and Easter presents, as well as money towards school books and transportation.
5 The kindergarten has been given to the local government but maintains close links with H2.
6 H2 is currently trying to sell the apartments it owns.
7 This company has scrapped no benefits but has reduced the extent of all of them.
8 Employees of H9 have access to their trade union's holiday camp.
9 Employees now only receive work clothes from H10.
10 H11 has extensively reorganised the provision of social services while maintaining their real value. The company has kept its holiday camp, arts' centres and hotels and has opened them up to outsiders. The PM claims that providing these benefits in kind to the employees rather than paying them higher wages to enable them to purchase them leads to tax savings on both the employees' and the employers side. However the company no longer provides medical services, childcare etc. Instead employees all get an equal per capital budget in the form of *vouchers* which they can use to purchase these service in the free market. The PM justifies this new arrangement that providing social services is not the task of the company in the first place. Apparently the workforce, after initial reluctance, now like this new system because it is *viewed as 'fairer and it gives them more choice'* (PM). The TUR points out that the budget for social service provision in the company is 5 billion HUF. The TUR would like to see an extension and fine-tuning of the voucher system. It should be noted that this extensive reorganisation in the provision of social benefits took place while the company was still predominantly state owned. Starred entries stand for services which are now provided in voucher form.
11 Percentage of German companies providing this service in 1990/96.

Table 4.3a East German data on the internal provision of social services

	D fdi	D coop	D socres	D leaving	D unemp	Dprofit 95	Dprofit 97	Dsize 90	Dsize 96	DDben num90	DDben num96	Ddel ben	Dms 90	Dms 96	Dexport 96
D1	1	1	1	70	45	1	1	2000	600	1	0	-1	100	3	0
D2	1	0.5	1	25	25	1	1	330	248	1	0	-1	100	10	0
D3	1	0	0	87	77	0	0	2021	270	5	1	-4	95	20	75
D4	1	1	1	92	60	0	1	9500	722	5	1	-4	100	20	75
D5	1	0	0	62	57	1	1	2700	1033	6	1	-5	10	2.6	15
D6	0	0	0	95	95	0	0	6500	320	5	3	-2	100	7.5	7
D7	0	1	1	88	28	1	1	6800	800	5	3	-2	100	4	0
D8	1	1	0	89	59	0	1	4500	500	5	0	-5	100	72.5	30
D9	1	1	1	78	40	0	1	3000	700	5	0	-5	100	0	95
mean	0.77	0.61	0.55	76	54	0.44	0.77	4150	577	4.2	1	-3.2	89	15.5	33

Table 4.3b Hungarian data on the internal provision of social services

	H fdi	H coop	H socres	H leaving	H unemp	Hprofit 96	Hsize 90	Hsize 97*	Hben num90	Hben num97	Hdel ben	Hsoc inc	Hsoc const	Hsoc reorg	Hms 90	Hms 97	Hexport 97
H1	1	1	1	70	60	1	2100	640	6	6	0	0	1	0	100	100	0
H2	1	1	1	52	52	0	2400	1396	7	7	0	1	1	1	90	80	0
H3	1	0	0	76	50	0	3400	800	6	5	-1	0	1	1	5	10	10
H4	1	1	1	56	49	1	4500	2750	7	7	0	1	1	0	75	25	38
H5a	0	1	1	30	0	1	5000	5100	7	7	0	0	1	0	78	78	42
H6	0	1	0	70	29	0	10500	7800	7	7	0	0	0	0	98	90	20
H7	1	1	1	30	14	1	14297	11952	6	6	0	0	1	0	78	85	87
H8	0	0	0	42	2	1	1000	940	3	4	1	1	1	0	45	60	6
H9	1	0	0	78	78	0	450	100	3	1	-2	0	0	0	5	3	0
H10	1	0	0	60	60	0	650	250	4	1	-3	0	0	0	25	5	0
H11	0	0	0	64	21	1	40000	14500	7	4	-3	0	1	1	100	85	15
Mean	0.63	0.54	0.45	57.1	37.7	0.54	4430 exc.H11 7663 inc.H11	3173 exc.H11 4203 inc.H11	5.72	5	0.72	0.27	0.72	0.27	60	56	20

Note

* This figure includes the employees which are now employed by newly founded independently run companies with which the parent company still has ownership ties. In organisational terms from the parent company's point of view these employees count as shed but not unemployed.

Table 4.4a Correlation matrix for the East German variables[1]

	Dfdi	Dcoop	Dsocres	Dleaving	Dunemp	Dprofit 95	Dprofit 97	Dsize90	Dsize96	Dben num90	Dben num96	Ddel ben	Dms90	Dms96	Dexport b96
Dfdi	1.00														
Dcoop	0.13	1.00													
Dsocres	0.06	0.71**nc	1.00												
Dleaving	-0.39	0.12	-0.30	1.00											
Dunemp	-0.19	-0.60**t	-0.76***t	0.59**t	1.00										
Dprofit95	-0.06	0.03	0.35	-0.64**t	-0.64**t	1.00									
Dprofit97	0.36	0.71**nc	0.60*nc	-0.38	-0.80***t	0.48*t	1.00								
Dsize90	-0.50*t	0.18	-0.01	0.66**t	0.33	-0.28	-0.07	1.00							
Dsize96	0.04	0.26	0.16	0.13	-0.29	0.33	0.60**t	0.23	1.00						
Dbennum90	-0.24	-0.24	-0.53*t	0.66**t	0.46	-0.50*t	-0.24	0.44	0.42	1.00					
Dbennum96	-0.93***t	-0.32	-0.19	0.48*t	0.35	0.00	-0.46	0.62**t	0.07	0.44	1.00				
Ddelben	-0.40	0.03	0.43	-0.37	-0.25	0.54*t	-0.07	-0.04	-0.41	-0.77***t	0.24	1.00			
Dms90	-0.20	0.50*t	0.42	0.23	-0.07	-0.38	-0.15	0.16	-0.62**t[2]	-0.37	0.00	0.40	1.00		
Dms96	0.25	0.22	-0.43	0.27	0.21	-0.45	0.04	0.19	-0.25	0.18	-0.28	-0.39	0.21	1.00	
Dexportb96	0.44	0.12	0.03	0.37	0.19	-0.73**t	-0.12	-0.01	0.03	0.43	-0.30	-0.68**t	0.15	0.10	1.00

Notes

1 In order to calculate the significance level of associations between two dummy variables contingency tables were used. A X^2 distribution with 1 degree of freedom has the following critical values: $X^2_{(critical\text{-}10\%)} = 2.7$, $X^2_{(critical\text{-}5\%)} = 3.84$, $X^2_{(critical\text{-}1\%)} = 6.63$. We find that the uncorrected X^2 statistic is significant at the 10% level for associations of 0.60 [$X^2 = 2.97$]. Associations of 0.71 are significant at the 5% level [$X^2 = 4.44$ dropping the 0.5 observation for Dsocres or $X^2 = 5.21$ assuming 0.5=1]. Using uncorrected X^2 statistics ignores the fact due to the very small number of cases in my data set we will not fulfil the requirement of having at least five observations in each cell of the relevant contingency table. If we allow for this by using Yate's correction for continuity, then we find that associations of 0.60 generate a corrected X^2 of 1.05 only and are hence insignificant. Associations of 0.71 yield a corrected test statistic of 2.26 which is significant at the 20% level only [$X^2_{(critical\text{-}20\%)} = 1.64$]. The significance levels reported in Table 3a refer to the uncorrected test statistics and should be therefore treated with some care. Associations between a dummy and a continuous variable as well as those between two continuous variables are tested using small sample t-tests. The relevant t-statistics are: $t^7_{0.15} = 1.11$, $t^7_{0.10} = 1.41$, $t^7_{0.05} = 1.89$, $t^7_{0.01} = 2.99$. We find that in both cases all associations above 0.48 (t = 1.44) are significant at the 10% level, associations above 0.59 (t= 1.93) are significant at the 5% level and associations above 0.75 (t = 3.00) are significant at the 1% level.

2 This result is entirely due to D5 who is an outlier both with respect to Dms90 and Dsize96 and is hence unlikely to reflect an underlying economic relationship.

Table 4.4b Correlation matrix for the Hungarian variables[1]

	Hfdi	Hcoop	Hsocres	Hleaving	Hunemp	Hprofit96	Hsize90	Hsize97	Hben num90	Hben num97	Hdel ben	Hsocinc	Hsoc const	Hsoc reorg	Hms90	Hms97	H export97
Hfdi	1.00																
Hcoop	0.07	1.00															
Hsocres	0.31	0.83***nc	1.00														
Hleaving	0.26	-0.39	-0.53**t	1.00													
Hunemp	0.76***t	-0.17	-0.10	0.75***t	1.00												
Hprofit96	-0.31	0.27	0.47*t	-0.57**t	-0.59**t	1.00											
Hsize90²	-0.44)	-0.12	-0.17	-0.02		-0.37	0.35	1.00									
	(-0.16	(0.58**t)	(0.28)	(-0.39)	(-0.48*t)	(0.22)											
Hsize97	-0.45	0.17	0.03	-0.30	-0.56	0.40	0.90	1.00									
	(-0.25)	(0.58**t)	(0.32)	(-0.53**t)	(-0.58**t)	(0.29)	(0.98***t)										
Hbennum90	-0.13	0.67**t		0.52**t	-0.13	-0.23	0.19	0.43	0.49	1.00							
							(0.51*t)	(0.45*t)									
Hbennum97	-0.17	0.84***t	0.67**t	-0.37	-0.41	0.34	0.06	0.26	0.81***t	1.00							
							(0.53**t)	(0.49*t)									
Hdelben	-0.13	0.62**t	0.52**t	-0.46*t	-0.42*t	0.34	-0.41	-0.16	0.18	0.72***t	1.00						
Hsocinc	0.04	0.15	0.26	-0.27	-0.08	0.15	-0.28	-0.32	-0.02	0.28	0.51*t	1.00					
Hsocconst	-0.04	0.26	0.56*nc	-0.46*t	-0.44*t	0.67**nc	0.21	0.19	0.42*t	0.56**t	0.45*t	0.38	1.00				
Hsocreorg	0.04	-0.26	-0.15	0.26	0.08	-0.26	0.41	0.17	0.37	0.09	-0.29	0.08	0.38	1.00			
Hms90	-0.36	0.71***t	0.53	-0.30	-0.39	0.49*t	0.47	0.56	0.72***t	0.70***t	0.33	0.11	0.36	0.03	1.00		
							(0.48*t)	(0.49*t)									
Hms97	-0.46*t	0.60**t	0.43	-0.38	-0.54**t	0.48*t	0.41	0.55	0.54**t	0.64**t	0.44*t	-0.02	0.40	0.03	0.89***t	1.00	
							(0.50*t)	(0.53**t)									
Hexport97	-0.03	0.49*t	0.48*t	-0.67**t	-0.54**t	0.49*t	0.26	0.61**t	0.36	0.43*t	0.30	-0.12	0.31	-0.27	0.28	0.28	1.00
							(0.84***t)										

Notes

1 In order to calculate the significance level of associations between two dummy variables contingency tables were used. A X^2 distribution with 1 degree of freedom has the following critical values: $X^2_{(critical\text{-}\ 10\%)} = 2.7$, $X^2_{(critical\text{-}\ 5\%)} = 3.84$, $X^2_{(critical\text{-}\ 1\%)} = 6.63$. We find that the uncorrected X^2 statistic is significant at the 10% level for associations of 0.56 [$X^2 = 3.3$]. Associations of 0.67 are significant at the 5% level [$X^2 = 4.94$]. Associations of 0.83 are significant at the 1% level [$X^2 = 7.2$]. Using uncorrected X^2 statistics ignores the fact due to the very small number of cases in my data set we will not fulfil the requirement of having at least five observations in each cell of the relevant contingency table. If we allow for this by using Yate's correction for continuity, then we find that associations of 0.56 generate a corrected

Table 4.4b cont'd

X^2 of 1.10 only and are hence insignificant. Associations of 0.67 yield a corrected test statistic of 2.37, which is significant at the 20% level only [$X^2_{(critical-20\%)} = 1.64$]. Associations of 0.83 generate a corrected test statistic of 3.91, which is significant at the 5% level. The significance levels reported in Table 3b refer to the uncorrected test statistics and should be therefore treated with some care. Associations between a dummy and a continuous variable as well as those between two continuous variables are tested using small sample t-tests. The relevant t-statistics are: $t^9_{0.10} = 1.38$, $t^9_{0.05} = 1.83$, $t^9_{0.01} = 2.82$. We find that for both types of associations all correlation coefficients above 0.42 ($t = 1.38$) are significant at the 10% level, associations above 0.52 ($t = 1.83$) are significant at the 5% level and associations above 0.69 ($t = 2.85$) are significant at the 1% level.

2 Values in parentheses indicates correlations obtained if H11 is excluded, which is a strong outlier with respect to size and is hence likely to bias the results obtained for Hsize90 and Hsize96.

Appendix E

Data and Tables for Chapter 5

Table 5.1 List of variables summarising the data on strategic restructuring

D(H)PRODCH	number of major product groups, both vertical and horizontal, which have been either closed down or have been newly introduced; this variable captures the overall restructuring activity with respect to the company's product range
D(H)PCLOSED (hor)	number of major horizontal product groups which have been closed down
D(H)PNEW (hor)	number of major new horizontal product groups which have been newly introduced
DΔhorint	H Pnew (hor) minus H Pclosed (hor): This variable captures the net effect on horizontal integration of the closure of (horizontal) product lines and the introduction of new ones
D(H)PRODMETH	number of new production methods which have been introduced since 1990: a given method is given the value of 1 if it was entirely new and 0.5 if its use has been significantly expanded
D(H)WORKORG	1 if the company introduced new methods of work organisation, 0 otherwise
D(H)INVS	accumulative investment between 1990 and 1996 divided by after tax sales for 1996
D(H)INVEST	accumulative investment between 1990 and 1996 in million DM
D(H)AGELIFE	average age of machinery divided by its expected technical lifetime; if there are several groups of machinery with differing average ages and lifetimes, then the overall

	figure is the average of these averages. Assume, for example, that there are two groups of machinery, G1 and G2, with a lifetime of L1 and L2 respectively. Then AGELIFE = (G1/ T1 + G2/ T2) /2. The smaller this number, the more up-to-date the machinery in a company
D(H)FDI	1 if the company has a foreign direct investor, 0 otherwise
D(H)IMPPR	1 if the investor was the most important force in determining changes in the product range; 0.5 if the investor and the company's 'old' management had roughly the same influence; 0 if the 'old' management was the main force in determining changes in the product range
D(H)IMPPM	1 if the investor was the most important force in determining changes in production methods; 0.5 if the investor and the company's 'old' management had roughly the same influence; 0 if the 'old' management was the main force in determining changes in production methods
D(H)KNOWH	sum of the areas in which more know-how is required; if interview partners placed particular emphasis on an area, then this area was counted twice
D (H)**96(7) investor**	number of functions (out of a maximum of 11) which are catered for by the investor (that is other companies in the acquiring conglomerate) in 1996
D(H)IMMT	1 if the investor was the main force in managerial training, 0 otherwise
D96%EGer	percentage of total inputs (physical and support services) procured in East Germany in 1996
H97%Hung	percentage of total inputs (physical and support services) procured in Hungary in 1997
D(H)%oldsup	percentage of current suppliers which pre-date 1990
D(H)Export 96(7) EurU	Percentage of the company's total output which was sold in the European Union – including West Germany – in 1996(7)
D(H)Δ Total Export	Total Export 96 minus Total Export 90: the increase (or decrease) in the company's overall export orientation since 1990

D profit 95	1 if the company is profitable in 1995, 0 otherwise
D profit 97	1 if the company is profitable in 1995 (97), 0 otherwise
H profit 96	1 if the company is profitable in 1995, 0 otherwise

Table 5.2 Functional integration with the investor in companies with FDI

Co.	Personnel	Design	Quality control	R&D	Procurement	Maintenance	Sales	Transportation	Marketing	Customer services	Computing facilities
D1	I	**INV**	I	None	I	E (sub)	I	E (sub)	I	quality guarantees	I
D2	I	None	I	None	I	E	None	I (logistics) E	word of mouth	quality guarantees	I
D3	I	None	I	None	I	I,E	I	I (logistics) E	I	no separate department	I
D4	I	**INV**	I	**INV**	**INV**	I	I	E	I	I	I, **INV**
D5	I	I, **INV**	I	I, **INV**	I	I	I	I (logistics) E	I	I	I
D8	I	I, **INV**	I	I, **INV**	I	E (sub)	I	E (sub)	I	I	**INV**, E
D9	I	None	I	I, **INV**	I	I	I	I, E	I, E	I	I, **INV**
Proportion	0	4/9	0	4/9	1/9	0	0	0	0	0	1/3
H1	I	I	I	I	I	I, E(sub)	I	I, E	I	I	I, E
H2	**INV**	(I), E	I, **INV**	I, **INV**	(I), **INV**	I, E	**INV**	E	**INV**	**INV**	**INV**
H3	I	I, (**INV**)	I, (**INV**)	I, **INV**	I, **INV**	I, E (sub)	I., (**INV**)	E (sub)	I, (**INV**)	I	I
H4	I	I	I	I, **INV**	I, **INV**	I, E (sub)	I, **INV** export only	E (sub)	I, (**INV**)	I	I, **INV**
H7	I	I, (**INV**)	I	I	I, **INV**	I	I	I, (**INV**)	I, **INV**	I	I
H9	I	I, **INV**	I	I	I	I	I	I	I	I	I
Proportion	1/9	1/3	2/9	1/3	4/9	0	1/3	1/9	4/9	1/9	2/9

Table 5.3a Summary of the East German data on strategic restructuring

	D1	D2	D3	D4	D5	D6	D7	D8	D9	mean
DPRODCH	3	1	2	2	3	2	1	2	4	2.2
DPCLOSED (hor)	2	0	2	1	2	1	0	0	0	1.4
DPNEW (hor)	1	1	0	0	0	1	0	1	3	0.77
DΔ horint	-1	1	-2	-1	-2	0	0	0	3	-0.28
DPRODMETH	2	1	2	1	0	0	0	3.5	3	1.3
DWORKORG	1	1	0	1	1	0	1	1	1	0.77
DINVS	0.2	0.08	0.014	0.29	0.97	0	0.05	0.66	0.47	0.30
DINVEST	30	2.9	1.0	40	250	0	10	80	100	57.1
DAGELIFE	0.5	0.4	0.6	0.62	0.4	0.86	0.4	0.35	0.66	0.53
DFDI	1	1	1	1	1	0	0	1	1	0.77
DIMPPR	0	0	0	1	0.5	0	0	0.5	1	0.33
DIMPPM	1	0	0	1	0	0	0	0.5	0.5	0.33
DKNOWH	4	4	4	4	3	3.5	3	3.5	2	3.44
D96 investor	1	0	0	3.5	1	0	0	1.5	1	0.88
D IMMT	1	1	0	1	0	0	0	1	1	0.55
D96%Eger	50	50	0	30	0	80	100	30	5	38.5
D%oldsup	8	5	0	70	35	80	17	35	2	28.0
Dexport 96(West)	0	0	75	75	15	7	0	30	95	33.0
DΔ total export	0	0	55	50	10	-20	0	20	95	23.2
DPROFIT 95	1	1	0	0	1	0	1	0	0	0.44
DPROFIT 97	1	1	0	1	1	0	1	1	1	0.77

Table 5.3b Summary of the Hungarian data on strategic restructuring

	H1	H2[1]	H3	H4	H5	H6	H7	H8	H9	H10	H11	mean
HPRODCH	1	3*	1	2	2	0	4	0	1	2	0	1.45
HPCLOSED (hor)	1	2*	1	1	1	0	3	0	0	0	0	0.81
HPNEW (hor)	0	1*	0	1	0	0	0	0	1	0	0	0.27
HΔ horint	-1	-1	-1	0	-1	0	-3	0	1	0	0	-0.54
HPRODMETH	3	2*	5.5	5	0	1.5	6.5	4.5	3	3	4	3.45
HWORKORG	0	1	0	0	1	0	1	0	1	1	1	0.54
HINVS	0.1058	0.3609	0.7425	0.4490	0.3514	0.001[2]	1.083	0.964	0.001	0.1913	0.6684	0.44
HINVEST	30.9	48	75	119	≈ 200[3]	0.22	1170[4]	93.6	0.01	4.4	2780	411

	H1	H2	H3	H4	H5	H6	H7	H8	H9	H10	H11	H12
HAGELIFE	0.32	0.57	0.57	0.56	0.37	0.45	1	0.54	0.44	0.6	1.2	0.59
HFDI	1	1	1	1	0	0	1	0	1	1	0	0.62
HIMPPR	0.5	1	0	0	0	0	1	0	1	1	0	0.41
HIMPPM	0.5	1	1	0	0	0	0.5	0	1	0	0	0.36
HKNOWH	3	1	4	5	4	0	4	2	4	4	5	3.3
H97 investor	0	6.5	3	2.5	0	0	2	0	0.5	0.66	0	1.26
H IMMT	0	1	0	0	0	0	1	0	1	1	0	0.36
H96%Hung	98	30	35	30	80	70	60	10	20	100	20	50
H%oldsup	100	95	25	25	95	80	76	70	20	60	80	66
Hexport 96 (EurU)	0	0	10	15	30	5	45	6	0	0	15	11.45
HΔ total export	0	0	27	5	0	5	25	9	-5	-12	5	5.36
HPROFIT 96	1	0	0	1	1	0	1	1	0	0	1	0.58

Notes

1 All starred values only refer to the Budapest factory visited and do not include H2's factory in Northern Hungary. Consequently the starred values are likely to be biased downwards compared to those which would include both factories.

2 Both in the case of H6 and H9 interview partners could not give precise investment figures but indicated that overall investment levels had been minimal. I hence use this value as a proxy for minimal investment figures and then calculate the overall investment figure which would result in such a low investment over sales figure. Consequently, the values given for overall investment in these two companies are also to be interpreted as merely proxying minimal values.

3 This is a minimum estimate (and hence biased downwards). Investment has been fairly stable around 65.5 million DM in 1995, 1996 and 1997, the years for which data is obtainable. I arrive at my estimate for investment between 1990 and 1996 by adding up the investment figures for the two years (1995 and 1996) in this period for which data is available and assuming that investment between 1990 and 1994 was only at about 66 million DM, that is the yearly figure of later years. This approach is likely to bias the overall figure downwards. However, from the interviews my impression is that due to the uncertainty concerning the ownership and future of H5a before 1995 lead to far less investment taking place before 1995 than after. Consequently, assuming that the post 1995 trend of about 65.5 million DM per annum also held before the company's flotation (an assumption which would yield a total investment figure of 393 million DM) is likely to have such a strong bias upwards that I decided to use the lower estimate.

4 The investment figures for H7 and H8 were calculated using an exchange rate of 1.8 DM per 1US$.

Table 5.4a Correlation matrix for the East German variables

	DPRODCH	DPCLOSED (hor)	DPNEW (hor)	DD horint	DPROD METH	DWORK ORG	DINVS	DIN VEST	DAGE LIFE	DFDI PR	DIMP	DIMP PM
DPRODCH	1.00											
DPCLOSED (hor)	0.31	1.00										
DPNEW (hor)	0.59**t	-0.45	1.00									
DD horint	0.20	-0.79***t	0.87***t	1.00								
DPRODMETH	0.41	-0.22	0.56*t	0.35	1.00							
DWORKORG	0.13	-0.37	0.16	0.28	0.17	1.00						
DINVS	0.53*t	0.09	0.09	-0.09	0.20	0.50*t	1.00					
DINVEST	0.56*t	0.24	0.02	-0.15	-0.03	0.40	0.94***t	1.00				
DAGELIFE	0.27	0.18	0.28	0.16	-0.13	-0.67**t	-0.41	-0.31	1.00			
DFDI	0.42	0.24	0.16	-0.08	0.60**t	0.36	0.47	0.37	-0.33	1.00		
DIMPPR	0.54*t	-0.21	0.35	0.31	0.35	0.44	0.57*t	0.48*t	0.10	0.44	1.00	
DIMPPM	0.40	0.10	0.20	0.03	0.46	0.44	0.12	-0.04	0.05	0.44	0.50	1.00

	DPRO DCH	DPCL OSED (hor)	DP NEW (hor)	DD hor int	D PROD METH	D WORK ORG	D INVS	DINV EST	D AGE LIFE	DF DI	D IMP PR	D IMP PM	D KNOW	D96 inves tor	D IM MT	D96% EGer	D% old sup	Dexp ort 96 (West)	DΔ total export	D PRO FIT 95	D PRO FIT 97
D KNOWH	-0.54 *t	0.38	-0.59 **t	-0.60 **t	-0.11	-0.25	-0.42	0.49 *t	-0.07	0.16	-0.46	0.18	1.00								
D96 investor	0.25	0.05	-0.08	-0.12	0.22	0.44	0.40	0.25	0.00	0.44	0.78 **t	0.78 ***t	0.11	1.00							
D IMMT	0.22	-0.37	0.52 *t	0.47	0.64	0.60 **t	0.13	-0.10	-0.19	0.60 *nc	0.46	0.73 **t	0.10	0.53 *t	1.00						
D96% EGer	-0.61 **t	-0.37	-0.16	0.14	-0.48 *t	-0.03	-0.58 *t	-0.57 *t	0.05	-0.83 ***t	-0.53 *t	-0.14	0.14	0.14	-0.18	1.00					
D%oldsup	-0.13	0.05	-0.27	-0.22	-0.42	-0.23	0.06	0.03	0.46	-0.39	0.22	0.12	0.16	0.44	-0.16	0.27	1.00				
Dexport 96 (West)	0.47	-0.01	0.31	0.20	0.50 *t	-0.12	0.11	0.07	0.37	0.44	0.71 **t	0.29	-0.28	0.44	0.22	-0.67 **t	-0.08	1.00			
DΔ total export	0.54 *t	-0.10	0.43	0.33	0.58 *t	0.09	0.20	0.16	0.18	0.52 *t	0.72 **t	0.30	-0.42	0.37	0.32	-0.69 **t	-0.32	0.95 ***t	1.00		
D PROFIT 95	-0.22	0.11	-0.27	-0.17	-0.46	0.48 *t	0.06	0.19	-0.61 **t	-0.06	-0.46	-0.18	0.08	-0.32	-0.10	0.31	-0.37	-0.73 **t	-0.54 *t	1.00	
D PROFIT 97	0.13	-0.37	0.16	0.28	0.17	1.00 ***t	0.50 *t	0.40	-0.67 **t	0.36	0.44	0.44	-0.25	0.44	0.60 *nc	-0.03	-0.23	-0.12	0.09	0.48	1.00

Note

In order to calculate the significance level of associations between two dummy variables contingency tables were used. A X^2 distribution with 1 degree of freedom has the following critical values: $X^2_{(critical\text{-}10\%)} = 2.7$, $X^2_{(critical\text{-}5\%)} = 3.84$, $X^2_{(critical\text{-}1\%)} = 6.63$. The test statistics reported were all obtained by dropping, where appropriate, 0.5 observations. This was done since I have insufficient observations to justify larger than 2x2 tables. The significance levels reported in Table 4b are based on uncorrected test statistics. Unless otherwise stated in this footnote the test statistics obtained using Yate's correction for continuity were all insignificant. Using uncorrected X^2 statistics ignores the fact due to the very small number of cases in my data set we will not fulfil the requirement of having at least five observations in each cell of the relevant contingency table. Consequently any inferences drawn from uncorrected X^2 values, especially when they are based on simplifying assumptions as in this case, should be interpreted with some care.

We find that the uncorrected X^2 statistic is insignificant for associations of 0.50 [$X^2 \approx 2.25$, significant at the 15% level only]. Associations of 0.57 [$X^2 \approx 2.94$] are significant at the 10% level, associations of 0.64 [$X^2 \approx 4.7$] and 0.66 [$X^2 \approx 5.95$, still insignificant corrected value] are significant at the 5% level. Associations of 0.95 are significant at the 1% level [$X^2 \approx 10$, corrected value of 6.25 significant at the 5% level]. Associations between a dummy and a continuous variable as well as those between two continuous variables are tested using small sample t-tests. The relevant t-statistics are: $t^9_{0.10} = 1.38$, $t^9_{0.05} = 1.83$, $t^9_{0.01} = 2.82$. We find that for both types of associations all correlation coefficients above 0.42 (t = 1.38) are significant at the 10% level, associations above 0.52 (t = 1.83) are significant at the 5% level and associations above 0.69 (t = 2.85) are significant at the 1% level.

Table 5.4b Correlation matrix for the Hungarian variables

	HPROD CH	HPCLOS ED (hor)	HPNEW (hor)	HΔ Horint	HPROD METH	HWORK ORG	HINVS	HINV EST	HAGE LIFE	HFDI	HIMPPR	HIMPPM	HKNO WH	H97 investor	H IMMT
HPRODCH	1.00														
HPCLOSED (hor)	0.86***t	1.00													
HPNEW (hor)	0.27	0.12	1.00												
HΔ horint	-0.69***t	-0.89***t	0.34	1.00											
HPRODMETH	0.17	0.32	-0.04	-0.32	1.00										
HWORKORG	0.48*t	0.21	0.15	-0.13	-0.23	1.00									
HINVS	0.23	0.43*t	-0.30	-0.55**t	0.71***t	-0.01	1.00								
HINVEST	-0.09	0.04	-0.27	-0.16	0.29	0.39	0.44*t	1.00							
HAGELIFE	0.14	0.21	-0.19	-0.28	0.54	0.41	0.61**t	0.91	1.00						
HFDI	0.59**t	0.46*t	0.46*t	-0.23	0.40	0.07	-0.10	-0.33	-0.11	1.00					
HIMPPR	0.62**t	0.38	0.34	-0.21	0.05	0.60**t	-0.18	-0.15	0.05	0.66**nc	1.00				
HIMPPM	0.29	0.39	0.43*t	-0.17	0.17	0.13	-0.05	-0.24	-0.14	0.64**nc	0.50	1.00			
HKNOWH	0.17	0.03	0.02	-0.02	0.41	0.28	0.26	0.42*t	0.39	0.26	-0.03	-0.08	1.00		
H97 investor	0.58**t	0.61**t	0.57**t	-0.32	0.16	0.13	0.16	-0.18	0.06	0.54**t	0.35	0.60**t	-0.18	1.00	
H IMMT	0.64**t	0.35	0.39	-0.16	0.07	0.69***t	-0.08	-0.10	0.15	0.57*nc	0.95***nc	0.46	-0.01	0.40	1.00

	HPROD CH	HPCLO SED (hor)	HP NEW (hor)	HΔ Hor int	H PROD METH	H WORK ORG	H INVS EST	H INV	H AGE LIFE	H FDI	H IMP PR	H IMP PM	H KNOW H	H97 inves tor	H IMMT	H97% Hung	H% old sup	H export97 (EurU)	HD total export	HPRO FIT 96
H97%Hung	0.23	0.10	-0.47*t	-0.30	-0.38	0.05	-0.42*t	-0.26	-0.33	0.13	0.20	-0.25	-0.07	-0.29	0.05	1.00				
H%oldsup	0.10	0.24	-0.42*t	-0.41	-0.47*t	0.19	-0.02	0.20	0.04	-0.41	0.03	-0.27	-0.44*t	-0.07	-0.09	0.44*t	1.00			
Hexport 97 (EurU)	0.52+	0.61+	-0.29	-0.71+	0.30	0.28	0.61**t	0.42*t	0.46*t	-0.14	-0.09	-0.20	0.38	-0.05	-0.01	0.06	0.14	1.00		
HD total export	0.15	0.51+	-0.30	-0.62+	0.68**t	-0.31	0.75**t	0.22	0.37	0.04	-0.28	0.25	0.08	0.22	-0.23	-0.30	-0.17	0.56**t	1.00	
HPROFIT 96	0.04	0.21	-0.26	-0.32	0.23	-0.10	0.48*t	0.43*t	0.27	-0.31	-0.37	-0.50	0.40	-0.36	-0.45*t	-0.02	0.32	0.56**t	0.19	1.00

Note

Throughout scattergrams were obtained for all the major associations in order to check that they are not entirely due to outliers. If a scattergram is not reported it confirmed the significance of the association being examined.

Scattergram for Hinvest and Hagelife

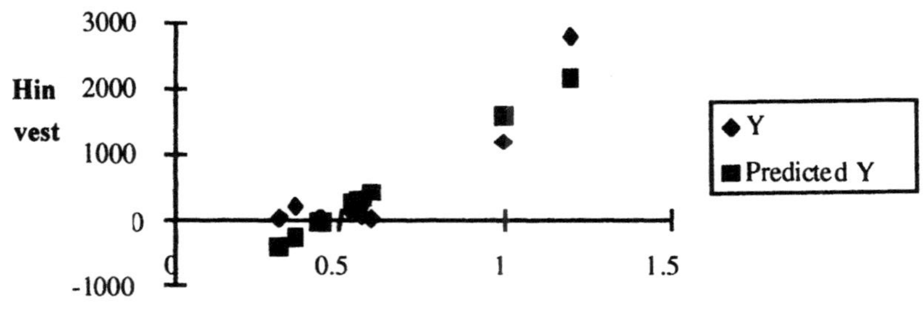

This highly counterintuitive association is entirely due to H11 and H7 who happen to be outliers both in terms of their total investment and the remaining life expectancy of their machinery. If these two companies are excluded we obtain a correlation coefficient of -0.12.

+ these associations are entirely due to H7, who is an outlier both in terms of its export performance as well as with respect to its overall reduction in horizontal integration. If this company is excluded we obtain correlation coefficients of -0.26 and 0.03 respectively.

Appendix F

Data and Tables for Chapter 6

Table 6.1 Data on changes in the geographical structure of supply relationships: the definition of the variables used

D90%Eger/ H90%Hung	percentage of total inputs (physical and support services) procured in East Germany/Hungary in 1990
D90%Wger	percentage of total inputs (physical and support services) procured in West Germany in 1990
D (H) 90%EEur	percentage of total inputs (physical and support services) procured in Eastern Europe in 1990
D90%EU	percentage of total inputs (physical and support services) procured in the European Union in 1990, excluding West Germany
H90%EU	percentage of total inputs (physical and support services) procured in the European Union in 1990, including West Germany
H90%WW	percentage of total inputs (physical and support services) procured worldwide in 1990, zero for all East German companies in 1990
D96%Eger/ H96%Hung	percentage of total inputs (physical and support services) procured in East Germany/ Hungary in 1996
D96%Wger	percentage of total inputs (physical and support services) procured in West Germany in 1996
D (H) 96%EEur	percentage of total inputs (physical and support services) procured in Eastern Europe in 1996
D96%EU	percentage of total inputs (physical and support services) procured in the European Union in 1996, excluding West Germany

H96%EU	percentage of total inputs (physical and support services) procured in the European Union in 1996, including West Germany
D96%WW	percentage of total inputs (physical and support services) procured worldwide Union in 1996
DΔEger	D96%EGer minus D90%EGer: the increase (or decrease) in the percentage of total inputs which are procured in East Germany
HΔHung	H96%Hung minus H90%Hung: the increase (or decrease) in the percentage of total inputs which are procured in Hungary
DΔWger	D96%WGer minus D90%WGer: the increase (or decrease) in the percentage of total inputs which are procured in West Germany
D (H) ΔEeur	D (H) 96%EEur minus D (H) 90%EEur: the increase (or decrease) in the percentage of total inputs which are procured in Eastern Europe
DΔEU	D96%EU minus D90%EU: the increase (or decrease) in the percentage of total inputs which are procured in the European Union, excluding West Germany
HΔEU	H96%EU minus H90%EU: the increase (or decrease) in the percentage of total inputs which are procured in the European Union, including West Germany
D (H) ΔWW	D (H) 96%WW minus D (H) 90%WW: the increase (or decrease) in the percentage of total inputs which are procured worldwide, since D90%WW is 0 for all companies DDWW equals D96%WW
D(H)%oldsup	percentage of current suppliers which pre-date 1990

Table 6.2a Hungarian data on changes in the geographical structure of supply relationships

	H1	H2	H3	H4	H5	H6	H7	H8	H9	H10	H11	mean	Significant differences between East German and Hungarian data?[1]
H90%Hung	100	0	20	40	80	75	50	30	80	100	25	54.5	Complete data set: YES Manufacturing only: NO
H90%Eeur	0	0	0	15	0	20	0	0	10	0	75	10.9	Complete data set: NO Manufacturing only: NO
H90%EU	0	15	60	40	20	5	40	70	10	0	0	23.6	Complete data set: YES Manufacturing only: NO
H90%WW	0	85	20	5	0	0	10	0	0	0	0	10.9	Complete data set: NO Manufacturing only NO
H96%Hung	98	30	35	30	80	70	60	10	20	100	20	50.2	Complete data set: NO Manufacturing only: YES
H96%Eeur	2	5	0	10	0	10	0	0	60	0	78	15	Complete data set: NO Manufacturing only: NO
H96%EU	0	10	45	30	20	20	30	90	20	0	0	24.1	Complete data set: YES Manufacturing only: YES
H96%WW	0	55	20	30	0	0	10	0	0	0	2	10.6	Complete data set: NO Manufacturing only: NO
HΔHung	-2	30	15	-10	0	-5	10	-20	-60	0	-5	-4.2	Complete data set: YES Manufacturing only:YES
HΔEeur	2	5	0	-5	0	-10	0	0	50	0	3	4.1	Complete data set: NO Manufacturing only: NO
HΔEU	0	-5	-15	-15	0	15	-10	20	10	0	0	0	Complete data set: YES Manufacturing only: YES
HΔWW	0	-30	0	25	0	0	0	0	0	0	2	-0.3	Complete data set: NO Manufacturing only: NO
H%oldsup	100	95	25	25	95	80	76	70	20	60	80	66	Complete data set: NO Manufacturing only: NO

Note

1 The critical values relevant to the complete pooled data set are: $t_{18\,(10\%)} = 1.33$, $t_{18\,(5\%)} = 1.73$, $t_{18\,(1\%)} = 2.55$. The critical values relevant to the pooled data set containing the Hungarian and German manufacturing companies only are: $t_{13\,(10\%)} = 1.35$, $t_{13\,(5\%)} = 1.77$, $t_{13\,(1\%)} = 2.65$.

Variables	t-statistic obtained for complete data set, reject or accept null of homogeneity between country data sets?	t-statistic obtained for manufacturing data set, reject or accept null?
90%Hung/90%Eger	-1.63, reject at 10% level	-0.85, accept
90%Eeur	-0.02, accept	-0.31, accept
90%EU / (90%EU + 90%WGer)	1.37, reject at 10%	0.62, accept
90%WW	1.28 accept	0.99, accept
96%Hung	0.78, accept	2.25, reject at 5%
96%Eeur	0.40, accept	-0.08, accept
96%EU/ (96%EU + 96%WGer)	-1.89, reject at 5%	-2.43, reject at 5%
96%WW	1.14, accept	0.61, accept
ΔHung, Δ Eger	2.85, reject at 1%	3.16, reject at 1%
ΔEeur	0.44, accept	0.15, accept
ΔEU/ ΔEU + ΔWger	-4.82, reject at 1%	-5.13, reject at 1%
ΔWW	-0.85, accept	-1.07, accept
%oldsup	2.84, reject at 1%	2.28, reject at 1%

Table 6.2b German data

	D1, c	*D2,c*	D3	D4	D5	*D6,c*	*D7,c*	D8	D9	mean, complete data	mean, manufacturing data only
D90%EGer	*100*	*100*	95	70	0	*80*	*100*	96	70	79	66
D90%WGer	*0*	*0*	0	20	50	*0*	*0*	4	5	8.7	16
D90%Eeur	*0*	*0*	5	0	50	*20*	*0*	0	25	11.1	16
D90%EU	*0*	*0*	0	10	0	*0*	*0*	0	0	1.1	2
D96%EGer	*50*	*50*	0	30	0	*80*	*100*	30	5	38.3	13
D96%WGer	*50*	*50*	15	28	50	*20*	*0*	40	60	34.7	39
D96%Eeur	*0*	*0*	85	0	5	*0*	*0*	0	0	10, (0.5 excl. D3)	18 *(1 excl. D3)*
D96%EU	*0*	*0*	0	40	40	*0*	*0*	20	20	13.3	24
D96%WW	*0*	*0*	0	2	5	*0*	*0*	10	15	3.5	6
DΔEger	*-50*	*-50*	-95	-40	0	*0*	*0*	-66	-65	-41	-52
DΔWger	*50*	*50*	15	8	0	*20*	*0*	36	55	26	23
DΔEeur	*0*	*0*	80	0	-45	*-20*	*0*	0	-25å	-1.1, (-10 excl. D3)	2 (-14 excl. D3)
DΔEU	*0*	*0*	0	30	40	*0*	*0*	20	20	12.2	22
DΔWW	*0*	*0*	0	2	5	*0*	*0*	10	15	3.5	6
D%oldsup	8	5	0	70	35	80	17	35	2	23	28

Table 6.3a Qualitative data on suppliers: the German cases

	What were the main reasons for stopping using 'old' suppliers?	Do you think that there are any significant differences between suppliers located in East Germany and those in West Germany?	How are your supply relationships going to develop in the next five years?
D1	D1 is aiming to obtain the ISO certificate for **quality** and for that reason has to insist on supplies which meet these requirements.	No significant ones, companies in East Germany accept the new rules of the game.	No significant changes are envisaged.
D2	The **quality** of some of the products offered by old suppliers was not sufficient. Others were offering a **too narrow product range** and were located at **too great a geographical distance**.	NONE.	NONE.
D3	They **stopped existing.** Furthermore the parent offers good **quality** at advantageous prices.	Not really, but there are not many left.	Essentially remain unchanged, would like the parent to improve product range, they do not think that the parent might use D3's dependence since D3 demands only a minimal fraction of the parent's overall output
D4	Quality problems.	NONE.	In principle no changes, but there might be new entrants with better prices, which might not be matched by old suppliers.
D5	Insufficient **quality, fraudulent labelling** by trading houses (e.g. claims that a product made by a no-name supplier was produced in Germany).	Today the company still uses its old suppliers of packaging materials. D5 claims that there is a sense of **Solidarity** between itself and suppliers in East Germany. However there has never been much inputs production for pharmaceuticals in the East Germany and chemicals production has been reduced drastically.	Even stronger concentration on a few input sources and stronger quality control requirements on suppliers. Each supply relationship requires a large investment, hence D5 needs to know suppliers well and needs personal contacts to communicate changes in production requirements.
D6	Insufficient **quality** and lack of **punctuality, bankruptcies**.	Initially large **price differentials** East Germany–West Germany. West German suppliers are seen as less cooperative than East German ones who have to acquire a good reputation	There are constant bankruptcies, D6 has to constantly find new suppliers.
D7	Many East German companies were too small to be able to offer competitive prices.	NONE – you find unacceptable behaviour with both.	The company is aiming to establish close relationships with a core set of suppliers while keeping a close look on market developments.
D8	1) Stopped existing. 2) Lacking technological and quality standards. 3) Uncompetitive prices (a problem in all of Germany).	Suppliers in Eastern Germany are more flexible and willing to cater for special requests.	The company is wanting to improve its risk management and thus be able to enter more price competitive (but also more risky) input markets.
D9	1) Companies ceased to exist. 2) Company D9 had no use for their product because it took over an entire product line together with the suppliers from the investor.	Companies in Eastern Germany have more modern machinery and production methods than those in West Germany.	The company is intending to consolidate its suppliers to a smaller core.

Table 6.3b Qualitative data on suppliers: the Hungarian cases

	What were the main reasons for stopping using 'old' suppliers?	**Do you think that there are any significant differences between suppliers located in Hungary and foreign ones?**	**How are your supply relationships going to develop in the next five years?**
H1	With respect to packaging materials many old suppliers were unable to meet H1's increased **quality** requirements. Foreign owned companies based in Hungary filled the gap very quickly, however.	NONE: most Hungarian packaging companies are foreign owned and are entirely up to Western standards. H8 supplies H1 with printed labels.	According to H1's MD the Hungarian packaging sector is competitive. This gives him a large enough choice of potential suppliers should the existing ones prove to be unsatisfactory.
H2	They were unable to offer competitive **prices** and a sufficient **quality.** There were also severe problems with **punctuality** in some instances.	YES: 'In the area of packaging materials, for example, foreign companies are better able to meet our increased **quality** requirements because they have a better technology. When we give tenders, we find that Hungarian companies have a lower amount of **experience and economic knowledge**. An exception to this previous statement are Hungarian companies with FDI, which are even more confused than those without an investor because their investors are constantly introducing new systems and procedures. In terms of the punctuality of deliveries foreign companies are just as unreliable as Hungarian ones.'	H2 is aiming at developing close partnerships with a small group of **core suppliers.** In these partnerships explicit account is taken of **'non-price benefits obtained through longer term contracts.** Partners tend to be more reliable than other suppliers. Until now we tended to test the market with every purchase. This is very work intensive. We will save these transaction costs with long-term suppliers, which leads to large savings even though we might not be buying at the cheapest price in every given instance. We re-evaluate the partners on a yearly basis and offer new tenders if we are not satisfied.'
H3	Many went **bankrupt**. In other cases no agreement concerning **payment methods** could be reached. **Quality** and lack of **punctuality** constituted further problems.	YES: 'Hungarian suppliers are close to us and work at least as hard. If the **Hungarian** supplier has the same technology we choose him anytime. They are **reliable, cheaper and open to suggestions.**'	H3 wants to **widen the circle of its suppliers** and wants to search out **direct suppliers** in order to cut intermediaries (wholesalers) out.
H4	**Bankruptcy** and **'ethical misendeavours'**.	YES: Some Hungarian suppliers are highly developed. The majority is, however, in dire need of investment which makes them ineffective and inflexible. Some suppliers have not yet been privatised, others have been unsuccessfully privatised and yet others were acquired for asset stripping purposes. Investors bought them, took their good products away and ran them to the ground.	H4 is aiming to establish more **direct supply relationships on an increasingly global scale** and to move to **longer-term (that is one year) contracts.** It is establishing a tender process which is very similar to that described in H2.
H5	Insufficient **quality and punctuality**.	Hungarian suppliers used to have more problems with **quality and punctuality**. Nowadays **these differences are disappearing fast**.	H5 aims to maintain its current supply arrangements.

H6	H6's output declined dramatically, so that a major reason for discontinuing pre-existing supply relationships was **H6's economic problems**. Russian suppliers especially had problems with **punctuality and quality**. Other **suppliers decided that they no longer wanted to supply H6** because they perceived better opportunities elsewhere. These latter companies tended to, however, approach H6 again subsequently.	'It is easier to stay in contact with Hungarian suppliers and to co-ordinate one's actions. Most foreign suppliers are more diligent in drawing up precise contracts and they require more payment guarantees. However, these trends are highly company specific, we had Western suppliers as well who lacked punctuality and flexibility.'	H6 is aiming to build more **long-term relationships and to engage in close co-operation** and daily contact with a core set of suppliers.
H7	Some suppliers **could not adjust to the new requirements** made by H7. Very seldom there were **quality** problems, but the quality of inputs was very high already before 1990. Some smaller suppliers suffered from **financial instability**.	Hungarian suppliers used to be **less financially stable** than Western ones, but their financial position has been strengthening. Their productivity has been lower but is rapidly growing. The **quality** of their products depends on their previous customers. Suppliers which had very export orientated customers before 1990 tend to be better. The **ancillary services** they provide tend to be very backwards.	H7 is intending to **increase its reliance on Hungarian suppliers**. 'WE are training local suppliers and bring them up to scratch rather than to depend on European suppliers. Some suppliers respond by fleeing in panic whereas others endorse our quality control methods etc. with enthusiasm.'
H8	**Unreliability.**	The main differences relate to the **quality** of the products offered, which can be lower in the case of Hungarian suppliers.	If there exists a Hungarian supplier who offer a quality price combination which is comparable to that offered by foreign suppliers, then H8 will always choose the Hungarian supplier. H8 is hoping for **more Hungarian suppliers** to develop who have a pro-active (customer focused) attitude and offer a high quality product.
H9	H9 **changed its product range** after a fire destroyed some of its product facilities. This was the main reason for changing suppliers.	Hungarian suppliers are approaching, although not yet entirely achieving, Western standards.	Remain **unchanged.**
H10	Some old suppliers were **unable to offer competitive prices** and to adjust to the new **quality** requirements and **needs of their customers**.	NA	H10's aim is to **continue avoiding becoming excessively dependent on any given supplier**.
H11	1) **Bankruptcy.** 2) **Lack of reliability** with respect to the products' quality and punctuality in delivery. 3) **Opportunism:** attempts to change prices after at tender has been won inevitably leads to a discontinuation of the business relationship.	NONE: All nationalities have black cats among them.	H11 is aiming to **reduce its dependency on Russia** and is open to developing relationships with new suppliers. Its long-term aim is to develop **close relationships with a core set of high quality suppliers**. In the interest of finding good new suppliers H11 is constantly keeping an eye on opportunities in this area and takes references from possible new business partners. H11 then enters into a **'trial marriage'** in which it starts with a low level of commitment and a low exposure to the new supplier.

Table 6.4 List of variables relating to product markets

D(H)hqual	1 if the availability of a highly qualified workforce is of high importance to the company's competitive success, 0.5 if this factor is of medium importance and 0 otherwise
D(H)cheap	1 if the availability of a cheap workforce is of high importance to the company's competitive success, 0.5 if this factor is of medium importance and 0 otherwise
D(H)custprox	1 if proximity to the company's most important customers is of high importance to the company's competitive success, 0.5 if this factor is of medium importance and 0 otherwise
D(H)inprox	1 if proximity to the company's most important input suppliers is of high importance to the company's competitive success, 0.5 if this factor is of medium importance and 0 otherwise
D(H)servprox	1 if proximity to the company's most important service suppliers is of high importance to the company's competitive success, 0.5 if this factor is of medium importance and 0 otherwise
D(H)randdprox	1 if proximity to local research institutions is of high importance to the company's competitive success, 0.5 if this factor is of medium importance and 0 otherwise
D(H)localgov	1 if a competent local government is of high importance to the company's competitive success, 0.5 if this factor is of medium importance and 0 otherwise
D(H)infrastr	1 if a well developed infrastructure is of high importance to the company's competitive success, 0.5 if this factor is of medium importance and 0 otherwise
D%out 90 EGer/ H%out90Hung	percentage of the company's total output which was sold in East Germany/Hungary in 1990
D(H)%out 90EEur	percentage of the company's total output which was sold in Eastern Europe in 1990
D%out 90WGer	percentage of the company's total output which was sold in West Germany in 1990
D (H) %out 90EU	percentage of the company's total output which was sold in the European Union (excluding West Germany for East German data, including West Germany for Hungarian data) in 1990
D(H)%out 90 WW	percentage of the company's total output which was sold worldwide (that is outside Europe) in 1990

D(H)Total Exp 90	sum of total sales realised outside East Germany/Hungary in 1990
D%out 96 EGer/ H%out96Hung	percentage of the company's total output which was sold in East Germany/Hungary in 1996
D(H) %out96 Eeur	percentage of the company's total output which was sold in Eastern Europe in 1996
D%out 96Wger	percentage of the company's total output which was sold in West Germany in 1996
D(H) %out 96EU	percentage of the company's total output which was sold in the European Union (excluding West Germany for East German data, including West Germany for Hungarian data) in 1996
D(H) %out 96 WW	percentage of the company's total output which was sold worldwide (that is outside Europe) in 1996
D(H) Total Exp 96	sum of total sales realised outside East Germany/Hungary in 1996
DΔ Total Exp	DTotal Export 96 minus DTotal Export 90: the increase (or decrease) in the company's export orientation since 1990
DΔ out Eger/ HΔ out Hung	D%out 96EGer minus D%out 90EGer: the increase (or decrease) in the percentage of total output which is sold in East Germany/Hungary
DΔ out Wger	D%out 96WGer minus D%out 90WGer: the increase (or decrease) in the percentage of total output which is sold in West Germany
D(H) Δ out Eeur	D%out 96EEur minus D%out 90EEur: the increase (or decrease) in the percentage of total output which is sold in Eastern Europe
DΔ out EU	D%out 96EU minus D%out 90Eur U: the increase (or decrease) in the percentage of total output which is sold in the European Union
D(H) Δ out WW	D%out 96WorldW minus D%out 90WorldW: the increase (or decrease) in the percentage of total output which is sold worldwide
D(H) MS 90	Market share of the company in 1990, 100% = the East German (Hungarian) market, except in the cases of D1, D2 and D7 where the relevant market is greater Berlin or, in the case of D2, only one quarter of Berlin
D(H) MS 96	Market share of the company in 1996, the same areas are taken as 100% as for Market Share 90
D(H) ΔMS	D(H)MS 96 minus D(H)MS 90

D (H) numcomp	1 if the company faces a large number of competitors, 0 otherwise. In the East German data this variable is 0 for Company D9 only
D (H) small comp	1 if the company mainly faces small competitors, 0 otherwise
D(H) big comp	1 if the company mainly faces large competitors, 0 otherwise. This variable is 1 for all the East German companies. If a company faces both large and small competitors, then both big comp and small comp equal 1
D(H) C Eger (Hung)	1 if important competitors are located in East Germany/ Hungary in 1996, 0 otherwise
DComp 96 Wger	1 if important competitors are located in West Germany in 1996, 0 otherwise
D(H) C Eeur	1 if important competitors are located in Eastern Europe in 1996, 0 otherwise
D(H) C EU	1 if important competitors are located in the European Union in 1996, 0 otherwise
D(H) C 96 WW	1 if important competitors are located in countries outside Europe in 1996, 0 otherwise
D(H) DiC price	Captures the extent to which price is an important dimension of competition in the company's main product markets. Interview partners ranked the importance of this factor on a sale of 1 (very important) to 6 (unimportant). Consequently the lower the numeric value for this entry, the more important a determinant of the company's competitive success price is
D(H) DiC quality	Captures the extent to which quality is an important dimension of competition in the company's main product markets. Interview partners ranked the importance of this factor on a sale of 1 (very important) to 6 (unimportant)
D(H) DiC punct	Captures the extent to which punctual delivery is an important dimension of competition in the company's main product markets. Interview partners ranked the importance of this factor on a sale of 1 (very important) to 6 (unimportant)
D(H) DiC design	Captures the extent to which design (including packaging and technical design) is an important dimension of competition in the company's main product markets Interview partners ranked the importance of this factor on a sale of 1 (very important) to 6 (unimportant)
D pr 95	1 if the company was profitable in 1995, 0 otherwise
Hpr 96	1 if the company was profitable in 1996, 0 otherwise

D pr97	1 if the company was profitable in 1997, 0 otherwise
D manufacturing/ H food	1 if the company belongs to the manufacturing/food sector, 0 if it belongs to the construction sector
D(H) IMPPR	1 if the investor was the main force determining the restructuring of the product range, 0 otherwise
D(H) FDI	1 if the company has FDI, 0 otherwise.

Table 6.5a Summary of the data on the East German companies' product markets

	D1	D2	D3	D4	D5	D6	D7	D8	D9	*mean*
Dhqual 1	1	1	1	1	1	1	1	1	*1*	
Dcheap	0[1]	0	0	0	0	0	0.5	0.5	0.5	*0.33*
Dcustprox	1	1	0.5	0	0	0.5[2]	1	0.5	0	*0.5*
Dinprox 1	1	0	0	0	0	0	0.5	0	*0.27*	
Dservprox	1	0	1	0	0.5[3]	0	0.5	1	0.5	*0.5*
Dranddprox	0	0	0	0	1	0	0	0	0	*0.1*
Dlocalgov	1[4]	0.5	0	1	1[5]	0	1[6]	0.5	0	*0.55*
Dinfrastr	0	0.5	1	1	0.5	1	0.5	1	1	*0.72*
D%out 90Eger	100	100	75	80	60	70	100	85	100	*85.55*
D%out 90Eeur	0	0	15	0	40	5	0	15	0	*8.33*
D%out 90Wger	0	0	10	6.6	0	0	0	0	0	*1.84*
D%out 90EU	0	0	0	6.6	0	0	0	0	0	*0.73*
D%out 90 WW	0	0	0	6.6	0	25	0	0	0	*3.51*
DTotal Exp90	0	0	25	20	40	30	0	15	0	*14.44*
D%out 96EGer	100	100	20	25	50	90	100	65	5	*61.66*
D%out96 EEur	0	0	5	0	35	3	0	5	0	*5.33*
D%out 96Wger	0	0	60	75	10	7	0	5	65	*24.66*
D%out 96EU	0	0	15	0	5[7]	0	0	25	30	*8.33*
D%out 96 WW	0	0	0	0	0	0	0	0	10	*1.11*
DTotal Exp 96	0	0	80	75	50	10	0	35	95	*38.33*
DΔ total Export	0	0	55	50	10	-20	0	20	95	*23.33*
DΔ out Eger	0	0	-55	-55	-10	20	0	-20	-95	*-23.8*
DΔ out Wger	0	0	50	68.4	10	7	0	5	65	*8.59*

DΔ out Eeur	0	0	-10	0	-5	-2	0	-10	0	*-3*
DΔ out EU	0	0	15	-6.6	5	0	0	25	30	*7.6*
DΔ out WW	0	0	0	-6.6	0	-25	0	0	10	*-2.4*
DM[8] S90	100	100	95	100	10	100	100	100	100	*89.44*
DM S 96	3[9]	10	20	20	2.6	7.5	4	72.5[10]	0[11]	*15.5*
DΔMS	-97	-90	-75[12]	-80	-7.4	-92.5	-96	-27.5	-100	*-73.9*
Dnumcomp	1	1	1	1	1	1	1	1	0	*0.88*
Dbigcomp	1	1	1	1	1	1	1	1	1	*1*
Dsmall comp	0	0	0	1	1	1	0	1	0	*0.44*
DC Eger1[13]	0	[14] 0	0	1	1	1	1	0	*0.55*	
DC Wger	1	1	0	1	1	1	1	1	1	*0.88*
DC Eeur	0	0	1	0	0	1	0	1	0	*0.33*
DC EU	0	0	1	0	0	1	0	1	0	*0.33*
DC WW0	0	0	0	0	1	0	0	0	*0.11*	
DDiC price	1	1	1	1	1	1	1	1	2	*1.11*
DDiC quality	2.5	3	2	1	1	1	2	1	1	1.61
DDiC punct	4	3	1.5	2	1	1	1	1	2	1.83
DDiC design	3[15]	3	5	2	3	1	3	3	6	3
Dpr95	1	1	0	0	1	0	1	0	0	0.44
Dpr97	1	1	0	1	1	0	1	1	1	0.77
Dmanufact	0	0	1	1	1	0	0	1	1	0.55
DIMPPR	0	0	0	1	0.5	0	0	0.5	1	0.33
DFDI	1	1	1	1	1	0	0	1	1	0.77

Table 6.5a cont'd

Notes

1 The personnel managers of companies D1 and D3 see stable and high wages as an important incentive increasing productivity. Hence he does not think that paying the lowest wages possible is desirable. Company D2 has made bad experience with cheap labour.

2 'Contacts are more important than geographical proximity.'

3 Here the manager in charge of procurement mentioned the proximity of service suppliers which had been separated out of the original *Kombinat* and are independent companies now.

4 'This would be highly desirable ... but there is no solidarity with East German products. The West German lobbies have more power in East German local government, than the lobbies representing local industry have' Company D2 has a similar opinion, stating that in practice the company receives no support from the local government.

5 Company D5 describes its relationship with the local government as good since it is one of the biggest employers in that quarter of Berlin and are thus in regular contact with the authorities.

6 The Senate is the main customer of company D7, thus its competence is very important to this company. A manager in company D9 however stated: 'If this was of any importance at all to our success, then we would have long left Brandenburg.'

7 D5 and D8 export to subsidiaries of the investor which are located in the European Union.

8 For both 1990 and 1996 the market share figures refer to the East German market or to relevant sub-segments of it. The three building companies D1, D2 and D7 had markets which only extended to the greater Berlin area or, in the case of D2, to a quarter of Berlin only. However, within each of these sub-markets the company in question still had a monopoly position.

9 Values for D1, D2 and D4 are estimates provided by interview partners when they were pushed to make a personal guess. In these companies the prevalent sentiment was that the relevant markets had changed so much beyond recognition that one could not really compare market shares. D2's relatively large market share refers to its position within the quarter of Berlin it was originally operating in. By 1997 D2 has extended its operations to the entire Berlin area, for which market its market share is very close to zero.

10 This summary statistic hides a share of the East German market of 60% for new turbines and 85% for servicing old ones. The company also has acquired a 30% market share in Eastern Europe for servicing turbines.

11 Although the East German market for gears ceased to exist with the traditional East German car industry, D9 has managed to acquired a 1.5 market share of the West German market. From what I gather the West German market seems to be a duopoly, so that D9 faces only one, but much larger, competitor there.

12 It should be noted that we are dealing with a rapidly shrinking market here. Before 1990, D3 had a market share of 2% in West Germany. By 1996 this has increased in 10%.

13 D1's main competitors are new subsidiaries of West German companies, there has been a 1 to 1 import of the West German market structure.

14 It is interesting in this context that D3 seems to be entirely unconcerned about competitors in West Germany, but very much about Scandinavian, Italian, Polish and Hungarian competitors. This probably indicates collusion in the (West) German steel processing sector.

15 Companies D1, D2 and D7 do not directly engage in design activities, but rather purchase these from architects, who work in separate companies. It is, however, of importance that the company collaborates with good architects.

Table 6.5b Summary of the data on the Hungarian companies' product markets

	H1	H2	H3	H4	H5	H6	H7	H8	H9	H10	H11	*mean*
Hhqual	1	1	1	1	1	0.5	1	0.5	1	1	1	*0.90*
Hcheap	1	0.5	0.5	0.5	1	0.5	0.5	0	0.5	0.5	0.5	*0.59*
Hcustprox	1	0.5	0.5	1	0.5	0.5	0.5	0.5	0.5	0.5	1	*0.63*
Hinprox	1	1	1	0.5	1	1	0.5	0.5	0.5	1	0	*0.72*
Hservprox	1	1	1	1	0.5	1	1[1]	1	0.5	0.5	1	*0.86*
Hranddprox	0[2]	0.5	0.5	1	0	0	1	0	0	0	1	*0.36*
Hlocalgov	0	0.5	0	1	0	0	0.5	0	0	0.5	1	*0.31*
Hinfrastr	1	1	1	1	0	0.5	1	1	0.5	1	1	*0.81*
H%out90Hung	40	97	92	40	50	15	35	93	75	87	90	*64.9*
H% out 90EEur	36[3]	3	1[4]	30	8[5]	80	10	4	20	10	3	*18.6*
H% out 90EU	0	0	4	10	30	0	30	3	0	0	7	*7.6*
H%90 out WW	24	0	3	20	12	5	25	0	5	3	0	*8.8*
H90Totol Exp	60	3	8	60	50	85	65	7	25	13	10	*35*
H% out 96Hung	40	97	65	35	50	10	10	84	80[6]	99	85	*59.5*
H% out 96EEur	60	3	25	27	8	70	3[7]	10	20	1	0	*20.6*
H%96 out EU	0	0	10	15	30	5	45	6	0	0	15	*11.5*
H%96 out WW	0	0	0	23	12	15	42	0	0	0	0	*8.3*
HtotalExp96	60	3	35	65	50	90	90	16[8]	20	1	15	*40.4*
HΔ total Export	0	0	27	5	0	5[9]	25	9	-5	-12	5	*5.4*
HΔ Hung	0	0	-27	-5	0	-5	-25	-9	5	12	-5	*-5.4*
HΔ Eeur	24	0	24	-3	0	-10	-7	6	0	-9	-3	*2*
HΔ EU	0	0	10	5	0	5	15	3	0	0	8	*4.18*
HΔ WW	-24	0	-3	3	0	10	17	0	-5	-3	0	*-0.45*
HMS90	100	90[10]	5[11]	75	78[12]	98	78	45	5	25[13]	100	*63.5*
HMS96	100	80	10	25	78	90[14]	85	60	3	5	85[15]	*56.5*
HΔ MS	0	-10	5	-50	0	-8	7	15	-2	-20	-15	*-7.00*
Hnumcomp	0	1	1	1	0	1	0	1	1	1	1	*0.72*
Hsmallcom	1	1	1	1	0	1	0	0	0	0	1	*0.54*
Hbigcomp	0	1	1	1	1	1	1	1	1	1	1	*0.90*
HCHung	1	1	1[16]	1	0	0	0	0	1	1	0	*0.54*
HCEEur	0	0	0	0	0	0	1	0	0	0	0	*0.09*
HCEU	0	1	1	1	1	1	1	1	1	0	1	*0.81*
HCWW	0	1	0	1	0	1	0	0	0	0	1	*0.36*
HdiCprice	1	1	1	1	2	1	1	2	2	2	1	*1.36*

HdiCquality	1	2	3	1	1	1	1.5	1	2	1	1	*1.41*
HDiC punct	4	3	3	2	1	2	1	1	1	1	2	*1.91*
HdiCdesign	2	1	2	3	1	2	3	4[17]	2	2	4.5[18]	*2.41*
Hpr96	1	0	0	1	1	0	1	1	0	0	1	*0.54*
Hfood	1	1	1	0	0	0	0	0	0	0	0	*0.27*
Hfdi	1	1	1	1	0	0	1	0	1	1	0	*0.63*
Himppr	0.5	1	0	0	0	0	1	0	1	1	0	*0.41*

Notes

1 H7 especially emphasises the importance of being close to the providers of ancillary services and of packaging materials as well as the importance of a well-developed regional infrastructure.

2 'We have our own internal R&D department.'

3 H1's MD is keen to stress that these exports went and continue to go to Central (the Czech Republic, Austria, Switzerland and the Ukraine) rather than Eastern Europe. The company's world wide exports went to Algeria and Egypt and although they have ceased to exist by 1996, the MD states that the company has no intention of rebuilding these exports.

4 H3 explains its low exports to Eastern Europe in 1990 by stating that it offers better quality at higher prices than local producers. The export growth experienced by 1996 in the Eastern European category has been mainly to Central Europe. Exports to the European Union are mainly via the investor.

5 H5a exported to the USSR not directly but via western intermediaries (and continues to do so). Its exports to the rest of the world are mainly to the USA and Asia.

6 By 2001 H9 is hoping to sell only 65% of its output in Hungary, 25% in Eastern Europe and regain the 5% world-wide sales it has lost.

7 The manager interviewed stated: 'They [that is business partners from the former Soviet Union] cannot pay and they cannot offer us anything worth bartering for.'

8 This includes direct exports by H8 only. Indirectly H8 exports about 50% of its output because the products packaged in H8's products are being exported.

9 H6's proportion of sales exported to its target markets have not changed dramatically, but its overall output has shrunk dramatically. At the company's low-point in 1996 output was at 500 buses, down from 12000 in the late 1980s. By 1997 output recovered to 1500-2000 buses. Throughout this period domestic demand has been fairly stable at 300 buses per annum, with the largest falls in orders and payment ability originating from the area of the former Soviet Union.

10 H2's high market share refers to the market for instant drinks only, that is to the products of the factory visited.

11 The factory which is the core of H3 was a relatively small player in the Hungarian sweets industry in 1990. Furthermore it has always produced a multitude of products, without having a dominant role in any product group except in edible Christmas decorations.

12 H5a's market share depends on its product groups. In petrochemicals (that is input production) it has a monopoly and imports account for 10% of the market only, while in plastic processing it has a market share of 67% only. 78% is the average of 90% and 67%.

13 H10's low market share in 1990 was due to the fact that the civil engineering sector had quite a few companies operating, typically on a regional basis, in it already. For the future the interview partner stated: 'We haven't got much of a chance in terms of market share really. We are big enough to be tolerated as a bystander by the cartel operated by Western firms' subsidiaries, but small enough for them not to see us as a threat and to do us in. If we grew any bigger, they would cease to tolerate us.'

14 H6's market share in the Eastern European market is still, depending on the country concerned, 50-100%. Consequently its large falls in total sales are due to large falls in demand, rather than the loss of market share to competitors.

15 In 1996/97 H11 still had a legal monopoly on the supply of gas. This is likely to change, but H11 seems overall unconcerned about the impending legal changes. In petrol its market share has fallen to 70% due to entry by multinationals who are building up petrol station networks. These multinationals have to frequently, however, buy petrol from H11 because of the high transportation costs and the import taxes they face. H11 has also invested into upgrading its own chain of petrol stations and is fairly confident that it will be, given favourable legislation, able to sustain its market share. The large number of competitors H11 faces refers to the petrol market. The small competitors originate from 'the illegal [blending] activities of individuals', which were especially rampant during the oil embargo during the Yugoslav war.

16 The Hungarian competitors are almost all subsidiaries of western companies. The same statement holds for H10 and for the Eastern European (especially Polish) competitors of H7.

17 Design is unimportant because it is usually supplied by the customer.

18 4.5 is the average of 6 for lubricants and 3 for petrol stations.

Table 6.6a Correlation matrix 1 for the German data: regional characteristics*

	Dcheap	Dcustprox	Dinprox	Dservprox	Dranddprox	Dlocalgov	Dinfrastr
Dcheap	1.00						
Dcustprox	0.00	1.00					
Dinprox	-0.19	**0.65*nc**	1.00				
Dservprox	0.29	0.17	0.16	1.00			
Dranddprox	-0.25	-0.43	-0.24	0.00	1.00		
Dlocalgov	-0.09	0.16	0.22	0.00	0.36	1.00	
Dinfrastr	0.23	**-0.60*nc**	**-0.63*nc**	-0.20	-0.23	**-0.64*nc**	1.00
D%out 90EGer	0.46	**0.57*t**	**0.53*t**	0.09	**-0.63**t**	0.08	-0.36
D%out 90EEur	-0.19	-0.43	-0.28	0.27	**0.88***t**	0.12	0.02
D%out 90Wger	-0.37	-0.25	-0.35	0.13	-0.18	-0.19	0.42
D%out 90EurU	-0.25	-0.43	-0.24	-0.43	-0.13	0.36	0.29
D%out 90 WW	-0.32	-0.11	-0.30	**-0.55*t**	-0.16	-0.35	0.36
DTotal Exp90	-0.46	**-0.57*t**	**-0.53*t**	-0.09	**0.63**t**	-0.08	0.36
D%out 96EGer	-0.10	**0.83***t**	**0.58*t**	-0.11	-0.11	0.35	**-0.64**t**
D%out96 EEur	-0.24	-0.45	-0.27	0.09	**0.98***t**	0.26	-0.13
D%out 96Wger	-0.03	**-0.68**t**	**-0.53*t**	-0.08	-0.17	-0.30	**0.61**t**
D%out 96EurU	**0.63**t**	-0.42	-0.20	**0.48*t**	-0.10	**-0.54*t**	**0.53*t**
D%out 96 WW	**0.50*t**	-0.43	-0.24	0.00	-0.13	-0.45	0.29
DTotal Exp 96	0.10	**-0.83***t**	**-0.58*t**	0.11	0.11	-0.35	**0.64**t**
DΔ total Export	0.31	**-0.62**t**	-0.38	0.18	-0.14	-0.35	**0.51*t**
DΔ out EGer	-0.29	**0.63**t**	0.38	-0.16	0.14	0.33	**-0.51*t**
DΔ out WGer	0.01	**-0.71**t**	**-0.53*t**	-0.10	-0.16	-0.30	**0.61**t**
DΔ out EEur	-0.06	0.17	0.16	**-0.60**t**	-0.17	0.31	-0.40
DΔ out EU	**0.63**t**	-0.32	-0.14	**0.53*t**	-0.08	**-0.57*t**	0.45
DΔ out WW	0.45	-0.05	0.18	**0.48*t**	0.10	0.15	-0.22
DMS 90	0.27	0.44	0.25	-0.02	-1.00	-0.34	0.21
DM S 96	0.33	-0.04	0.13	0.37	-0.21	-0.08	0.42
DΔMS	-0.01	-0.41	-0.14	0.27	**0.75***t**	0.25	0.09
Dnumcomp	-0.50	0.43	0.24	0.00	0.13	0.45	-0.29
Dsmall comp	-0.16	-0.55	-0.33	-0.27	0.40	0.14	0.40
DC Eger	0.16	0.27	0.06	0.27	0.32	0.37	-0.40
DC Wger	0.25	0.00	0.24	-0.43	0.13	0.45	-0.29
DC Eeur	0.00	0.00	-0.19	0.29	-0.25	**-0.63**t**	**0.57*t**
DC EU	0.00	0.00	-0.19	0.29	-0.25	**-0.63**t**	**0.57*t**
DC WW	-0.25	0.00	-0.24	-0.43	-0.13	-0.45	0.29
DDiC price	**0.50*t**	-0.43	-0.24	0.00	-0.13	-0.45	0.29
DDiC quality	-0.27	**0.83***t**	**0.72**t**	0.09	-0.29	0.15	**-0.65**t**
DDiC punct	-0.35	0.41	**0.78***t**	0.07	-0.29	0.21	**-0.62**t**
DDiC design	**0.57**t**	-0.22	0.00	0.33	0.00	-0.20	0.00
Dpr95	-0.16	0.55	0.48	0.00	0.40	**0.65*nc**	**-0.91***nc**
Dpr97	0.38	0.00	0.36	0.00	0.19	**0.68**nc**	-0.43
Dmanufacturing	0.16	**-0.82***nc**	-0.48	0.27	0.32	-0.14	0.58
DFDI	-0.19	-0.33	0.36	0.33	0.19	0.07	-0.04
DIMPPR	0.29	**-0.83***nc**	-0.38	-0.17	0.14	0.05	0.46

Note

The associations involving Dranddprox merely reflect D5 rather than more general trends. I treated the regional variables as 0, 0.5, 1 dummies. When obtaining significance levels for associations involving two dummies I have to either merge the 0.5 cells of the relevant contingency table with another row or entirely drop them. This is a consequence of the very low number of observations, allowing only for 2 by 2 tables. For the regional dummies I make the simplifying assumption that 0.5 = 0. The intuitive justification is that interview partners usually had a firm opinion on which factors were clearly important to their competitive success, but were frequently more hesitant in distinguishing between unimportant and slightly important factors. Generally several simplifying assumptions were tested for the 0.5 observations of other dummies, they are explicitly referred to. A X^2 distribution with 1 degree of freedom has the following critical values: $X^2_{\text{(critical- 10\%)}} = 2.7$, $X^2_{\text{(critical- 5\%)}} = 3.84$, $X^2_{\text{(critical- 1\%)}} = 6.63$. I find that generally all association below 0.60 tend to be insignificant. For associations of 0.65 uncorrected test statistics were obtained which oscillated between the 10% and 5% significance level, depending on the simplifying assumption. Associations of 0.66 generated uncorrected test statistics of 3.95 [5% level], while the corrected ones were insignificant. Associations of 0.73 generate test statistics of 5.10 [5% - obtained by dropping 0.5 observations]. Associations of 0.76 generate uncorrected test statistics of about 5.19 [5%]. Associations above 0.82 generate uncorrected test statistics of at least 7.14 [1%] and their corrected test statistics are also significant at the 10% and for the 0.91 association at the 5% level [0.5 = 0]. For associations between continuous & dummy variables as well as between two continuous variables the relevant test statistics are: $t^7_{0.10} = 1.41$, $t^7_{0.05} = 1.89$, $t^7_{0.01} = 2.99$. I find that in both cases all associations above 0.48 (t = 1.44) are significant at the 10% level, associations above 0.59 (t = 1.93) are significant at the 5% level and associations above 0.75 (t = 3.00) are significant at the 1% level.

Correlation matrix 2: the geographical distribution of sales in 1990 and 1996

	D%out 90Eger	D%out 90EEur	D%out 90WGer	D%out 90EurU	D%out 90 WorldW	DTotal Export 90	D%out 96EGer	D%out 96 EEur	D%out 96WGer	D%out 96EurU	D%out 96 WorldW
D%out90EGer	1.00										
D%out90EEur	-0.77***t	1.00									
D%out90WGer	-0.31	0.03	1.00								
D%out90EU	-0.14	-0.23	0.47	1.00							
D%out 90 WW	-0.42	-0.15	-0.06	0.14	1.00						
DTotal Exp90	-1.00***t	0.77***t	0.31	0.14	0.42	1.00					
D%out96EGer	0.29	-0.22	-0.57*t	-0.36	0.18	-0.29	1.00				
D%out96EEur	-0.72***t	0.95***t	-0.11	-0.18	-0.12	0.72**t	-0.15	1.00			
D%out96WGer	-0.12	-0.13	0.71**t	0.59**t	-0.05	0.12	-0.91***t	-0.17	1.00		
D%out96EU	0.09	0.14	0.03	-0.26	-0.33	-0.09	-0.63**t	-0.02	0.38	1.00	
D%out 96 WW	0.35	-0.23	-0.18	-0.13	-0.16	-0.35	-0.56*t	-0.18	0.47	0.68**t	1.00
DTotal Exp 96	-0.29	0.22	0.57*t	0.36	-0.18	0.29	-1.00***t	0.15	0.91***t	0.63**t	0.56*t
DΔ total Export	0.13	-0.08	0.45	0.28	-0.37	-0.13	-0.91***t	-0.14	0.87***t	0.71**t	0.74**t
DΔ out EGer	-0.12	0.09	-0.47	-0.32	0.36	0.12	0.92***t	0.14	-0.89***t	-0.69**t	-0.72**t
DΔ out WGer	-0.09	-0.14	0.65**t	0.58*t	-0.05	0.09	-0.91***t	-0.17	1.00***t	0.41	0.54*t
DΔ out EEur	0.51*t	-0.62**t	-0.39	0.26	0.16	-0.51*t	0.29	-0.35	-0.04	-0.48*t	0.26
DΔ out EU	0.11	0.17	-0.05	-0.42	-0.33	-0.11	-0.53*t	0.01	0.26	0.99***t	0.66**t
DΔ out WW	0.49*t	0.05	-0.01	-0.17	-0.94***t	-0.49*t	-0.36	0.05	0.21	0.53*t	0.49*t
DMS 90	0.64**t	-0.90***t	0.14	0.13	0.17	-0.64**t	0.14	-0.99***t	0.15	0.09	0.13
DM S 96	-0.11	0.15	0.11	0.07	-0.11	0.11	-0.07	-0.08	-0.05	0.44	-0.26
DΔMS	-0.65**t	0.90***t	-0.05	-0.07	-0.23	0.65**t	-0.17	0.83***t	-0.17	0.22	-0.29
Dnumcomp	-0.35	0.23	0.18	0.13	0.16	0.35	0.56*t	0.18	-0.47	-0.68**t	-1.00***t
Dsmall comp	-0.73***t	0.47	-0.05	0.40	0.50*t	0.73**t	-0.10	0.45	-0.01	-0.07	-0.32
DC Eger	-0.20	0.32	-0.58*t	-0.40	0.21	0.20	0.60**t	0.34	-0.75***t	-0.23	-0.40
DC Wger	0.26	-0.19	-0.81***t	0.13	0.16	-0.26	0.41	0.01	-0.42	-0.21	0.13
DC Eeur	-0.44	0.19	0.30	-0.25	0.43	0.44	-0.07	-0.07	-0.02	0.31	-0.25
DC EU	-0.44	0.19	0.30	-0.25	0.43	0.44	-0.07	-0.07	-0.02	0.31	-0.25
DC WW	-0.38	-0.09	-0.18	-0.13	0.97***t	0.38	0.28	-0.08	-0.21	-0.26	-0.13
DDiC price	0.35	-0.23	-0.18	-0.13	-0.16	-0.35	-0.56*t	-0.18	0.47	0.68**t	1.00***t
DDiC quality	0.57*t	-0.37	-0.01	-0.29	-0.37	-0.57*t	0.55*t	-0.34	-0.38	-0.41	-0.29
DDiC punct	0.58*t	-0.48*t	-0.07	0.06	-0.28	-0.58*t	0.24	-0.39	-0.06	-0.25	0.06
DDiC design	0.49*t	-0.07	-0.17	-0.28	-0.64**t	-0.49*t	-0.47	-0.05	0.31	0.71**t	0.85***t
Dpr95	0.28	0.12	-0.47	-0.32	-0.40	-0.28	0.64**t	0.29	-0.66**t	-0.56*t	-0.32
Dpr97	0.48*t	-0.07	-0.48*t	0.19	-0.61**t	-0.48*t	0.10	0.07	-0.16	0.04	0.19
Dmanufacturing	-0.43	0.50*t	0.47	0.32	-0.31	0.43	-0.89***t	0.38	0.68**t	0.66**t	0.32
DFDI	0.02	0.25	0.28	0.19	-0.61**t	-0.02	-0.50*t	0.19	0.38	0.39	0.19
DIMPPR	-0.08	0.05	0.08	0.58*t	-0.14	0.08	-0.74**t	0.10	0.66**t	0.48*t	0.58*t

Correlation matrix 3: changes in the companies' sales and export orientation and market share

	Dtotal Export 96	DΔ total Export	DΔ out EGer	DΔ out WGer	DΔ out Eeur	DΔ out EU	DΔ out WW	DMS 90	DMS96	DΔMS	Dnum comp
DTotal Exp 96	1.00										
DΔ total Export	0.91***t	1.00									
DΔ out EGer	-0.92***t	-1.00***t	1.00								
DΔ out WGer	0.91***t	0.89***t	-0.91***t	1.00							
DΔ out EEur	-0.29	-0.10	0.09	0.00	1.00						
DΔ out EU	0.53*t	0.62**t	-0.59**t	0.29	-0.50*t	1.00					
DΔ out WW	0.36	0.59**t	-0.58*t	0.23	-0.05	0.53*t	1.00				
DMS 90	-0.14	0.12	-0.12	0.15	0.21	0.06	-0.10	1.00			
DM S 96	0.07	0.03	-0.03	-0.07	-0.69**t	0.41	0.01	0.21	1.00		
DΔMS	0.17	-0.09	0.09	-0.18	-0.65**t	0.22	0.10	-0.75***t	0.49*t	1.00	
Dnumcomp	-0.56*t	-0.74**t	0.72**t	-0.54*t	-0.26	-0.66**t	-0.49*t	-0.13	0.26	0.29	1.00
Dsmall comp	0.10	-0.22	0.20	-0.01	-0.28	-0.13	-0.55*t	-0.38	0.43	0.63**t	0.32
DC Eger	-0.60**t	-0.70**t	0.71**t	-0.74**t	-0.11	-0.15	-0.33	-0.30	0.13	0.35	0.40
DC Wger	-0.41	-0.33	0.32	-0.35	0.61	-0.22	-0.10	-0.07	-0.07	0.01	-0.13
DC Eeur	0.07	-0.10	0.11	-0.06	-0.76***t	0.34	-0.47	0.22	0.59**t	0.20	0.25
DC EU	0.07	-0.10	0.11	-0.06	-0.76***t	0.34	-0.47	0.22	0.59**t	0.20	0.25
DC WW	-0.28	-0.45	0.45	-0.20	0.09	-0.22	-0.90***t	0.13	-0.13	-0.21	0.13
DDiC price	0.56**t	0.74**t	-0.72**t	0.54*t	0.26	0.66**t	0.49*t	0.13	-0.26	-0.29	-1.00***t
DDiC quality	-0.55*t	-0.32	0.33	-0.41	0.24	-0.34	0.22	0.28	-0.26	-0.43	0.29
DDiC punct	-0.24	-0.01	0.01	-0.05	0.48*t	-0.24	0.27	0.30	-0.30	-0.47	-0.06
DDiC design	0.47	0.72**t	-0.69**t	0.36	0.09	0.72**t	0.86***t	0.00	-0.15	-0.10	-0.85***t
Dpr95	-0.64**t	-0.54*t	0.55*t	-0.66**t	0.39	-0.47	0.24	-0.38	-0.45	0.04	0.32
Dpr97	-0.10	0.09	-0.10	-0.11	0.40	0.00	0.60	-0.15	0.04	0.17	-0.19
Dmanufacturing	0.89***t	0.74**t	-0.74**t	0.68**t	-0.55*t	0.57**t	0.39	-0.34	0.39	0.57*t	-0.32
DFDI	0.50*t	0.52*t	-0.52*t	0.37	-0.26	0.34	0.60**t	-0.20	0.25	0.34	-0.19
DIMPPR	0.74**t	0.72**t	-0.73**t	0.71**t	0.10	0.35	0.32	-0.13	0.14	0.21	-0.58*t

Correlation matrix 4: origin of competitors and the main dimensions of competition

	Dsmall comp	DC EGer	DC WGer	DC EEur	DC EU	DC WW	DDi price	DDi quality	DDi punct	DDi design	Dpr95	Dpr97	Dmanu facturing
Dsmallc	1.00												
DC Eger	0.35	1.00											
DC WG	0.32	0.40	1.00										
DC EEu	0.32	0.16	-0.50	1.00									
DC EU	0.32	0.16	-0.50	1.00***nc	1.00								
DC WW	0.40	0.32	0.13	0.50	0.50	1.00							
DdiC pri	-0.32	-0.40	0.13	-0.25	-0.25	-0.13	1.00						
DdiCqu	-0.74**t	-0.17	-0.19	-0.27	-0.27	-0.29	-0.29	1.00					
DdiC pu	-0.52*t	-0.26	0.12	-0.47	-0.47	-0.29	0.06	0.67**t	1.00				
DdiCdes	-0.54*t	-0.36	0.00	-0.38	-0.38	-0.57	0.85**t	0.00	0.18	1.00			
Dpr95	-0.35	0.35	0.32	-0.63*nc	-0.63*nc	-0.32	-0.32	0.62**t	0.37	0.00	1.00		
Dpr97	-0.06	0.06	0.66*nc	-0.76**nc	-0.76**nc	-0.66*nc	0.19	0.08	0.31	0.43	0.48	1.00	
DIMPPR	-0.06	-0.48	-0.19	-0.19	-0.19	-0.66*nc	0.19	0.08	0.45	0.43	-0.06	0.36	0.60
DFDI	0.37	-0.37	0.29	-0.29	-0.29	-0.29	0.58**t	-0.68**t	-0.14	0.44	-0.46	0.44	0.73**nc

Table 6.6b Correlation matrix 1 for the Hungarian data: regional characteristics*

	Hhqual	Hcheap	Hcustprox	Hinprox	Hservprox	Hranddprox	Hlocalgov	Hinfrastr
Hhqual	1.00							
Hcheap	**0.54**nc**	1.00						
Hcustprox	0.29	0.29	1.00					
Hinprox	-0.03	0.42	-0.42	1.00				
Hservprox	-0.29	-0.29	0.38	-0.20	1.00			
Hranddprox	0.40	-0.15	0.43	**-0.58**nc**	**0.52*nc**	1.00		
Hlocalgov	0.39	-0.15	**0.55**nc**	**-0.57**nc**	0.24	**0.81***nc**	1.00	
Hinfrastr	0.10	-0.45	0.35	-0.25	**0.61**nc**	0.48	0.47	1.00
H%out90Hung	0.18	**-0.43*t**	-0.18	-0.17	-0.13	0.00	0.10	0.35
H% out 90EEur	**-0.49*t**	0.17	0.12	0.26	0.16	-0.28	-0.22	-0.26
H% out 90EU	0.26	0.31	-0.11	-0.14	-0.13	0.35	0.11	-0.38
H%90 out WW	0.32	**0.51*t**	0.38	0.04	0.14	0.25	0.08	0.02
H90Totol Exp	-0.18	**0.43*t**	0.18	0.17	0.13	0.00	-0.10	-0.35
H% out 96Hung	0.19	-0.30	-0.12	-0.10	-0.33	-0.18	0.11	0.22
H% out 96EEUr	-0.40	0.29	0.22	0.39	0.29	-0.36	**-0.43*t**	-0.15
H%96 out EU	0.20	0.16	-0.06	-0.27	0.06	**0.52*t**	0.21	-0.20
H%96 out WW	0.03	0.05	-0.03	-0.16	0.20	**0.51*t**	0.26	-0.06
HtotalExp96	-0.19	0.30	0.12	0.10	0.33	0.18	-0.11	-0.22
HΔ total Export	-0.07	-0.23	-0.11	-0.15	**0.61**t**	**0.51*t**	-0.05	0.27
HΔ Hung	0.07	0.23	0.11	0.15	**-0.61**t**	**-0.51*t**	0.05	-0.27
HΔ Eeur	0.17	0.25	0.22	0.27	0.27	-0.17	**-0.44*t**	0.23
HΔ EU	0.02	-0.26	0.02	-0.40	**0.53**t**	**0.71***t**	0.29	0.34
HΔ WW	-0.27	**-0.43*t**	**-0.42*t**	-0.26	0.14	**0.45*t**	0.28	-0.10
HMS90	-0.11	0.35	**0.49*t**	-0.09	**0.48*t**	0.28	0.33	-0.02
HMS96	-0.24	0.30	0.23	-0.02	**0.47*t**	0.08	-0.02	-0.09
HΔ MS	-0.30	-0.08	**-0.54*t**	0.15	0.01	-0.41	**-0.73***t**	-0.16
Hnumcomp	-0.29	**-0.69**nc**	-0.08	-0.20	0.08	0.04	0.24	0.29
Hsmallcom	0.04	0.16	**0.56*nc**	0.08	**0.67**nc**	0.35	0.28	0.34
Hbigcomp	-0.15	**-0.56**t**	-0.52	-0.26	-0.19	0.27	0.26	-0.18
HCHung	**0.52**t**	0.16	0.15	0.35	-0.15	-0.08	0.04	0.34
HCEEur	0.15	-0.06	-0.19	-0.22	0.19	**0.47*t**	0.15	0.18
HCEU	-0.22	-0.38	-0.24	-0.39	0.24	0.40	0.08	-0.27
HCWW	-0.13	-0.13	0.39	-0.24	**0.46*t**	**0.46*t**	**0.60**t**	0.13
HdiCprice	-0.13	-0.13	**-0.46*t**	0.05	**-0.81***t**	**-0.64**t**	-0.38	**-0.45*t**
HdiCquality	0.30	-0.11	-0.40	0.21	0.07	0.12	-0.25	0.14
HDiC punct	0.19	0.37	**0.47*t**	0.34	**0.56**t**	0.08	-0.04	0.37
HdiCdesign	-0.26	**-0.57**t**	**0.44*t**	**-0.85***t**	**0.43*t**	**0.47*t**	**0.46*t**	**0.48*t**
Hpr96	0.04	0.16	**0.56**nc**	**-0.48*t**	0.26	0.35	0.28	0.05
Hfood	0.29	0.29	0.08	**0.51*nc**	0.38	-0.04	-0.24	0.35
Hfdi	**0.62**t**	0.13	0.04	0.24	-0.04	0.20	0.13	**0.45*t**
Himppr	0.41	0.03	-0.32	0.13	-0.34	-0.06	0.03	0.19

Note

See also the comments in the footnote to Table 4a concerning the simplifying assumptions needed to produce 2 by 2 tables for associations of two dummy variables. A X^2 distribution with 1 degree of freedom has the following critical values: $X^2_{(critical\text{-}20\%)} = 1.64$, $X^2_{(critical\text{-}10\%)} = 2.7$, $X^2_{(critical\text{-}5\%)} = 3.84$, $X^2_{(critical\text{-}1\%)} = 6.63$. The significance levels for associations involving continuous variables are as before in the Hungarian data.

Dummies	Association	Assumption concerning 0.5	chi-square statistic	Significance level
Hfood and Hinprox	0.51	1) 0.5 = 0 2) dropping 0.5	1) **3.43**, 2) 1.34	**10%** level **Uncorrected**
Hservprox and Hranddprox, Hmanuf	0.52	drop Hservprox=0 column since it contains no observations, furthermore assume Hranddprox 0.5=1	3.43	**10%** level
Hcustprox and Hlocalgov, Hhqual and Hcheapemp	0.54, 0.55	1) 0.5 = 0 2) dropping 0.5	1) 6.54, 2) 4.43, corrected: 1.6, insignificant	**5%** level
Hinprox and Hlocalgov	0.57	0.5 = 0	2.94	**5%** level
Hservprox and Hinfrastr	0.61	drop Hservprox=0 column since it contains no observations, for Hinfrastr,1) 0.5 = 0, 2) dropping 0.5	1) 3.24, 2) 3.94	**5%** level
HFDI and HIMPPR	0.66	drop HIMPPR=0.5 column since only one observation in this column	5.95, corrected: 2.01, insignificant	**5%** level
Hranddprox and Hlocalgov	0.81	0.5= 0	6.54, corrected: 2.85 (10% level)	**1%** level

Correlation matrix 2: the geographical distribution of sales in 1990 and 1996

	H%out 90Hung	H% out 90EEur	H% out 90EU	H%90 out WW	H90 Total Exp	H%out 96Hung	H%out 96EEUr	H%96 out EU	H%96 out WW	HΔ total Export
H%out90Hung	1.00									
H% out 90EEur	**-0.77***t**	1.00								
H% out 90EU	-0.36	-0.25	1.00							
H%90 out WW	**-0.72***t**	0.23	**0.51*t**	1.00						
H90Total Exp	**-1.00***t**	**0.77***t**	0.36	**0.72***t**	1.00					
H%out 96Hung	**0.93***t**	**-0.64**t**	**-0.46*t**	**-0.73***t**	**-0.93***t**	1.00				
H%out96EEUr	**-0.65**t**	**0.88***t**	-0.36	0.29	**0.65**t**	**-0.59**t**	1.00			
H%96out EU	-0.38	-0.22	**0.96***t**	**0.51*t**	0.38	**-0.54**t**	-0.33	1.00		
H%96out WW	-0.68	0.21	**0.72***t**	**0.68**t**	**0.68**t**	**-0.78***t**	0.00	**0.81***t**	1.00	
HTotalExp96	-0.93	**0.64**t**	**0.46*t**	**0.73***t**	**0.93***t**	**-1.00***t**	**0.59**t**	**0.54**t**	**0.78***t**	1.00
HΔ total Export	-0.10	-0.16	0.39	0.22	0.10	**-0.44*t**	0.00	**0.56**t**	**0.46*t**	**0.44*t**
HΔ Hung	0.10	0.16	-0.39	-0.22	-0.10	**0.44*t**	0.00	**-0.56**t**	**-0.46*t**	**-0.44*t**
HΔ Eeur	0.21	-0.20	-0.23	0.12	-0.21	0.08	0.30	-0.25	**-0.43**	-0.08
HΔ EU	-0.18	-0.09	0.43	0.25	0.18	**-0.47*t**	-0.11	**0.66**t**	**0.63**t**	**0.47*t**
HΔ WW	-0.23	0.07	**0.49*t**	-0.04	0.23	-0.36	-0.28	0.61	**0.70***t**	0.36
HMS90	**-0.49*t**	0.37	0.22	0.34	**0.49*t**	**-0.42*t**	0.26	0.24	0.31	**0.42*t**
HMS96	-0.41	0.26	0.28	0.27	0.41	-0.41	0.24	0.29	0.24	0.41
HΔ MS	0.16	-0.21	0.13	-0.14	-0.16	0.01	-0.02	0.13	-0.13	-0.01
Hnumcomp	**0.51*t**	0.02	**-0.69***t**	**-0.76***t**	**-0.51*t**	**0.52**t**	-0.08	**-0.60**t**	**-0.45*t**	**-0.52*t**
Hsmallcom	-0.10	0.34	-0.41	-0.02	0.10	-0.15	**0.49*t**	-0.31	-0.17	0.15
Hbigcomp	0.28	-0.25	0.22	**-0.51*t**	-0.28	0.20	**-0.54**t**	0.26	0.20	-0.20
HCHung	0.27	-0.10	**-0.53**t**	0.04	-0.27	0.34	0.10	-0.58	-0.38	-0.34
HCEEur	-0.34	-0.12	**0.64**t**	**0.55**t**	0.34	-0.50	-0.24	0.77	**0.81***t**	**0.50*t**
HCEU	0.02	-0.09	0.33	-0.24	-0.02	-0.15	-0.20	0.39	0.30	0.15
HCWW	-0.12	0.35	-0.23	-0.21	0.12	-0.07	0.14	-0.15	0.07	0.07
HDiCprice	0.31	-0.28	0.04	-0.31	-0.31	**0.45*t**	-0.36	-0.13	-0.31	**-0.45*t**
HDiCquality	**0.42*t**	-0.35	-0.15	-0.25	**-0.42*t**	0.20	-0.12	-0.09	-0.18	-0.20
HDiC punct	-0.02	0.17	-0.43	0.14	0.02	-0.06	**0.51*t**	-0.39	-0.32	0.06
HDiCdesign	0.14	-0.15	-0.01	-0.06	-0.14	0.03	-0.20	0.17	0.10	-0.03
Hpr96	-0.27	-0.17	**0.57**t**	**0.55**t**	0.27	-0.31	-0.13	**0.56**t**	0.37	0.31
Hfood	0.25	-0.15	-0.35	0.01	-0.25	0.15	0.23	-0.36	-0.39	-0.15
Hfdi	0.08	-0.17	-0.16	0.37	-0.08	0.06	-0.05	-0.14	0.09	-0.06
Himppr	0.15	-0.20	-0.08	0.11	-0.15	0.24	-0.30	-0.09	0.06	-0.24

Correlation matrix 3: changes in the companies' sales and export orientation and market share

	HΔ total Export	HΔ Hung	HΔ EEur	HΔ EU	HΔ WW	HMS90	HMS96	HΔ MS	Hnum comp
HΔ total Export	1.00								
HΔ Hung	-1.00***t	1.00							
HΔ EEur	0.32	-0.32	1.00						
HΔ EU	0.87***t	-0.87***t	-0.05	1.00					
HΔ WW	0.42*t	-0.42*t	-0.71***t	0.61**t	1.00				
HMS90	-0.05	0.05	-0.20	0.05	0.09	1.00			
HMS96	0.12	-0.12	-0.03	0.11	0.06	0.89***t	1.00		
HΔ MS	0.37	-0.37	0.38	0.13	-0.05	-0.19	0.27	1.00	
Hnumcomp	-0.16	0.16	-0.20	-0.10	0.12	-0.38	-0.53**t	-0.35	1.00
Hsmallcom	0.16	-0.16	0.32	0.11	-0.21	0.45*t	0.26	-0.39	0.26
Hbigcomp	0.15	-0.15	-0.62**t	0.27	0.78***t	-0.33	-0.38	-0.13	0.52**t
HCHung	-0.28	0.28	0.39	-0.38	-0.56**t	-0.42*t	-0.59**t	-0.38	0.26
HCEEur	0.56**t	-0.56**t	-0.25	0.71***t	0.57**t	0.13	0.25	0.27	-0.52**t
HCEU	0.48*t	-0.48*t	-0.23	0.41	0.64**t	0.01	0.05	0.08	0.24
HCWW	-0.11	0.11	-0.40	0.05	0.29	0.58**t	0.28	-0.62**t	0.46*t
HDiCprice	-0.50*t	0.50*t	-0.18	-0.54**t	-0.12	-0.54**t	-0.42*t	0.24	0.04
HDiCquality	0.48*t	-0.48*t	0.45*t	0.26	-0.01	-0.58**t	-0.43*t	0.29	0.23
HDiC punct	0.13	-0.13	0.68**t	-0.07	-0.57**t	0.33	0.29	-0.07	-0.06
HDiCdesign	0.28	-0.28	-0.11	0.48*t	0.20	0.09	0.07	-0.04	0.24
Hpr96	0.19	-0.19	0.08	0.22	-0.02	0.49*t	0.48*t	0.00	-0.56**t
Hfood	0.20	-0.20	0.76***t	-0.11	-0.54**t	0.03	0.12	0.20	-0.08
Hfdi	0.04	-0.04	0.25	0.03	-0.23	-0.36	-0.46*t	-0.23	-0.04
Himppr	-0.28	0.28	-0.22	-0.15	-0.02	-0.21	-0.17	0.08	-0.12

Correlation matrix 4: origin of competitors and the main dimensions of competition

	Hsmall com	Hbig comp	HC Hung	HC EEur	HCEU	HCWW	HDiC price	HDiC quality	HDiC punct	HdiC design	Hpr96	Hfood	Hfdi	Himppr
Hsmallcom	1.00													
Hbigcomp	-0.29	1.00												
HCHung	0.27	-0.29	1.00											
HCEEur	-0.35	0.10	-0.35	1.00										
HCEU	0.04	0.67	-0.43*t	0.15	1.00									
HCWW	0.69***t	0.24	-0.07	-0.24	0.36	1.00								
HdiCprice	-0.83***t	0.24	-0.07	-0.24	-0.13	-0.57**t	1.00							
HdiCquality	0.16	0.20	0.45*t	0.05	0.30	-0.19	-0.19	1.00						
HDiC punct	0.83***t	-0.66**t	0.47*t	-0.29	-0.28	0.26	-0.69***t	0.28	1.00					
HdiCdesign	0.01	0.12	-0.42*t	0.18	0.18	0.15	-0.11	-0.32	-0.22	1.00				
Hpr96	-0.10	-0.29	-0.47*t	0.29	0.04	-0.07	-0.07	-0.56**t	-0.08	0.52*t	1.00			
Hfood	0.56**t	-0.52**t	0.56**t	-0.19	-0.24	-0.04	-0.46*t	0.57**t	0.88***t	-0.43*t	-0.26	1.00		
Hfdi	0.07	-0.24	0.83***t	0.24	-0.36	-0.21	-0.21	0.49*t	0.31	-0.33	-0.31	0.46	1.00	
Himppr	-0.37	-0.06	0.41	0.40	-0.34	-0.26	0.15	0.20	-0.12	-0.34	-0.37	0.12	0.66**nc	1.00

For Product Safety Concerns and Information please contact our EU representative GPSR@taylorandfrancis.com Taylor & Francis Verlag GmbH, Kaufingerstraße 24, 80331 München, Germany

Batch number: 10725923

Printed by Printforce, the Netherlands